The Practical
SQL
Handbook

Fourth Edition

The Practical
SQL
Handbook
Using SQL Variants

Fourth Edition

Judith S. Bowman
Sandra L. Emerson
Marcy Darnovsky

Addison-Wesley

Boston • San Francisco • New York • Toronto • Montreal
London • Munich • Paris • Madrid
Capetown • Sydney • Tokyo • Singapore • Mexico City

Many of the designations used by manufacturers and sellers to distinguish their products are claimed as trademarks. Where those designations appear in this book, and Addison-Wesley, Inc. was aware of a trademark claim, the designations have been printed with initial capital letters or in all capitals.

The authors and publisher have taken care in the preparation of this book, but make no expressed or implied warranty of any kind and assume no responsibility for errors or omissions. No liability is assumed for incidental or consequential damages in connection with or arising out of the use of the information or programs contained herein.

The publisher offers discounts on this book when ordered in quantity for special sales. For more information, please contact:

Pearson Education Corporate Sales Division
One Lake Street
Upper Saddle River, NJ 07458
(800) 382-3419
corpsales@pearsontechgroup.com

Visit AW on the Web: www.awl.com/cseng

Library of Congress Cataloging-in-Publication Data

Bowman, Judith S.
    The practical SQL handbook : using SQL variants / Judith S. Bowman, Sandra L.
  Emerson, Marcy Darnovsky.--4th ed.
        p. cm.
    Includes bibliographical references and index.
    ISBN 0-201-70309-2 (alk. paper)
    1. SQL (Computer program language) 2. Relational databases I. Emerson, Sandra L.,
1947- II. Darnovsky, Marcy. III. Title.

QA76.73.S67 B688 2001
005.75′6--dc21   2001022698

ISBN 0-201-70309-2
Text printed on recycled paper
1 2 3 4 5 6 7 8 9 10—MA—0504030201
First printing, June 2001

Dedication

To our mothers: Mary Jo Coogan Bowman, Alma E. Emerson, Betty Schwarcz

Contents

Chapter 1: SQL and Relational Database Management   1

Chapter 2: Designing Databases   21

List of Figures

Foreword to the Fourth Edition

This book made me happy! If you are already using a SQL-compliant database, or are just starting to learn, I bet this book will make you happy too.

When I first picked up *The Practical SQL Handbook*, I had been a database consultant for several years, yet I was having trouble getting a moderately complicated query (a "self-join") to work. I scanned the Table of Contents and immediately found the chapter I needed. In the Third Edition, this was "Chapter 7: Joining Tables for Comprehensive Data Analysis." As I read Chapter 7, I was impressed with the clarity of the language, the effective use of examples and figures, and the thoroughness of the chapter. It started by explaining how to extract information from several tables, using simple and accessible language. The chapter didn't stop with the basics, though; it explained advanced queries with the same grace and clarity I was learning to expect from the book.

After I solved my immediate problem, I took a day to further my education and read several chapters: "Solving Business Problems" and "Mistakes and How to Avoid Them." Wow! These chapters (combined in the Fourth Edition) really expanded my understanding of how to use SQL.

This book explained a number of things that none of the many other database books I'd read covered. I think the power of this book is that it explains things from the standpoint of an expert teaching a new learner, *practically*, how to do the things that everyone needs to do. It is like being in a kitchen, getting folk wisdom passed down from a master chef, not like a series of instructions for the refrigerator, oven, and blender.

In my capacity as technical director for the Institute for Global Communications, a San Francisco–based global network for activists, I mentored beginning programmers on how to integrate SQL databases into their work. I started by asking them to read the beginning chapters of *The Practical SQL Handbook*. Once they had read the chapters "Designing Databases," "Creating and Filling a Database," and "Selecting Data from the Database," they had a solid foundation. From this base, we programmed network applications in Cold Fusion, Perl, PHP, and Microsoft Access.

I recommend this book to both programmers and nonprogrammers and people using Microsoft SQL Server, Oracle, or any other SQL-compliant database. It is written so that *anyone* using SQL will find it helpful. Whether you are using Microsoft SQL Server, Oracle, or even a database not specifically supported by this book, such as the open-source *mysql* server, 95 percent of this book will be applicable to you. Programmers can use *The Practical SQL Handbook* to learn how to create, query, and modify SQL databases. Nonprogrammers will rapidly be able to understand how and why databases are the way they are, how to improve them, and how to extract the information they need from their organization's databases.

The Fourth Edition looks even better than the third, with more information on specific database servers, more example code, and explanations further honed by years of feedback from the enthusiastic readers of the past editions.

I suggest buying this book if you are using SQL or if you want to learn how to use SQL. *The Practical SQL Handbook* is well organized and well written and teaches what people need to know to use SQL to its fullest. It will jumpstart a novice and will provide hundreds of excellent examples and tips for the expert. Good luck!

Michael de Beer

Former Technical Director, Institute for Global Communications

http://www.igc.org/madebeer

February 2001

Michael de Beer is a consultant to the Association for Progressive Communications (APC), an international coalition of progressive computer networks reaching non-governmental organizations and citizen activists in more than 130 countries.

Preface

Why New Editions?

Many things have changed since this book was first published in 1989, and SQL is no exception. The SQL language has expanded tremendously, both in numbers of users and in numbers of commands. Sales of relational databases continue to rise at a strong and steady rate.

When we wrote the first edition of *The Practical SQL Handbook*, the American National Standards Institute (ANSI) had already approved the 1986 SQL standard. The International Standards Organization (ISO) adopted it in 1987. Both ANSI and ISO helped create the 1989 version. The 1986 standards were skimpy, lacking features that most commercial vendors offered. The 1989 standards were more complete but still left many important elements undefined.

For the first edition, we felt we should focus on industry practice: As always, each vendor was keeping a wary eye on what the others were doing and making core offerings similar enough to attract both customers migrating from competitors, as well as new users looking for database systems they could build on. Because of this, we left both the not-quite-jelled ANSI standards and particular vendor implementations to the experts in those fields and concentrated on the common ground: generic or "industry-practice" SQL. Our goal was to offer the intelligent amateur practical information on how to use the actually available SQL of that time.

The 1992 ANSI standard (often called SQL-2 or SQL-92) represented a new stage in SQL development. This standard was more comprehensive than the 1989 standard: In written form it contained more than four times as many pages as the earlier version. Database vendors have adopted large parts of the 1992 standard. With the widespread adoption of the SQL-92 standard, the industry practice and the ANSI/ISO standards began to converge.

Despite vendor-specific differences, there is a general, industrywide core of SQL commands that all users need to understand. Adopting standards doesn't happen overnight; it is a long process. At any point, vendors will have varying levels of conformance and will continue to produce vendor-specific variations. This book aims to give SQL users a mastery of the fundamentals of the language, with a side glance at the specifics of particular implementations.

Changes for Recent Editions

The changes for recent editions have been threefold:

- To include more real-world examples
- To emphasize the SQL-92 features that most vendors have implemented
- To provide software for hands-on practice

Include More Real-World Examples

In talking to new and developing SQL users, we heard over and over of their need for more examples to follow, change, narrow, and broaden. Accordingly, the bulk of the added material in the second edition consisted of code "recipes." Chapter 11, Solving Business Problems, is a selection of code samples based on questions and answers that came over computer newsgroups. We reproduce interesting problems and solutions in terms of the sample bookbiz database used throughout the book. The chapter includes examples of using the CASE function for conditional logic, formatting results, and finding date data. A few samples fall into a different category. They aren't so much solutions to problems as indications of common errors. They include issues with DISTINCT and misunderstandings of what SQL can do.

Emphasize SQL-92

With the third edition, we revised the book to incorporate the SQL-92 features that most vendors had adopted. These include new datatypes, additions to the CREATE TABLE statement that allow built-in integrity constraints, modifications to the ORDER BY and GROUP BY clauses, the new escape character for the LIKE keyword, and changes to GRANT and REVOKE, among others.

Provide Software for Hands-On Practice

With the fully usable trial version of Sybase's Adaptive Server Anywhere (ASA) on the CD that accompanies this book, you can run the examples (and your variants) on a PC. We've always felt that the secret to learning SQL is practice. Now you can experiment to your heart's content, trying out code samples with data you know and checking the results to see if they are what you expect. When you're stumped by complicated code, break it into small, meaningful pieces and run the pieces separately to make sure you understand what each segment does. Then put them together in increasingly complex combinations—and have fun!

The Sybase Adaptive Server Anywhere software on the CD is a 60-day full-feature version that allows you to create objects as well as to query existing objects. ASA is built with an updated version of the bookbiz database: For the fourth edition, we increased book prices and made dates more recent. Also included on the CD are scripts to create the database on ASA (in case you damage the original) and on the other systems discussed in the book.

The Fourth Edition

The Practical SQL Handbook, fourth edition, continues to focus on industry-practice SQL, but the information included is at once more general and more specific than earlier editions. For the fourth edition, we had two objectives:

- To expand our test base, running the examples on five different database systems
- To show vendor-specific differences among systems

Test on More Systems

For the fourth edition, all examples were run on *five* systems (Sybase Adaptive Server Anywhere, Adaptive Server Enterprise, Microsoft SQL Server, Oracle, Informix), rather than on Sybase systems only, as in the third edition. This expanded test base makes the information more universal. We are no longer limited to what we can explore or verify on a particular system. If an important feature doesn't exist on Adaptive Server Anywhere (ASA, the RDBMS included on the CD), we can show code and results from Oracle or SQL Server.

Show Examples of Vendor-Specific Differences

On the other hand, this edition is more specific. It includes information on specific idiosyncrasies of the five SQL dialects, warning readers where to look for differences. In this, it reflects the real world—lots of database users are working with multiple systems, either sequentially or simultaneously. Interesting SQL differences are flagged as SQL Variants, in-text sections that show details of differences in SQL use by different vendors. For example, how single and double quotes are used, or database users added, or outer joins specified. You won't see code for every one of the five systems every time, but you'll get an introduction to the kind of differences that are likely in a particular area.

Acknowledgments

We would like to thank the following people for their contributions to this book: Donna Jeker and Stu Schuster for supplying timely support and encouragement; Jeff Lichtman and Howard Torf for offering advice, examples, anecdotes, and reality checks; Tom Bondur, Susie Bowman, John Cooper, and Wayne Duquesne for providing resource materials and other information; Paul Winsberg for reviewing the database design chapter in the first edition; Robert Garvey for technical review of the second edition; Karen Ali for facilitating the third edition's SQL Anywhere CD; and Theo Posselt for technical review of the third edition.

For the fourth edition, we would like to acknowledge Mike Radencich of iAnywhere Solutions (a Sybase Company), for providing the software and permissions for the Adaptive Server Anywhere CD; Lance Batten of Tilden Park Software and Sanford Jacobs of Paragon Software for comments and corrections; our reviewers, on whom we rely for timely and detailed feedback: Vijay-anandan Venkatachalam, curriculum director of Oracle Corporation; David McGoveran of Alternative Technologies; Roger Snowden; Amy Sticksel of Sticksel Data Systems; Paul Irvine of Emerald Solutions; and Karl Batten-Bowman.

Introduction

The Beginnings of SQL

In the beginning was IBM, and IBM created SQL.

SQL, originally an acronym for "Structured Query Language," is a unified language for defining, querying, modifying, and controlling the data in a relational database. Its name is officially pronounced "ess-cue-ell" (according to the American National Standards Institute), but many people say "sequel." In this book, we use the term SQL as if it were pronounced "sequel."

The relational model of database management was proposed in 1970 by Dr. E. F. Codd at the IBM Research Laboratory in San Jose, California, and developed during the following decade in universities and research laboratories. SQL, one of several languages that grew out of this early work, continues to dominate the world of relational database languages. Vendors of relational database management systems all support SQL, albeit with many vendor-specific variations. National and international standards organizations have collaborated on several versions of the SQL standard, and standards work continues.

During the early years (roughly 1970–1980), the poor performance of relational database management systems hampered their commercial viability. The relational model's important strengths—mathematical soundness and intuitive appeal—could not overcome the fact that the management of large databases with early relational systems was slow and difficult—practically speaking, sometimes impossible. Two factors changed this situation: the availability of faster, larger-capacity computers, and the development of superior data retrieval, data storage, and data access methods to support the "back end" functions of relational systems.

In 1981, IBM announced its first commercial SQL-based product, SQL/DS. During the early 1980s, Oracle, Relational Technology, and several other vendors also announced SQL-based relational database management systems. By 1989, there were more than seventy-five SQL or SQL-like database management systems, running on computers of all sizes and shapes—from single-user micros to machines that handled hundreds of users. Today, SQL is entrusted with "mission-critical" information management and data processing tasks on the global networks of corporate, government, and public interest organizations.

The emergence of a highly competitive marketplace for relational database management systems helped produce an array of SQL implementations, each representing that vendor's best effort to develop a complete and highly expressive language for the relational model. With the widespread adoption of the SQL-92 standard, vendors' SQL implementations began to converge. Many implementations have a core set of commands that are similar in syntax and semantics. On the other hand, many vendors regularly extend their versions of SQL, which still makes the language a moving target.

SQL continues to evolve—for several reasons. SQL's original design was vague in a number of areas (and the database industry didn't wait for those fuzzy areas to be cleared up). Even as the industry implements more of the SQL standard, standards work continues into areas that "push the envelope" for SQL implementations. Finally, and most important, the role of databases in Internet-based applications means that SQL has had to step up to managing multimedia objects, securely, in a worldwide public arena.

Fortunately, SQL is flexible and easy to extend. As the chief language of relational (and object-relational) databases, SQL can keep on changing to meet the demands of the market.

The Commercialization of SQL

In addition to conforming to standards, SQL implementations have converged *because of* competition among the top RDBMS vendors. (There used to be many more database vendors, but the industry has consolidated as a result of mergers, acquisitions, and other market forces.) Naturally, companies try to offer prospective customers the same "checklist" of SQL functions and extensions. Companies are also constantly trying to attract customers of other relational systems and to minimize the cost of converting from one SQL-based system to another.

These forces, as well as standards, continue to push commercial implementations closer together. After all, both commercial interests and the standards committees are producing a SQL that

- implements an increasingly complete relational model;
- minimizes incompatibility and implementation dependence; and
- carefully adds language for new functions in order to maintain compatibility with earlier implementations.

This book (and the CD containing a time-limited version of Adaptive Server Anywhere) can help you teach yourself basic SQL. Then you can apply what you've learned to other SQL dialects you may be using. Once you understand the fundamentals, you'll find it easy to make adjustments for different versions.

Who Should Use This Book

The Practical SQL Handbook is meant for you if you use a relational database system—whether you're sharing that system with other users or going it alone on a single-user personal computer. It assumes that you're an intelligent amateur—whether you're an end user in a large company, government office, or nonprofit agency; the owner of a small business; the manager of a small organization; a home computer user working on a personal project; or a student learning about database technology. You may be moving to a relational database system from a PC file manager, making the transition to SQL from a non-SQL-based database management system, or taking up database management for the first time.

We do take for granted that you have a nodding acquaintance with computers and computer tools. Of course, some degree of familiarity with database systems will help.

If you're planning to develop a sophisticated database application, you may need to embed SQL in a programming language (such as C++ or Java) or use it with a scripting language (such as XML or JavaScript). But you need never have written a single line of programming or scripting code to use *The Practical SQL Handbook* successfully to learn the basics of SQL and to get a good grasp on a variety of more advanced topics.

Theoreticians are not our intended audience; we assume that the fine points of relational theory and the intricacies of ISO-ANSI debates are not of primary interest to our readers. On the other hand, we think you should be aware of the major SQL controversies—at least in their broad outlines—so that you'll be alert to the tricky areas of SQL use. In short, we think you want to know what really works, or at least the fastest way to find it out.

Accordingly, this book concentrates on teaching you to use SQL interactively—typing the commands and receiving results directly on a screen, as opposed to embedding them in a programming language. Every commercial implementation of SQL has an interactive interface for use in learning the language initially and writing ad hoc queries. Most implementations also provide a suite of tools such as a report writer, an administrative console, or a high-level scripting language that can be used in association with SQL to develop applications of moderate complexity.

The Focus of This Book

This book focuses on the real world of commercial SQLs—"industry SQLs"—rather than on the more abstract SQL represented by the ANSI standard. We chose to focus here because industry SQLs provide a better teaching tool in the areas of notation, target audience, and overall functionality:

- The syntax notation used to document most industry SQLs is reasonably clear and intuitively understandable. The ISO-ANSI publications, on the other hand, use BNF (Backus Naur Form) notation, which is very precise but difficult to read and understand.
- All the industry SQLs support an interactive interface for the beginning or casual user; the ISO-ANSI standard is largely concerned with the embedded SQL interface for programmers and applications developers.
- Vendors of relational database systems implement the features their customers ask for, including some originally offered only by competitors. Adoption of ANSI SQL features varies from SQL to SQL. By taking the industry practice (rather than the ANSI standard) as the basis for this book, we can focus on features available today.

The ANSI standard is a forbidding document, bristling with clauses, caveats, and footnotes; its BNF notation is best suited for capturing the function of each language element, rather than its exact syntax. If you want to undertake your own investigations, we recommend that you take a guide along: C. J. Date's *A Guide to the SQL Standard.* Date is one of the major theoreticians of the relational model and one of the most prolific writers on relational matters. His book explains how to read BNF and provides a concise exposition of his opinions on the merits and deficiencies of the standard and of SQL in general.

After ruminating on the ISO-ANSI document for a while, even with the assistance of Date's guide, you're likely to turn for enlightenment to the closest relational database management system's user's manual. But user's manuals have their own drawbacks and limitations.

While some user's manuals are adequate for learning the basics of SQL, a great many are either overly simple or overly obscure. Perhaps more problematic, user's manuals (including several written by the authors of this book) unavoidably focus on the details of syntax and the eccentricities of one particular dialect—often at the expense of the conceptual picture.

The Practical SQL Handbook is meant to take up where even the best SQL user's manual leaves off. It takes you step-by-step through the basics of SQL and then introduces you to the issues involved in designing SQL-based database applications. *The Practical SQL Handbook* covers topics that are usually neglected or given short shrift in user's manuals: database design, indexes, nulls, joins, subqueries, views, performance, and data integrity.

How to Learn SQL with This Book

Let's begin with a few expectations. First of all, we expect you to read large parts of this book while sitting at your terminal. Second, we expect you to study and reproduce the examples. Third, we expect you to practice, test, and explore. There's no substitute for interactive practice, even if your ultimate intention may be to program a highly sophisticated application.

From there, a lot is up to you. Learning styles differ: Some people absorb new material through carefully considering prose explanations; others take in concepts just by looking at pictures. We expect this book to be helpful whether you choose to read every word of it or you choose to scan the text briefly and rely mainly on the examples. Words and phrases in **boldface** indicate the first mention of an entry that is defined in the glossary.

Some of the hundreds of examples in *The Practical SQL Handbook* are deliberately simple in order to illustrate basic concepts; others are more difficult. At the most complex end of the range you'll find SQL statements that may serve as models for your own applications. Wherever their complexity warrants, examples are dissected and explained in detail.

The fact that every version of SQL is different from every other version, at least in some details, means that no general-purpose book on SQL can guarantee all of its examples to work exactly as presented. The good news is that our decision to base *The Practical SQL Handbook* on a variety of widely available commercial SQLs makes the "translation" process more straightforward. With the reference materials supplied with your SQL product, the list of cross-system analogies in keywords and operators in Appendix B, and a little detective work, you'll be able to test most of our examples on whatever SQL or SQL-like system you're using. The systems used to test the code are listed in Figure I.1. All the examples in *The Practical SQL Handbook* are guaranteed to work in the systems on which they were tested. We don't claim to represent in depth any single implementation of SQL. We do cover (in broad strokes) the major areas of commonality among industry SQLs.

With very few exceptions, all examples are derived from our sample database, called the `bookbiz` database. Chapters 2 and 3 explain the sample database. You don't have to use the same sample data we do, but that's the best approach. It will help you to see more quickly whether your results are correct.

The `bookbiz` database is very small. Its size and simplicity will allow you to become comfortable using a database before you tackle an enterprise-level

Vendor	Software	Version	Tool	Notes
Sybase	Adaptive Server Anywhere (ASA) also known as SQL Anywhere	6.0.3	Interactive SQL	Included on CD
Sybase	Adaptive Server Enterprise (ASE)	11.5	SQL Advantage	}Transact-SQL
Microsoft	SQL Server	7.0	Query Analyzer	
Oracle	Personal Oracle	8.1.7	SQL Plus	
Informix	Informix	7.30	dbaccess	

Figure I.1 Relational Database Management Systems Used in This Book

project. You can use the copy of bookbiz provided on the Adaptive Server Anywhere CD as you work through the examples in the book and later re-create the database on your own system. On the other hand, bookbiz is complex enough to illustrate important points about significant relational issues.

The Structure of This Book

Each chapter in *The Practical SQL Handbook* presents one SQL feature or a cluster of related features. The discussion follows a pattern:

- Definition: what it does
- Minimal syntax: a simple "vanilla" version of the command, one that is stripped of most optional clauses and extensions that tend to vary from SQL to SQL. See Chapter 3 for an explanation of syntax conventions.
- A simple example

Following this initial description of syntax and usage, we elaborate on the role of this feature in the relational model and its possible use in database applications.

If necessary, we then provide additional syntax—optional clauses offering additional functions or fine-tuning capabilities—and more-complex examples. In this way, each new feature has a complete description and example.

Where possible, each example builds on previous ones. However, the examples in each chapter stand alone so that you can complete a chapter at one sitting. Learning SQL is like learning any other foreign language: The learning process begins with imitation, proceeds through comprehension, and should end with fluency. At each of these stages, the key to success is practice.

How to Use This Book

Interactive practice with SQL will be more pleasant and efficient if you follow some simple time-saving procedures:

Save your practice SQL statements in operating system files (Your   system should provide a method for doing this.) If you are not certain that a SQL query (data retrieval operation) is producing the desired results, save the results for off-line examination. Keep a log or record of what worked and what didn't, and save the error message, too, if you can.

Save your successes Keep elegant SQL solutions on file: You may want to imitate them for other purposes later on.

Structure an application's queries into separate modules or subroutines Like modern structured programming, good SQL applications should be made of many subroutines and be open to constant reapplication and recycling.

Make yourself a crib sheet Even if your system has provided you with a quick reference card, make your own list and quick sketches of favorite commands. This will reinforce learning. You will soon find that you use some SQL commands much more often than others.

Improve on our solutions In our experience, the more you work at expressing yourself in SQL, the simpler and more elegant your statements become.

The point of learning SQL and practicing it interactively is to be able to express any desired operation properly so that you get the results you want. In order to achieve this level of proficiency, you'll have to explore and test-drive your relational system's SQL until you're sure you can trust it. You don't want to find out when you're running a high-volume multiuser system that your results have been invalidated by a SQL error (or a logic error).

SQL requires practice because it's a foreign language, and the entity that speaks it best—your system's parser—isn't human. Although SQL has a limited number of keywords and operators and is relatively easy to read, there are areas that are tricky. Like many other high-level languages for computers, SQL has a definite grammar and structure and a fair number of specific syntax rules. SQL may be like English, but it's still far from being a natural language. Sooner or later, you'll come across some operations that SQL simply cannot perform.

The Practical SQL Handbook will help you understand SQL's strengths and limits. It will assist in heading off potential disasters caused by poor database design or unwieldy and unmaintainable SQL-based applications, and it will make the learning of SQL as quick and painless as possible.

An Overview of the Book

Chapter 1: SQL and Relational Database Management This chapter briefly defines and informally illustrates the relational model. It presents the chief features of the SQL language as the voice of the relational model.

Chapter 2: Designing Databases Database design is often an intimidating prospect. This chapter surveys the most helpful techniques, using the sample database to illustrate the analysis of data and the decision making involved in database design. It discusses primary and foreign keys, entity-relationship modeling, and the normalization rules, which can act as guidelines for good database design.

Chapter 3: Creating and Filling a Database The design proposed in the previous chapter becomes a reality here as the SQL commands for creating databases, tables, and indexes, and for adding, changing, and deleting data, are examined in detail. An explanation of our SQL syntax conventions accompanies this initiation into hands-on use of the SQL language.

Chapter 4: Selecting Data from the Database With this chapter, you can start using the Adaptive Server Anywhere CD to run examples. The chapter presents the basic elements of the SELECT command. It explains how to retrieve particular rows and columns from a single table and covers computed values, comparison operators, and logical operators.

Chapter 5: Sorting Data and Other Selection Techniques Other clauses in the SELECT statement allow you to sort your data, eliminate duplicates from the results, or use aggregate functions to report averages, sums, or counts.

Chapter 6: Grouping Data and Reporting from It   The SELECT statement also includes language for grouping data and reporting from it using the aggregate functions described in the previous chapter. This chapter also returns to the controversial topic of how a relational database management system should handle null values (missing information).

Chapter 7: Joining Tables for Comprehensive Data Analysis   The join operation is one of the hallmarks of the relational model. This chapter explains how to use the join operation to retrieve data from one or more tables. A complex variant on simple selection, joins confront users with significant issues in analyzing and verifying the results of data retrieval.

Chapter 8: Structuring Queries with Subqueries   This chapter deals with the proper use and application of nested queries or subqueries. The correlated subquery (notorious for causing confusion) is explained, using many examples.

Chapter 9: Creating and Using Views   This chapter discusses views (virtual tables) and their use in providing customized access to data. Views can also provide data security because you can grant other users access to specified portions of a table for specified operations. The thorny issue of updating views is described in some detail.

Chapter 10: Security, Transactions, Performance, and Integrity   This chapter is devoted to considerations encountered in real-world database management. It explains the SQL commands for specifying permissions, returns to the subject of indexing to discuss its use in boosting performance, and covers mechanisms for transaction management. It also describes extensions to the SQL language that provide database consistency and referential integrity.

Chapter 11: Solving Business Problems   Here's where you can practice the skills you learned in earlier chapters, with SQL code samples based on questions and answers found on the Internet and reproduced in terms of the `bookbiz` database. You'll learn about CASE and other conditional functions, write code to pull column data apart and put it back together, convert from one datatype to another, and become familiar with date issues. The chapter ends with a section on avoiding mistakes.

Appendix A: Syntax Summary for the SQL Used in This Book   These notes on SQL conventions used in the book conclude with a list of SQL statements.

Appendix B: Industry SQL Equivalents   Comparison charts let you see the differences among five RDBMSs in naming conventions, datatypes, and SQL functions.

Appendix C: Glossary   Important terms (**bold** on first appearance in the text) are listed here in alphabetical order for your convenience.

Appendix D: The* bookbiz *Sample Database   This appendix includes charts of tables with data, data structure diagrams, and CREATE and INSERT statements.

Appendix E: Resources   Lists of useful books, Web sites, and newsgroups are provided.

Chapter 1

SQL and Relational Database Management

In This Chapter

- Relational Database Management
- The Relational Model: It's All Tables
- Independence Forever
- A High-Level Language
- Relational Operations
- Alternatives for Viewing Data
- NULLs
- Security
- Integrity
- SQL Functions

Relational Database Management

SQL is the language in which one "speaks" relational database. But just what is a relational database management system?

All database management systems store and manipulate information. The relational approach to database management is based on a mathematical model that includes formidable-sounding components such as relational algebra and relational calculus. Most working definitions of relational database management, however, rely on descriptions and functional specifications rather than on theoretical precision.

Relational expert C. J. Date gives this informal definition of a relational database management system, or DBMS:

- It represents all information in the database as tables.
- It supports the three relational operations, known as **selection**, **projection**, and **join**, for specifying exactly what data you want to see (and it can carry out these operations without requiring the system to store its data physically in any particular form).

Dr. E. F. Codd, the inventor of the relational model, has developed a detailed list of criteria that implementations of the relational model must meet. A comprehensive explanation of this list, often called "Codd's rules," would introduce terminology and theoretical issues not really within the scope of this book. We do touch on many of these issues, however, in subsequent chapters. Here we summarize the features of Codd's twelve-rule test for relational systems and use these, in combination with Date's more basic definition, to come up with a general definition (don't worry if the vocabulary is not familiar—each topic is explored in the following sections). To be considered fully relational, a relational database management system must

- Represent all information in the database as tables
- Keep the logical representation of data independent from its physical storage characteristics
- Use one high-level language for structuring, querying, and changing the information in the database (theoretically, any number of database languages could fit this bill; in practice, SQL is *the* relational language)
- Support the main relational operations (selection, projection, join) and set operations such as union, intersection, difference, and division
- Support views, which allow the user to specify alternative ways of looking at data in tables
- Provide a method for differentiating between unknown values (**nulls**) and zero or blank
- Support mechanisms for security and authorization
- Protect data integrity through transactions and recovery procedures

The rest of this chapter gives an overview of these points; most of them are discussed further in subsequent chapters. A section on SQL functions is also included. After reading the brief explanations here, you'll begin to understand the lay of the relational land. Check Appendix E for a list of resources with additional information.

The Relational Model: It's All Tables

Codd's very first rule says that all information in a relational database is represented by values in **tables**. In a relational system, tables have (horizontal) **rows** and (vertical) **columns** (see Figure 1.1). All data is represented in table format—there's no other way to see the information in the database.

A note on terminology: Because table, row, and column are the common terms used in commercial relational database management systems, they're the ones we'll use in this book. The parallel relational model terms are **relation**, **tuple**, and **attribute**. The related general data processing terms are **file**, **record**, and **field**.

A set of related tables forms a **database**. The tables in a relational database are separate but equal. There is no hierarchical ranking of tables and, in fact, no necessary physical relationship among them.

Each table consists of a set of rows and columns. Each row describes one occurrence of an **entity**—a person, a company, a sale, or some other thing. Each column describes one characteristic of the entity—a person's name or address, a company's phone number or president, a sale's items sold or quantity or date.

Each data element, or **value**, can be identified as the intersection of a row (the horizontal element) and a column (the vertical element). To zero in on the exact data element you want, you need to know the name of its table, what column it's in, and the value of its row's **primary key**, or unique identifier. (As we'll discuss in Chapter 2, it is necessary that each row be uniquely identified by one of its values.)

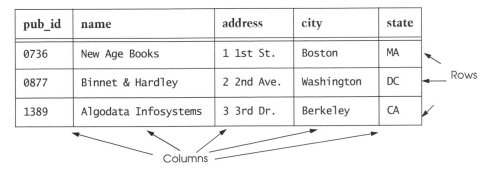

Figure 1.1 **The** publishers **Table**

For example, suppose you want to know which street a particular publisher is on. To instruct the system to show you that particular piece of information, you tell it to fetch Binnet & Hardley's address from the table called `publishers`. The column name is `address` (or some such thing); the name *Binnet & Hardley* is the value identifying that row (see Figure 1.2).

There are two types of tables in a relational database: **user tables** and **system tables**. User tables contain the information that is the database management system's *raison d'être*—information on sales, orders, personnel schedules, and the like. The system tables, also known as the **system catalog** (or data dictionary), contain the database description. System tables are usually kept up-to-date by the DBMS itself, but they can be accessed just like any other table. Being able to access the system tables as if they were any other table is another of Codd's rules for relational systems.

To reiterate: All the information in the database, whether it's system data or user data, is represented as tables.

Independence Forever

In database management, as in certain other aspects of life, independence is something to strive for. Data independence is a crucial aspect of database management: It lets applications change without affecting database design, and it lets database design change without affecting applications. A database management system should not force you to make irrevocable decisions about what data you'll store, how you'll access it, or what your users will require. You don't want to be stuck with a system that's become obsolete because your work requirements have changed.

pub_id	name	address	city	state
0736	New Age Books	1 1st St.	Boston	MA
0877	Binnet & Hardley	2 2nd Ave.	Washington	DC
1389	Algodata Infosystems	3 3rd Dr.	Berkeley	CA

The intersection of Binnet & Hardley's row and the **address** column is Binnet & Hardley's street address.

Figure 1.2 Locating a Specific Piece of Data in a Table

The relational model provides data independence on two important levels: *physical* and *logical*. Physical storage is an architectural issue: It differs from vendor to vendor and often from version to version. **Physical data independence** means that the representation of the data—the user's eye view—is completely independent of how the data is physically stored. As a consequence, physical storage can be changed or rearranged without affecting either your view of the data or the logical database design.

In addition, local changes can become necessary or desirable, especially in large multiuser systems. For example, when you run out of storage space, you'll need to add physical storage. When a storage device breaks down, you'll have to replace it—in a hurry. Usually, less urgently, you may want to improve performance, efficiency, or ease of use by changing the method by which the system locates the physical data. (These methods are referred to generically as **access strategies**, which often make use of **indexes**.)

A second type of independence provided by relational systems, known as **logical independence**, means that relationships among tables, columns, and rows can change without impairing the function of application programs and ad hoc (on-the-fly) queries. You can split tables between rows, or between columns, without disrupting applications or queries. You can also get an answer to any ad hoc question that you ask the system about the database, even though the database's logical design has changed.

Physical and logical data independence account for two more of Codd's twelve rules.

A High-Level Language

The definition of a relational system and Codd's rules, require that a single language—sometimes called a **comprehensive data sublanguage**—be able to handle all communications with the database. In the commercial world of relational database management, that language is SQL.

SQL is used for three kinds of operations:

- Data manipulation
- Data definition
- Data administration

Every manipulation, definition, or administrative operation is expressed as a SQL **statement** or **command**. SQL is called a high-level language because its English-like commands are far from the 1's and 0's of the low-level (close to the machine) commands you find in more basic languages.

Data Manipulation

There are two varieties of **data manipulation** operation, collectively called **DML**, data manipulation language:

- **Data retrieval:** finding the particular data you want
- **Data modification:** adding, removing, or changing the data

Data retrieval operations (often called **queries**) search the database, fetch information you've requested in the most efficient way possible, and display it. All SQL queries are expressed using the keyword SELECT.

The rest of this chapter includes some simple SQL queries. Don't worry about the syntax right now: it'll be fully explained in Chapter 3 before you're expected to sit down at a computer terminal and replicate anything you see here. For now, just glance at the examples and results to get the flavor of SQL and an impression of what the statement is doing.

Following is a SELECT statement that shows you all the data in the `publishers` table, part of the `bookbiz` database. The asterisk (*) is a shorthand device for asking for every column in the table:

```
SQL
select *
from publishers
pub_id pub_name                 address             city            state
====== ======================== =================== =============== =====
0736   New Age Books            1 1st St.           Boston          MA
0877   Binnet & Hardley         2 2nd Ave.          Washington      DC
1389   Algodata Infosystems     3 3rd Dr.           Berkeley        CA
[3 rows]
```

Data modification operations are accomplished using the INSERT, DELETE, and UPDATE keywords, respectively. You can add a row to the `publishers` table like this:

```
SQL
insert into publishers
values ('0010', 'Pragmatics', '4 4th Ln.', 'Chicago', 'IL')
[1 row]
```

When you look at the data again with a SELECT statement, you see the new row:

SQL
```
select *
from publishers
pub_id pub_name               address              city              state
====== ===================== ==================== ================= =====
0736   New Age Books          1 1st St.            Boston            MA
0877   Binnet & Hardley       2 2nd Ave.           Washington        DC
1389   Algodata Infosystems   3 3rd Dr.            Berkeley          CA
0010   Pragmatics             4 4th Ln.            Chicago           IL
[4 rows]
```

You can remove the row with a DELETE statement.

SQL
```
delete from publishers
where pub_id - '0010'
[1 row deleted]
```

Data Definition

Other SQL commands, classified as **data definition** language or **DDL**, perform data definition operations, such as creating or removing objects like tables, indexes, and views. This statement sets up a table called `test` with two columns: one called `id` that holds integers, and another called `name` that holds up to fifteen characters.

SQL
```
create table test
(id  int,
name char (15) )
[table created]
```

You can SELECT from the `test` table, even before it has any data in it:

```
SQL
select *
from test
          id name
=========== ===============

[0 rows]
```

Data Administration

In the final category of SQL statements are **data administration**, or **data control**, commands. They allow you to coordinate the use of the database and maintain it in its most efficient state.

One important aspect of administration in a shared database system is the ability to control access to the data. The SQL keyword GRANT, controlling which users can access data, is a good example of an administrative command. Following is a GRANT statement that gives members of the `public` group (which includes all users) permission to select data from the `test` table:

```
SQL
grant select
on test
to public
[command executed]
```

Before we go on to consider the relational operations, remember that these remarks are strictly introductory—don't try to learn the details of SQL syntax yet.

Relational Operations

Three specific data retrieval (or query) operations are part of the definition of a relational database management system. The relational operations allow you to tell the system exactly what data you want to see.

- Projection selects columns.
- Selection (also called **restriction**) chooses rows.
- Join brings together data in related tables.

The physical and logical independence described earlier in this chapter means that you don't have to worry about where the data is physically stored, or how to find it—that's the database management system's problem. SQL is considered a **nonprocedural language** because it allows you to express what you want without specifying any of the details about where it's located or how to get it.

All three of the data retrieval operations are expressed with the SQL keyword SELECT. This can be confusing: In SQL, you use SELECT not only for the selection operation, but also for projections and joins.

To give you a bit more of the flavor of the all-important SELECT statement, here's a simplified version of its syntax:

SYNTAX

```
SELECT select_list
FROM table_list
WHERE search_conditions
```

The next subsections explain how this deceptively simple-looking statement is used to express all three relational operations.

Projection

The projection operation allows you to list (in the SELECT list) which *columns* you want to see. For example, if you want to see all the rows in the table that contain information about publishers, but only the columns that contain the publishers' names and identification numbers, you'd write this data retrieval statement:

SQL
```
select pub_id, pub_name
from publishers
```

Here are the results you would get:

Results
```
pub_id pub_name
====== ======================================
0736   New Age Books
0877   Binnet & Hardley
1389   Algodata Infosystems
[3 rows]
```

Once again, don't concern yourself with the SQL syntax at this point. Focus on understanding the conceptual point: *A projection specifies a subset of the columns in the table.* Note that the results of this projection (or any other relational operation) are displayed as a table. Result tables are sometimes called **derived tables** to distinguish them from the **base tables**, which contain the raw data.

Selection

The selection operation allows you to retrieve a subset of the rows in a table. To specify the rows you want, put conditions in a WHERE clause. The SELECT statement's WHERE clause specifies the criteria that a row must meet in order to be included in the selection. For example, if you want information about publishers located in California only, here's what you'd type:

```
SQL
select pub_id, pub_name, address, city, state
from publishers
where state = 'CA'
```

Here are the results you would get:

```
Results
pub_id pub_name               address             city            state
====== ==================== ================== =============== =====
1389   Algodata Infosystems  3 3rd Dr.          Berkeley        CA
[1 row]
```

You can combine projection and selection in many ways to zero in on just the columns and rows in a table you want to see.

Join

The join operation works on two or more tables at a time, combining the data so that you can compare and contrast information in your database. The join operation gives SQL and the relational model a good deal of their power and flexibility. You can find any relationship that exists among data elements, not just the relationships you anticipated when you designed your database.

When you "join" two tables, it's as if you're melding them together for the duration of the query. The join operation combines data by comparing values in specified columns and displaying the results.

The easiest way to understand the join operation is with an example. Let's suppose you want to know the names and publishers of all the books in the database. The name of each book is stored in the `titles` table. So is a good deal of other information about each book, including the identification number of its publisher (see Figure 1.3). However, the publisher's name isn't in the `titles` table—that information is in the `publishers` table.

The problem can be solved because both the `publishers` table and the `titles` table contain the publishers' identification numbers (`pub_id`). You can join the two tables in order to display the publisher's name along with the book's title (see Figure 1.4).

The system tests for every instance in which the two `pub_id` columns are the same; whenever there is a match, it creates a new row—containing columns from both tables—as the result of the join. Here's the query:

SQL
```
select title, pub_name
from titles, publishers
where publishers.pub_id = titles.pub_id
```

The `title` column in the SELECT clause comes from the `titles` table; the `pub_name` column comes from the `publishers` table. Projection can specify

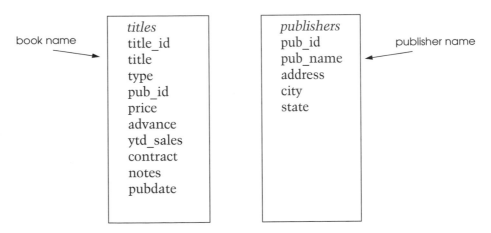

Figure 1.3 Columns in the `titles` **and** `publishers` **Tables**

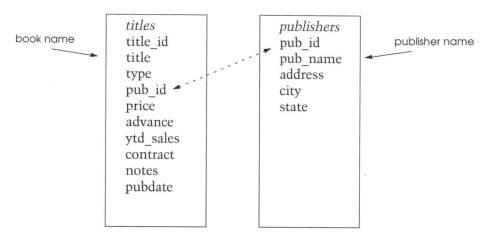

Figure 1.4 Shared Columns in titles **and** publishers

columns from several tables in the SELECT list. The FROM clause indicates the two tables that are to be joined; the WHERE clause says that rows in these tables are to be linked when the identification numbers in the two pub_id columns are the same.

Here are the results:

```
Results
title                                                    pub_name

======================================================  ==================
Emotional Security: A New Algorithm                     New Age Books
Prolonged Data Deprivation: Four Case Studies           New Age Books
You Can Combat Computer Stress!                          New Age Books
Is Anger the Enemy?                                      New Age Books
Life Without Fear                                        New Age Books
Computer Phobic and Non-Phobic Individuals:
   Behavior Variations                                  New Age Books
Silicon Valley Gastronomic Treats                       Binnet & Hardley
Sushi, Anyone?                                          Binnet & Hardley
Fifty Years in Buckingham Palace Kitchens               Binnet & Hardley
The Gourmet Microwave                                   Binnet & Hardley
Onions, Leeks, and Garlic: Cooking Secrets
   of the Mediterranean                                 Binnet & Hardley
The Psychology of Computer Cooking                      Binnet & Hardley
```

```
Secrets of Silicon Valley                    Algodata Infosystems
The Busy Executive's Database Guide          Algodata Infosystems
Cooking with Computers: Surreptitious
Balance Sheets                               Algodata Infosystems
But Is It User Friendly?                     Algodata Infosystems
Straight Talk About Computers                Algodata Infosystems
Net Etiquette                                Algodata Infosystems
[18 rows]
```

At this point in the discussion you might wonder if we're overselling the importance of the join operation. Why not just put all those columns in the same table in the first place? If the table gets big and unwieldy, why not simply use the projection operation to limit the number of columns that are displayed at one time?

Those are reasonable questions. The answer is that the number of columns in a table must often be limited for reasons of consistency (minimizing redundancy), convenience, and performance. The discussion of database design in the next chapter sets out guidelines for deciding which columns to put into which tables.

Alternatives for Viewing Data

A **view** is an alternative way of looking at the data in one or more tables. Views are sometimes called **virtual tables** or derived tables, as opposed to base tables.

A view is a frame through which you can see only the particular data that concerns you. You can derive a view from one or more database tables (or, for that matter, from other views), using any desired selection, projection, and join operations. Views allow you to create customized tables tailored to special needs. In effect, you capture a cluster of selection, projection, and join operations to use as the foundation for future queries.

The data you see when you look at a view (or "through" a view, as it's often put) is not actually stored in the database the way data in "real" or base tables is. It's important to realize that a view is not a copy of the data in another table. When you change data through a view, you're changing the real thing. Like selection results, a view looks like an ordinary database table, but it is a virtual, derived construct.

Views are set up with the SQL CREATE VIEW statement. You can make virtually any SELECT statement into a view simply by incorporating it into a

CREATE VIEW command. To make the previous example into a view, you would use the CREATE VIEW command shown here:

```
SQL
create view Books_and_Pubs
as
select title, pub_name
from titles, publishers
where publishers.pub_id = titles.pub_id
[view created]
```

When you select from the view, it displays results based on the query that you used to create it. In the following example, the SELECT statement WHERE clause constrains the results further so you see just one row. You don't need to include the join between publishers and titles in the query. It is part of the underlying view.

```
SQL
select *
from Books_and_Pubs
where title = 'Sushi, Anyone?'
title                     pub_name
========================  ==================
Sushi, Anyone?            Binnet & Hardley
[1 row]
```

In the ideal relational system, you would be able to display a view and operate on it almost exactly as you could any other table. In the real world, different versions of SQL place limitations on view manipulation, particularly with respect to updates. One of Codd's rules explicitly addresses view updatability, stipulating that a true relational system should allow all updates that are "theoretically" possible. Most relational database management systems fall short of his standards on this one.

Chapter 9 is devoted to views and includes a discussion of what a "theoretically updatable" view means.

NULLs

In the real world of information management, data is often missing or incomplete: You forgot to ask for a phone number; a respondent to a questionnaire refuses to divulge his age; a book has been contracted, but the publication date has not been set. Such missing information leaves gaping holes in your set of tidy tables.

The unsightliness of these holes is not the real problem, of course. The danger is that they might introduce inconsistencies into your database. In order to preserve the integrity of your data, the relational model, and Codd's rules, use the concept of **nulls** to handle missing information.

"NULL" does not mean zero or blank. Rather, it indicates that a value is unknown, unavailable, or inapplicable. Essentially the use of nulls changes two-valued logic (yes/no or something/nothing) into three-valued logic (yes/no/ maybe or something/nothing/not sure).

In the opinion of some, NULLs are not the perfect solution to the problem of missing information. However, they are an integral part of both the official SQL standard and the de facto industry standard. NULLs are such an important topic that they are covered in several chapters: Chapter 3 explains how to set up tables that allow nulls in certain columns; Chapter 4 touches on issues in selecting nulls; Chapter 5 considers nulls with ordering and aggregate functions; and Chapter 6 summarizes the issues regarding nulls in database management.

Security

The security issue can be summarized as the need to control who can use what data and for what purpose. The SQL GRANT and REVOKE commands allow certain privileged users to choose who will be authorized to look at or change database information. In most SQL implementations, access and data modification **permissions** can be controlled on the levels of both tables and columns.

The privileged users who bestow these permissions are the **owners** of databases and database objects (tables and views). A user owns a database or one of its objects by virtue of having created it with one of the SQL CREATE commands; some systems allow ownership to be transferred from the creator to another user.

Most multiuser systems designate another privileged user, higher on the totem pole than owners, who is often called the **system administrator** or **database administrator**. The user in this role often possesses wide powers to grant

and revoke permissions (and is also responsible for a variety of other maintenance and administrative tasks).

Views can be used as an additional security mechanism: Users can be
granted permission to access only the particular subset of data that's included
in a view. Views are covered in Chapter 9; the GRANT and REVOKE commands are covered in Chapter 10.

Integrity

Integrity is a serious and complex issue in relational database management.
In general, it means the consistency of the data in the database. Inconsistencies in data arise in several ways. System failure—a hardware problem, a
software bug, or a logical error in an application program—can introduce one
kind of inconsistency. Relational database management systems that protect
data from this type of inconsistency do so by guaranteeing that SQL commands either run to completion or are canceled. The processes by which this
guarantee is enforced are often called **transaction management**. Transactions
and SQL's method of handling them are discussed in Chapter 10.

Another kind of integrity, **entity integrity**, is a design issue. Entity integrity
requires that no primary key be allowed to have a null value.

A third variety of data integrity, **referential integrity**, is consistency among
pieces of information that are repeated in more than one table. For example, if
you correct an employee's improperly entered Social Security number in one
table, other tables that include employee information probably still reference
the old number, so you have to update them, too. *It's vital that when information is changed in one place, it is also changed in every other place it appears.*

Codd's rules firmly state that relational database management systems
should support not only entity and referential integrity but also additional
integrity constraints reflecting business policies or government regulations
and so forth. Furthermore integrity constraints must be

- Definable in the same high-level language used by the rest of the system
- Stored in the system catalogs, not in application programs

In the early days, only a few implementations of SQL met Codd's integrity
criteria, but this is changing. The 1992 ANSI SQL standard provides for **constraints** in the CREATE TABLE statements that can enforce referential integrity and business rules. Most vendors have implemented these new features in
some form. Constraints are covered in Chapter 3.

SQL Functions

Most commercial relational database management systems (and the ANSI standard, to a more limited extent) support SQL functions to work with character, numeric, and date data, as well as to convert from one datatype to another and to perform some conditional operations. These are covered in Chapter 11. There is also a group of functions for working with set results, and they are discussed in Chapters 5 and 6.

Here's an example of a query using the LENGTH function to find out how long each book title is. (The ORDER BY sorts the results by size to show how LENGTH works.)

SQL
```
select  title, length (title) as size
from titles
order by length(title)
```

title	size
Net Etiquette	13
Sushi, Anyone?	14
Life Without Fear	17
Is Anger the Enemy?	19
The Gourmet Microwave	21
But Is It User Friendly?	24
Secrets of Silicon Valley	25
Straight Talk About Computers	29
You Can Combat Computer Stress!	31
Silicon Valley Gastronomic Treats	33
The Psychology of Computer Cooking	34
The Busy Executive's Database Guide	35
Emotional Security: A New Algorithm	35
Fifty Years in Buckingham Palace Kitchens	41
Prolonged Data Deprivation: Four Case Studies	45
Cooking with Computers: Surreptitious Balance Sheets	52
Onions, Leeks, and Garlic: Cooking Secrets of the Mediterranean	63
Computer Phobic and Non-Phobic Individuals: Behavior Variations	63

[18 rows]

You can combine functions to get sophisticated results. The following example shows using the LENGTH function as a parameter of the MAX function to find the maximum title size. You could then use this value to decide how many characters of the title you need to display in reports (the defined length is 80 characters).

```
SQL
select max( length (title) )
from titles
max(length(titles.title))
==========================
                        63
[1 row]
```

Summary

This chapter introduces basic relational database concepts. A relational database management system must

- Represent all information in the database as tables
- Keep the logical representation of data independent from its physical storage characteristics
- Use one high-level language for structuring, querying, and changing the information in the database
- Support the main relational operations (selection, projection, join) and set operations such as union, intersection, difference, and division
- Support views, which allow the user to specify alternative ways of looking at data in tables
- Provide a method for differentiating between unknown values (nulls) and zero or blank
- Support mechanisms for security and authorization
- Protect data integrity through transactions and recovery procedures

In addition, most relational databases support features needed in the commercial world: stored procedures, triggers, and SQL functions. We do not treat the first two topics in any detail here because they vary so much from vendor to vendor. SQL functions are more standard. You'll find information about them in Chapter 11.

Now that you have a basic understanding of relational database systems, you may be impatient to get started. But before you can do any data retrieval or modification, you have to get data into the database. And before you can do that, you have to decide what the database should look like. Although creating a database and tables is very easy, designing a well-functioning database takes some skill. We cover the rules and practices for designing databases in Chapter 2.

Chapter 2

Designing Databases

In This Chapter

- Design Considerations
- Data Entities and Relationships
- The Normalization Guidelines
- Reviewing the Database

Design Considerations

The process of deciding what the database will look like is called **database design.** Designing a database involves choosing

- The tables that belong in the database
- The columns that belong in each table
- How tables and columns interact with each other

Database design is concerned with the *logical* structure of the database. In the relational model, decisions about logical design are completely independent of the database's *physical* storage and structure. The logical structure is also independent of what the end user eventually sees. That can be customized with views created by the designer (see Chapter 9 for details) or with front-end application programs.

Database design using the relational model offers some important advantages over the design process used in other database models:

- The independence of the logical design from both the physical design and the end user's view
- The flexibility of the database design—design decisions don't limit the questions you can ask about the data in the future

Because the relational model does not require you to define access paths among your data, you can query about any kind of logical relationship the database contains, not just the relationships for which you originally planned. (In this chapter, we assume that "you" are the database designer.)

On the other hand, relational systems have no *built-in* protections against poor design decisions, no automatic way to distinguish a good design from a bad one. There is simply no set of automated tools that can substitute for your understanding of relational design principles and procedures.

Database design, like some of the other issues touched on in this book, is a very large subject. Professional careers have been devoted to it, and hundreds of articles and dozens of books have been written about it—some of them extremely technical and bristling with jargon and abstract terminology, others aimed at casual users of personal computers. (The ones we've found most helpful are listed in Appendix E.)

While the discussion in this chapter is brief, and decidedly practical rather than theoretical, it is meant to give you enough understanding to design a moderately complex database. It will acquaint you with the jargon and the issues so that you'll be able to tackle more technical discussions of database design if you need to do so. The basic principles are the same whether the database you're designing is simple or complex.

Do You Need an Expert?

If you're working with a single-user system, the database is likely to be straightforward enough so that, with the help of this chapter, you can bootstrap yourself to design competence.

If you're working in a multiuser situation, on the other hand, the design and creation of the database is usually the job of a specialist. This is especially true if your application is critical to the mission of your organization and involves sharing data with other users. This specialist—who might be called system administrator, database administrator, or MIS specialist—is qualified by his or her experience in and understanding of the local computing environment, the organization's business policies, and the rules of relational database design. A database designer who is knowledgeable about all of these factors is more likely to provide a database that is easy to use and maintain, as well as conducive to efficiency and consistency.

Even if you'll be relying on an expert for database design, this chapter will help you become a better SQL user by showing you how to analyze the relationships among the data. A grasp of relational design issues is invaluable both in learning and practicing SQL and in maintaining, updating, or querying a database that someone else has set up. Furthermore, when it comes time to ask the design guru for help, knowledge of the ground rules will make your questions and requests more intelligent.

Data Definition and Customization

Like the rest of *The Practical SQL Handbook*, this chapter uses the `bookbiz` database as its main example. Once you've worked your way through this chapter and have come to understand how `bookbiz` is designed, you'll need to know how to put it online with the SQL CREATE commands—a process called data definition. We discuss data definition in Chapter 3.

Other issues connected to database design and data definition include customization (setting up views tailored to each end user's needs—see Chapter 9), security (deciding whom to authorize for what options on what data—see Chapter 10), and integrity (guaranteeing the consistency of related data items—mentioned here and treated in more detail in Chapters 3 and 10).

How to Approach Database Design

Discussions of database design for relational systems—this one included— often seem schizophrenic. On the one hand, you're told that the relational model makes database design intuitive and easy; on the other hand, you're told that unless your database is "simple" (whatever that is), you'll either have to refer to other sources (which sounds ominous), or let the gurus do it for you. So why bother to wade through endless explanations?

Recognizing this confusion, one relational theorist postulates that database design is often easier to do than to explain exactly what it was you did. In our attempt to explain exactly what to do when you design a database, we will encourage and educate your intuitive impulses, as well as briefly discuss two design aids: **normalization** and **entity-relationship modeling**.

Educating the intuition is mostly a matter of demonstrating a few mistakes that beginning designers are likely to make. Once the flaws have been pointed out, the correct structures become obvious by comparison.

As for the formal design methodologies, most experts stress that they are guidelines rather than rigid rules. The best way to describe the existence of real-world objects and the relationships among them is, to some degree, a subjective matter—almost as much in database design as in natural language. Often there's more than one correct solution to a design problem, and there is sometimes good reason to violate even the most basic design rule.

But this doesn't mean that the theories of database design are not useful. Even as a beginner, it's important that you understand the basics. As your experience grows, you will probably rely on the formal methodologies more and more, but don't let them tyrannize you.

Getting Started   Many discussions of relational database design focus almost entirely on how to apply the normalization rules. Basically, normalization means protecting your data integrity by avoiding duplicate data. This often results in splitting a table that initially seems to "make sense" into two or more related tables that can be "put back together" with the join operation. The technical term for this process is **non-loss decomposition**, which simply means splitting a table into several smaller tables without losing any information.

The normalization guidelines are most valuable as an after-the-fact check on your work. Once you have a pretty good idea which columns go into which tables, you can analyze them according to the normalization rules in order to make sure you haven't committed any database design *faux pas*. An understanding of normalization can also guide you as you build your design, but it's not a recipe for creating a database structure from scratch.

So how do you figure out what columns go where in the first place? What *is* the recipe? The answer is that there is no very precise method. However, you can get a good deal of help from entity-relationship modeling, analyzing the data in terms of

- The entities (objects or things) it describes
- The relationships (one-to-one, one-to-many, or many-to-many) between those entities

In practice, designing a database requires combining a thorough understanding of the world you're trying to model with the analysis techniques of entity-relationship modeling and normalization. Then you examine your results and do it again. Database design is usually an iterative process in which you keep getting closer and closer to what you want, but you often move back a step or two and redo earlier work as you refine your idea of what you need.

To give you a more concrete idea, here's an example of some steps you might follow when you design a database:

1. Investigate and think about the information environment you're modeling. Where will the information come from and in what form? How will

it be entered into the system and by whom? How frequently will it change? What is most critical in terms of response time and availability? How much of the universe of data do you actually need?

Examine all paper and online files and forms that are currently used to store and track the organization's data; consider also what kind of output is needed from the database—reports, purchase orders, statistical information—and for whom. In a shared database environment, you'll need to collect information by interviewing other people in the organization, either individually or in groups. Don't forget anyone who will be involved in any way with the data—generating it, handling it, changing it, querying it, making reports from it, and so on.

2. Make a list of the entities (things that are the subjects of the database), along with their properties or attributes. The entities are likely to wind up being tables (each row describing one thing, such as a person or a company or a book); the properties are likely to be columns in those tables (the person's salary, the company's address, the book's price). Of course, you can list all possible attributes first and then group them into entities, rather than starting with entities. Whichever method you choose, keep reviewing your work. Do the attributes really belong where you put them, or would they make more sense attached to a different entity? Do you need additional entities? More or different attributes? Are these entities really needed, or are they in some way outside the scope of this particular database?

3. As you work, find a systematic way to record the design decisions you're making, either on paper or with a text editor. Designers generally start with lists and then move to sketches of the tables and the relationships among them, called **data structure diagrams** or **entity-relationship (E-R) diagrams**.

4. Once you have made preliminary decisions about the entities and their attributes, make sure that each entity has an attribute (or group of attributes) that you can use to identify uniquely any row in the future table. This unique identifier is often called the logical primary key. If the natural primary key (author name, book title, company name) is not unique, you may have to look for a different attribute that fills this purpose (Social Security number for an author, ISBN number for a book) or add a column to serve as a surrogate key (assign unique company identifiers or generate incremental order numbers, for example).

5.   Next, consider the relationships between the entities. Are they one-to-many (one publisher has many titles, but each title has only one publisher) or many-to-many (an author can write multiple books, and a book can have multiple authors)? Do you have ways to join the data in one proposed table to that in other related tables? **Foreign keys** (columns that match a primary key in a related table) serve this function. While `pub_id` in `publishers` is a primary key, `pub_id` in `titles` is a foreign key.

6.   After you have a draft of the database design, look at it as a whole and analyze it according to the normalization guidelines (discussed later in this chapter) to find logical errors. Correct any violations of the normal forms—or make a conscious decision to override the normalization guidelines in the interests of ease of comprehension or performance. Document the reasons for such decisions.

7.   Now you're ready to put the database online and add some prototype data, using SQL for both steps. Experiment with some of the queries and reports you think you'll need. You may want to make some benchmark tests (see Chapter 10) to try out a few variations on the design.

8.   Reevaluate what you've done in light of how satisfied you are with the results. You'll probably find you need to add some entities you overlooked. You may be able to do without some that "logically" belong but actually play no role in the applications using this data.

Most of the rest of this chapter is devoted to an explanation of how we approached the design of the `bookbiz` database. This detailed, step-by-step discussion should help you understand the database design process.

The Characteristics of a Good Design   What is a good database design—a "clean" design, as the jargon has it? Broadly speaking, a good design

*   Makes your interactions with the database easier to understand
*   Guarantees the consistency of the database
*   Paves the way for the highest performance your system can deliver

Some factors that make a database easy to understand are not technically part of database design. Practically speaking, wide tables (many columns) are difficult to read and understand because they don't fit on your computer screen or on a printed page. On the other hand, splitting data into many small tables makes it hard to see relationships. Settling on the right number of columns is a compromise between ease of comprehension and adherence to the normalization guidelines.

A well-designed database helps prevent the introduction of inconsistent information and the unintentional deletion of information. It accomplishes these ends by minimizing the unnecessary duplication of data within tables and making it possible to support referential integrity among tables. The perils of data inconsistency are explained in more detail later in this chapter.

Finally, a well-designed database is a prerequisite for satisfactory performance. Again, the number of columns in a table is important: The retrieval of data can be slower if results have to come from many tables rather than from one table. On the other hand, huge tables can require the system to handle more data than may be absolutely necessary to answer a particular query. In other words, the number and size of tables affect performance. (Also crucial for performance purposes are appropriate choices about which columns to index and what kind of indexes to put on them. Indexing is a matter of physical design rather than logical database design; it is discussed in Chapters 3 and 10.)

These are some of the benefits of good database design. A bad design, on the other hand, can

- Return incorrect query results
- Foster misunderstandings of query results
- Increase the risk of introducing inconsistencies in the data
- Force redundant data entry
- Make life difficult if you need to change the structure of the tables that you've built and filled with data

No single solution can fully satisfy all the objectives of good design. Frequently, you juggle trade-offs, making choices based on the needs and uses of the application for which the database is being designed.

Introducing the Sample Database

The bookbiz database is not a real-world database but simply a learning tool. Its primary purpose is to provide you with a small collection of interesting data to manipulate as you study SQL syntax and semantics.

The bookbiz database is about a fictitious publishing company that has three subsidiary publishing lines. The database stores information that editors, administrators, and executives might want about books, their authors, their editors, and the company's financial arrangements. This database can produce many kinds of reports summarizing current sales, comparing different book lines, discovering which editors work with which authors, and so on. In real life, the database would probably support many other uses and many more reports.

Users of the bookbiz database can pose many different questions, including these:

- Which authors live in California?
- Which business books cost more than $19.95?
- Who has written the greatest number of books?
- How much do we owe the author of *Life Without Fear*?
- What's the average advance paid for all the psychology books?
- How would increasing the price of all the cookbooks by 10 percent affect royalty payments?
- How are sales of the computer subsidiary doing?
- Which books are most popular?

As the database designer, don't try to just imagine which questions are most important to the future users of the database you're designing. You need to research users' needs by reviewing current data collection and retrieval methods and by interviewing your users individually, in groups, or both.

TIP

One important area of investigation is the organization's business rules and policies that affect the data. The policies of the publisher for which bookbiz is being designed include these:

- An author may have written more than one book.
- A book may have been a collaborative project of more than one author.
- The order of the authors' names on the title page is crucial information, as is the percentage of the royalties each will collect.
- An editor may be working on more than one book, and a single book may be assigned more than one editor.
- A sales order may be for one or many titles.

Data Entities and Relationships

We begin designing bookbiz using a somewhat simplified version of entity-relationship modeling. At the most basic level, entity-relationship modeling (also called entity modeling) means identifying

- The things—entities—about which information will be stored in the database system
- The properties of these entities
- The relationships among the entities

Entities: Things with an Independent Existence

Let's start by considering some of the bookbiz database entities. If we ignore for the moment most of the financial information that bookbiz tracks, a preliminary list of entities might look like this:

- The authors who have written books published by the company
- The books themselves
- The editors working for the company
- The subsidiary publishing houses owned by the company

Each item in this list is an entity with an independent existence in the world under consideration, that is, the world of the bookbiz database. Each is represented in the database by a table. (Other kinds of data elements are also represented by tables, but that's jumping ahead.)

The entities have certain properties that are to be recorded in the database. Among the properties are

```
book's name
book's price
book's publication date
author's name
author's address
author's telephone number
editor's name
editor's address
editor's phone number
publisher's name
publisher's address
```

Each property or attribute of the entity in question (the author, book, editor, or publishing subsidiary) is a potential column in the database. Column names should be selected for clarity, to describe the kinds of values the column holds, and brevity, to minimize both typing and the width of displays.

The list of entities and properties we've identified can be seen as a first tentative step in deciding on the tables and columns to be included in the database. You might sketch these decisions like this:

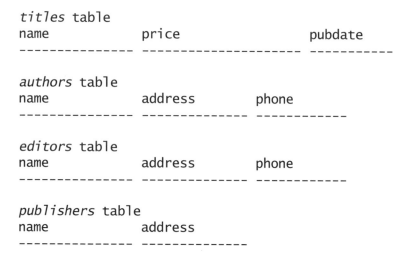

```
titles table
name                   price                    pubdate
--------------         --------------------     -----------

authors table
name                   address         phone
--------------         --------------  ------------

editors table
name                   address         phone
--------------         --------------  ------------

publishers table
name                   address
--------------         --------------
```

Diagramming Entities and Attributes   Another way to view the information is in an entity-relationship diagram, as shown in Figure 2.1. The usual convention is to display each table as a box with columns listed inside.

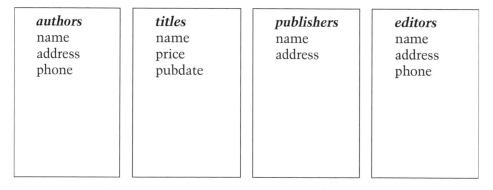

Figure 2.1 A Preliminary bookbiz **Sketch**

This sketch of four tables, each with several columns, is a first stab at the structure of the database; you can imagine that the tables will contain multiple rows of data. Each row in a table represents an **occurrence** (or **instance**) of the entity, that is, a single book, author, editor, or publishing company.

Primary Keys   One of the jobs of the database design is to provide a way to distinguish among entity occurrences so that the system can retrieve a particular row. As you might have guessed, rows (representing occurrences of entities) arc distinguished from each other by the values of the table's primary key. In fact as we've said, the (informal) definition of a primary key is the column or combination of columns that uniquely identifies the row.

What is the primary key for each of these tables? Consider the authors table. Of the columns identified so far, name is the obvious candidate for the primary key: An author's name distinguishes him or her from other authors, but the name column is problematic as a primary key for several reasons. First, the value in name is made up of the author's first name and last name. Combining first and last names in one column is a bad idea, if only because it would be difficult (in many systems, impossible) to sort authors alphabetically by last name. So the first necessary change is to split the name column (in both authors and editors) into two columns (see Figure 2.2).

Now, with regard to the question of identifying the primary key of the authors table, it might seem as though the combination of the columns au_lname and au_fname is the right choice. In fact, that combination would work pretty well, until the table grew large enough to contain duplicate names. Once there are two Mary Smiths, for example, the au_lname-au_fname combination would no longer uniquely identify each author.

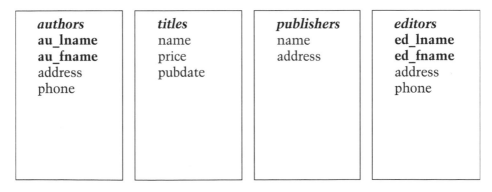

Figure 2.2 Splitting the Authors' and Editors' Names into Two Columns

Another problem with using values like names as unique identifiers is the frequency with which they are entered incorrectly. It's easy to misspell names: Imagine a data entry clerk on the phone entering a new record about Anne Ringer, or is it *Ann* Ringer? Other kinds of proper names, like names of companies or organizations, are even worse. How many variations on data entry might there be on a company name, for example: AT&T, A.T. and T., Ma Bell, and so on. To a computer, these different names are all different companies.

Finally, consider volatility. Personal names are likely to change, due to marriage or divorce. Company names may succumb to rebranding or acquisition.

For these reasons, it's usually a good idea to create a separate column explicitly designed to serve as the primary key. Real-world examples of such unique identifiers are common: Social Security numbers, employee identification numbers, license plate numbers, purchase order numbers, student identification numbers, airline flight numbers, and so on.

In the `authors` and `editors` tables, we'll use Social Security numbers. For the `titles` and `publishers` tables, we'll arbitrarily assign some identifying codes. As a recordkeeping convention, we'll underline these columns to show they are primary keys (see Figure 2.3).

Choosing and setting up the column(s) for a table's primary key is one of the crucial steps in database design.   **TIP**

Despite the importance of primary keys, early versions of SQL had no syntax for designating them. The 1992 ANSI standard for SQL, now adopted by

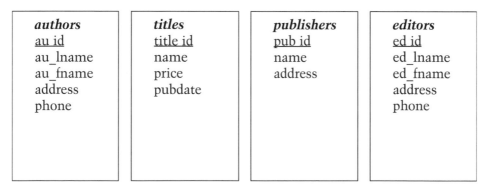

Figure 2.3 Defining Primary Keys

most vendors, supports the PRIMARY KEY clause in the CREATE TABLE statement (see Chapter 3 for details). Vendors have also developed their own implementation-specific methods to deal with this important concept.

One-to-Many Relationships

At this point we have structures for four tables in the `bookbiz` database: `authors`, `titles`, `editors`, and `publishers`. Some of the properties of each of the entities described by the tables have been specified, and a primary key has been identified for each table.

However, you may have noticed that certain important relationships among the data are not yet represented in the proposed design. For example, there's nothing in these four tables that tells you about the connection between a particular publisher and the books it puts out.

The relationship between publishers and books can be described as **one-to-many**: Each book has only one publisher, while each publisher can produce many books. One-to-many relationships among data are often written as *1-to-N* or *1:N*.

Representing the Relationship How can you represent this one-to-many relationship? In the `bookbiz` database, a first impulse might be to add a column for `title_id` in the `publishers` table, as shown in Figure 2.4.

The `title_id` column in the `publishers` table is a foreign key. You can use it to point to specific rows in the `titles` table and join title and publisher information. Unfortunately, this proposed solution sends your database design off in the wrong direction. Remember the data relationship we're mod-

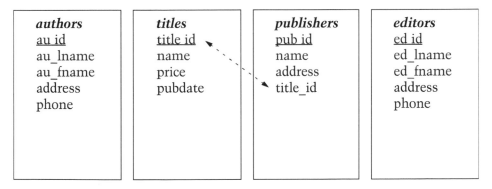

Figure 2.4 Adding a Foreign Key

eling—one publisher, many books—and consider what happens whenever a new book is published. You'll add a new row to `titles`, with book name, price, and so on.

title_id	title	price	date
BU2075	You Can Combat Computer Stress!	2.99	6/30/85

For each row in `titles`, you'll have to add a row to `publishers`. The `publishers` row will repeat three columns of existing information (publisher number, name, and address) and add one column of new information (`title_id`) to point to the fuller description in the `titles` table.

pub_id	pub_name	address	**title_id**
0736	New Age Books	1 1st St. Boston MA	**BU2075**

Recall that one of the goals of database design is to control redundancy because redundancy introduces opportunities for error. A better solution is to add a `publishers` foreign key to the `titles` table (see Figure 2.5).

When a new book comes out, add a row (with a `pub_id` column) to the `titles` table. You don't need to do anything to the `publishers` table unless the company takes on a new subsidiary.

title_id	title	price	date	**pub_id**
BU2075	You Can Combat Computer Stress!	2.99	6/30/85	**0736**

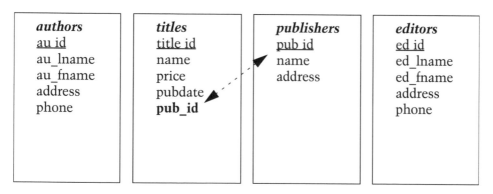

Figure 2.5 Changing the Foreign Key

With these changes a structure begins to emerge:

- The `publishers` table has one row for each publisher.
- The `titles` table has one row for each book.
- Publisher ID numbers are repeated in the `titles` table because there are many books for each publisher, but that's far less redundancy than would occur with other options.

You can use the logical connection between the `pub_id` columns in `titles` and `publishers` for joining the two tables. In other words, *this design is planned with the join operation in mind to allow users to retrieve information about publishers and titles in one query.*

In the `publishers` table, `pub_id` is the primary key. In the `titles` table, the `pub_id` column is a foreign key. The relational model requires that one-to-many relationships be represented by means of primary key/foreign key pairings.

Foreign Keys   Like the concept of primary key, the concept of foreign key is crucial in database design. Informally, a foreign key is a column (or combination of columns) in one table, the values of which match those of the primary key in some other table.

A consideration of the logical relationship between the information in the primary and foreign key columns introduces some further questions. What happens in the `pub_id` column of the `titles` table if the row describing the publisher is deleted from or changed in the `publishers` table? Should the description of a book be allowed to refer to a publisher ID number if that publisher no longer exists in the database? It doesn't make sense logically, and it violates the definition of a foreign key, which requires the value in a foreign key column(s) to match the value in a primary key column somewhere in the database. However, this is not an unusual situation in real life. How you handle it depends on your business rules.

A complete database design should include planning for primary key/foreign key consistency (or referential integrity). For example,

- When a publisher's ID number is updated in or deleted from the `publishers` table, the system should automatically reproduce the change in the `titles` table, either by updating all corresponding values in the `titles` table `pub_id` column or by cascading (propagating) the deletions in `publishers` to `titles` rows with matching `pub_id`s.
- When a new title is added, the system should have a way of verifying that the associated `pub_id` is valid, that is, that it exists in the `publishers` table.

At this point, just make a note of these issues. The next chapter gives hints on how to handle some primary key/foreign key issues with the REFERENCES constraints in the CREATE TABLE statement. Vendors also have introduced implementation-specific ways to control integrity, such as SQL extensions for procedural code that can be executed in the database, often called procedures or triggers (discussed in Chapter 10).

Many-to-Many Relationships

After identifying all the one-to-many relationships in the `bookbiz` database and associating them with primary key/foreign key pairings, the next step is to consider other kinds of data relationships. For example, how are authors and books related?

Some books are written by more than one author, and some authors have written more than one book. In other words, authors and books have a **many-to-many** relationship (often written as *N-to-N*, or *N:N*, and sometimes called an **association**). According to entity-relationship theory, associations in relational databases should be represented as tables of their own. In other words, the `bookbiz` database needs a table for authors, a table for titles, and a table to represent the association between them, as shown in Figure 2.6.

The `titleauthors` table represents the many-to-many relationship between authors and books. It is a base table just like `titles` and `authors`, but it is an association rather than an independent entity. When a user of the `bookbiz` database wants information about who wrote which books, he or she writes a join query that uses the `titleauthors` table as a connecting table between `titles` and `authors`.

The `titleauthors` and `titles` tables join on their respective `title_id` columns; `titleauthors` and `authors` join on each table's `au_id` column. In other words, `title_id` in `titleauthors` is a foreign key whose matching primary key is `title_id` in `titles`; `au_id` in `titleauthors` is the foreign key whose matching primary key is `au_id` in `authors`.

What is the primary key in `titleauthors`? Neither the author ID nor the title ID uniquely identifies rows in `titleauthors`: The IDs of titles with more than one author are repeated, as are the IDs of authors who have written more than one book. However, each title ID/author ID combination *is* unique. The primary key of `titleauthors`, then, is the combination of `title_id` and `au_id`.

The `editors` and `titles` tables have a similar relationship. An editor can work on more than one book, and a book can have multiple editors. This many-to-many relationship also calls for a connecting table.

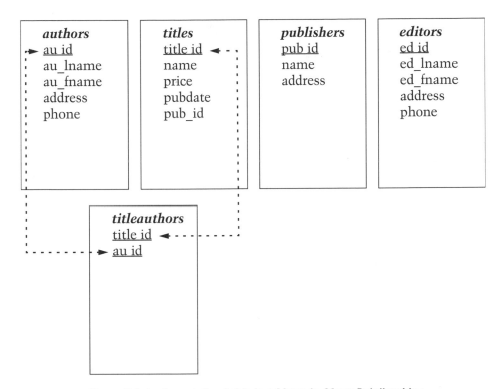

Figure 2.6 An Associating Table in a Many-to-Many Relationship

One-to-One Relationships

Take a final look at the entities. If you find a one-to-one (1:1) relationship between two tables, you might be better off collapsing them into one table. However, maintaining a 1:1 relationship could improve response speed in queries. For example, if you have information about titles that you seldom use (notes on copyright information, lists of change pages, for example), you might want to keep it in a separate table so that you don't have to access the information when running common queries. Generally speaking, you should avoid 1:1 structures when you first design a database, unless you know your data very well.

The Entity-Relationship Approach Summarized

Entity-relationship modeling is much larger, more precise, and more detailed than the procedures that we discussed so briefly here indicate. However, the approach just outlined can help you design a good database that checks out against the next design methodology to be considered, the normalization rules. Before we turn to that topic, here is a review list of the basic steps discussed so far:

1. Represent each independent entity (book, author, publisher, editor, employee, department, student, course, company, and so on) as a base table.

2. Represent each property of an entity (author's address, book's price, and so on) as a column of the entity's table.

3. Make sure each table has a primary key. The key may be an existing property (a name) or an artificial one that you add (a Social Security number, an order number), or a combination of two or more properties. At any rate, it must uniquely describe each row.

4. Locate one-to-many relationships between tables. Check that there is a foreign key column(s) in the "many" table pointing to the primary key column(s) in the "one" table. Consider the referential integrity constraints associated with each foreign key.

5. Represent each many-to-many relationship (or association) as a "connecting table" between the two tables that participate in the association. Include in this connecting table foreign keys that point to the entity tables. The primary key of the connecting table is often the combination of those foreign keys.

6. Collapse 1:1 relationships into a single table, where appropriate.

After each pass, look at your needs again. Have you incorporated the business rules? Can you get the information you need? Such a check against the bookbiz requirements reveals a few shortcomings: There's no way to record author order or royalty split. There's also no notation for contracts, and you need to keep track of advances. Sales are another topic not covered in this design. With these points in mind, you might modify the E-R diagram as in Figure 2.7, adding new attributes and entities, and using arrows to show the relationships between tables. If you're not sure where an attribute (such as

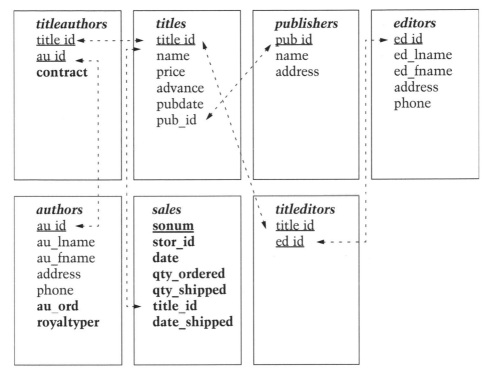

Figure 2.7 A Fuller E-R Diagram

author order) goes, don't worry. Get it listed. You'll go through more analysis—attributes, entities, and relationships—before you settle on a final form.

The Normalization Guidelines

Basically, the normalization guidelines are a set of data design standards called the **normal forms**. Five normal forms are widely accepted, although many more have been proposed. Making your tables match these standards is called normalization.

The normal forms progress in order from first through fifth. Each form implies that the requirements of the previous forms have been met. If you follow normalization rule number one, your data will be in first normal form. If you follow normalization rule number three, your data will be in third normal form as well as in first and second normal form.

Following the normalization guidelines usually means splitting tables into two or more tables with fewer columns, designing primary key/foreign key relationships into the new, smaller tables so that they can be reconnected with the join operation.

One of the main advantages of splitting tables according to the normalization guidelines is the reduction of data redundancy within tables. This may seem confusing when the existence of matching primary key/foreign key hooks means that these columns are duplicated. But *controlled duplication* is not the same thing as redundancy. In fact, the maintenance of intentional duplication (that is, consistency) between primary and foreign keys is a major purpose of referential integrity.

The normalization guidelines, like entity-relationship modeling, were developed as part of the academic work on database theory. While they are extremely useful, they can be followed too slavishly. Most database designers find that putting their data in third or fourth normal form is usually as far as they need to go.

First Normal Form

First normal form requires that at each row-and-column intersection, there must be one and only one value and that value must be atomic. There can be no repeating groups in a table that satisfies first normal form.

This design principle reveals a problem with the new `sales` table. How will you handle a single sales order that includes multiple books, as shown in Figure 2.8? The general information is at the top of the sales order form: the order

---

Bookbiz Sales Order Form

Order # **14**   Store **7131**   Date: 5/29/2000

Item #	Title	# Ordered	# Shipped	Fulfillment
1.	PS1372	20	20	May 29 2000
2.	PS2106	25	25	Apr 29 2000
3.	PS3333	15	10	
4.	PS7777	25	25	Jun 13 2000
5.				
6.				

Figure 2.8 A bookbiz Sales Order Form

number, store number, and order date. Each numbered line contains details on a title. Lines used varies from order to order.

Recording multiple book numbers in one `title_id` column, as shown in Figure 2.9, violates first normal form. Adding columns like `title1` or `title2` is just a disguise for repeating groups and leaves you with the same problems. It's not a great solution, practically speaking; as soon as a sales order includes a third book, you'll have to restructure the table again, adding a `title3` column. Since all data must be represented in regular rectangular tables, multiple entries just don't fit the model.

Where there are repeating columns, the correct design involves a **master table** (`sales`) for the sales order as a whole and a **detail table** (`salesdetails`) to hold information for individual order lines in the sales order (Figure 2.10). Notice that entity-relationship principles would have led to the same conclusion since this is a one-to-many structure (one sales order, many lines).

While you're looking at repeating fields, also make a note to break up any compound columns into their elements: `address` needs to have separate columns for `city` and `state`, for example.

Second Normal Form

The second normalization rule applies only in tables whose primary keys consist of multiple columns. It states that *every non-key column must depend on the entire primary key.* A table must not contain a non-key column that pertains to only part of a composite primary key. Putting a table into second normal form requires making sure that all the nonprimary key columns (the columns that give information about the subject but do not uniquely define it) relate to the entire primary key and not just to one of its components.

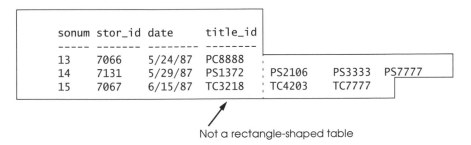

Not a rectangle-shaped table

Figure 2.9 Tables Must Be Rectangular

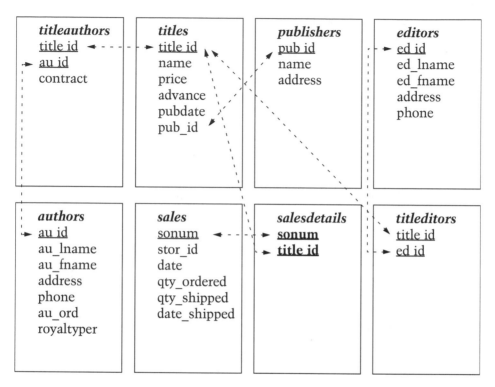

Figure 2.10 Breaking the sales **Table into** sales **and** salesdetails

To illustrate, look at the `contract` column in the `titleauthors` table (Figure 2.10). Does it apply to each author-title combination? If each author on a book has a separate contract, it does, but if the company signs contracts only when all authors are in agreement, it doesn't.

In this case, your company's legal division informs you that a contract is about a book, not about each individual author, and you move the column to the `titles` table (Figure 2.11). This illustrates why database design is tricky: Your decisions often depend on the particular business model your company uses.

To summarize: Second normal form requires that *no non-key column be a fact about a subset of the primary key.* It applies when the primary key is made up of more than one column and is irrelevant when the primary key is one column only.

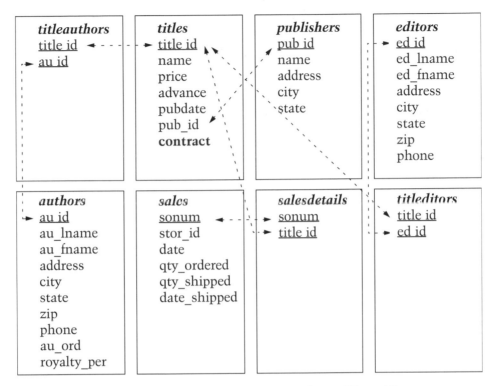

Figure 2.11 The bookbiz E-R Diagram after Second Normal Form

Third Normal Form

Third normal form applies the principle addressed by second normal form in a more general way: It's not limited to composite primary keys. Third normal form requires that *no non-key column depend on another non-key column.* Each non-key column must be a fact about the primary key column.

In the `authors` table, the primary key is `au_id`. When you check each column, you find that `au_ord` (the position of an author's name on a multi-author book) is not about an individual author (`au_id`) because an author might have several books and might occupy a different position on each (first, second, or third author). Author order really concerns each author-title relationship. The same is true of `royaltyper`. Both of these columns belong in the `titleauthors` table.

The `qty_ordered` and `qty_shipped` columns in the `sales` table also illustrate this principle. They concern individual line items, not the whole sales order, and should be moved to the `salesdetails` table.

The `date_shipped` column is more of a puzzle:

- If orders are shipped only when all line items are ready, `date_shipped` applies to the order as a whole and should go in the `sales` table.
- If items are shipped as they become available, the column belongs in the `salesdetails` table.

Since books are often out of print or otherwise unavailable, we'll assume the second model. The revised diagram is shown in Figure 2.12.

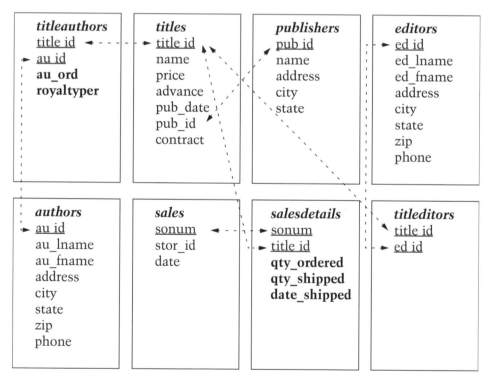

Figure 2.12 The `bookbiz` **E-R Diagram after Third Normal Form**

Analyzing the structures of these tables, you'll see that they satisfy both second and third normal forms:

- They satisfy second normal form because every non-key column is a fact about the entire primary key.
- They satisfy third normal form because no non-key column is a fact about another non-key column.

To summarize: Every non-key column must describe the key, the whole key, and nothing but the key.

Fourth Normal Form

Fourth normal form forbids independent one-to-many relationships between primary key columns and non-key columns. We'll use a rather unlikely example as an illustration: One author can have many cars and many pets, but there is no connection between cars and pets, even though each is legitimately related to a particular author.

```
au_lname    car                         pet
----------  --------------------------  --------
Ringer      1987 Chevy Nova             Rover
Ringer      1994 Volvo Station Wagon
Bennet      1990 VW Rabbit              Spot
Green                                   Valiant
Green       1989 Toyota Corolla         Fluffy
Green                                   Sam
```

Putting these two different kinds of information in the same table can lead to unsightly blanks where there are more pets than cars (as in Green's case) or more cars than pets (as in Ringer's case). Deleting a car or a pet (if a car dies or a pet moves to another home) could also cause blanks in rows.

The problem here is with the spurious relationship that seems to exist between cars and pets by virtue of their positional association in the row. It is better to put each of these entities in a separate table and to record their relationship to an author by using the author ID as a foreign key column. For example,

```
car                     au_id
----------------------- ----------
1987 Chevy Nova          998-72-3567
1994 Volvo Station Wagon 998-72-3567
1990 VW Rabbit           409-56-7008
1989 Toyota Corolla      213-46-8915

pet      au_id
-------  --------------------
Rover    998-72-3567
Spot     409-56-7008
Valiant  213-46-8915
Fluffy   213-46-8915
Sam      213-46-8915
```

You can go further with normal forms (fifth normal form and Boyce-Codd normal form), but these topics are beyond the scope of this book.

Reviewing the Database Design

Let's review the process by which the design of the bookbiz database was developed. We started by proposing four tables: authors, titles, publishers, and editors. It seems intuitive to design a table for each of these things; the entity-relationship approach states explicitly that each independent entity be represented by a base table. Entity-relationship theory also called for two more base tables—one to model the association among titles and authors (titleauthors), and one for the association among titles and editors (titleditors). We later added the sales and salesdetails tables.

That leaves only one bookbiz table undescribed: the roysched table, which lists the royalty rate to which authors are entitled as a function of the starting rate and the number of books sold. The roysched table is a **lookup table** used primarily for reference purposes. Its data will not change unless the royalty schedule itself changes—which would happen only if an author's contract were renegotiated or a new title added.

That makes nine tables in all.

Before we go into more detail about the full bookbiz database, take a look at the final data structure diagram (Figure 2.13). Each box in the diagram represents a table, with its name and the names of its columns inside it. The lines connecting the boxes represent relationships among the tables, showing the

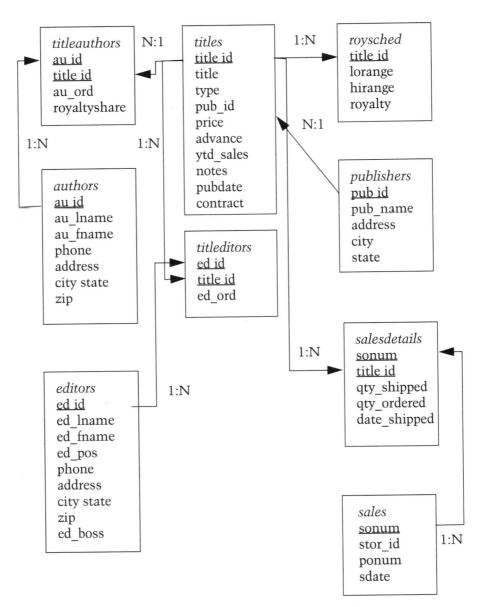

Figure 2.13 Data Structure Diagram for bookbiz

anticipated joins between them. (Other joins are also possible—these are just the explicitly planned ones.)

The arrowhead on one end of the line between two tables indicates a many-to-one relationship between the tables. For example, there can be many titles to one publisher, but there can't be many publishers to one title, so the arrowhead is on the `titles` side. The N:1 notation near the line means the same thing (many titles, one publisher). Some diagrams use a multiheaded arrow on the "many" side of the line.

Summarizing the `bookbiz` Database

Let's take a closer look at the nine tables in the `bookbiz` database to better familiarize you with the material on which the examples in the rest of *The Practical SQL Handbook* are based. (There are more `bookbiz` details in Appendix D.)

The `bookbiz` database keeps track of the activities of three subsidiary publishing companies. Since the fiscal arrangements of the subsidiaries are not independent, the parent publisher has chosen to maintain a single database.

The `publishers` table contains information about the three publishing lines: their identification numbers, names, and addresses.

For each author under contract with any of the publishers, the `authors` table contains an identification number (Social Security number), first and last name, and address information. The `editors` table contains similar information about each editor, with the addition of a position column that describes the type of work the editor does (acquisitions or project management).

For each book that has been or is about to be published, the `titles` table contains an identification number, name, type, publisher identification number, price, advance, year-to-date sales, contract status, comments, and publication date. The numbers in the `ytd_sales` column, which will change as more books are sold, might be kept current in one of several ways:

- By making periodic entries using the data modification commands
- By coding logic into an application program that automatically updates `ytd_sales` whenever a sale is entered into the `salesdetails` table
- By using SQL to define a **trigger** that accomplishes the same automatic updating. (Triggers, not covered in the 1992 ISO-ANSI SQL standard, are provided as extensions by a number of relational database management systems. See Chapter 10.)

The titles and authors are represented in separate tables that can be linked with a third table, the `titleauthors` table. For each book, `titleauthors` contains a row for every author involved, with information on the title ID, the author ID, the author cover credit order (which name comes first), and the royalty split among the authors of a book. The `titleditors` table similarly links the titles and their editors. Instead of cover credit order, it lists editing order so that it's possible to find who was the first or last editor.

The `roysched` table lists the unit sales ranges and the royalty connected with each range. The royalty is some percentage of the net receipts from sales. The percentage is used to calculate the amount due each author based on sales of his or her book.

The `sales` table has top-level information about each purchase order received from bookstores: sales order number (assigned by the publisher), store identification, purchase order number (assigned by the store), and date. The `salesdetails` table contains information about each line in the purchase order (assuming any purchase order may involve more than one book): title, quantity ordered, quantity shipped, and date shipped.

Of course, a real publisher's database would be much more complex, with tables for stores, employees, distributors, production costs, vendors, subcontractors, and the like. (As an exercise, you might try sketching some of these tables and deciding how they would relate to the tables already in `bookbiz`.) However, these nine tables do present enough material to work with for learning SQL, and they are used throughout this book.

Testing Your Database Design

Once you've come up with a proposed design for your database, you should create the tables and insert some data. (The next chapter gives detailed information on these procedures.) Then you should test your design by running queries and updating the data. Your tests may reveal oversights in the design.

TIP

Database designs are seldom satisfactory when based entirely on theory. It's essential to play with your design interactively before undertaking serious production efforts—especially if you plan to use it in an application that will involve thousands of lines of programming code and tens of thousands of rows of data. Don't wait until you've invested hundreds of hours in a flawed design: You can avoid problems by working interactively with a prototype of the database.

Other Database Definition Considerations

If you were about to put a real-world database online, you'd have several additional critical issues to consider before proceeding: indexing, security, and integrity.

Deciding which columns to index and what kind of index is best for each column is an important part of database implementation. It is covered in Chapter 3.

Security is discussed in Chapter 10.

Planning for data integrity is a major part of database design. It involves setting up a system to make sure changes to one piece of data apply to all copies of that data anywhere in the database, so that you won't end up with orphans or inaccuracies. An example using bookbiz might be discovering that an author's ID number was incorrect. If you changed it only in the authors table, you'd never again be able to find out what books that author had written because that author's ID number in titleauthors would no longer match the ID number in authors. In order to access the information in titleauthors, you'd have to make sure that when the author ID changed in authors, it also changed in titleauthors.

We'll assume you've considered these issues as you developed your design and made some mental notes. You'll learn how to implement SQL-92 referential constraints in the next chapter. Other integrity issues, not yet supported by all vendors, are deferred to Chapter 10.

Summary

This chapter walks you through the steps of database design, using the sample database bookbiz:

- You start off looking at some basic considerations for database design, including characteristics of good and bad design.
- Next, you look at how you define attributes and entities and what their relationships to each other mean.
- To make sure every column is in the right table, you check columns and tables closely against the normalization rules.
- Finally, you look at the database as a whole. Does it work? Can you get the reports you need?

Once the database design is in place, you can create the database and its tables and add data. Chapter 3 covers the SQL DDL and DML commands for creating objects and adding data.

Chapter 3

Creating and Filling a Database

In This Chapter

- From Theory to Practice
- Working with Databases
- Creating Simple Tables
- Creating Indexes
- Creating Tables with SQL-92 Constraints
- Changing and Deleting Databases and Objects
- Adding, Changing, and Removing Data

From Theory to Practice: Installing bookbiz

Once you've designed your database on paper, as discussed in the previous chapter, you're ready to put it online. Using the SQL CREATE commands, you can tell your relational database management system the name, structure, and other characteristics of your database objects. You add data to the database with the INSERT command.

If you use the Sybase Adaptive Server Anywhere compact disc distributed with this book (with full create and query capabilities for 60 days), you won't need to type the CREATE or INSERT commands: The bookbiz database has already been set up for you. Just load the program on your PC.

The CD also contains the scripts (sets of SQL commands) used to create the bookbiz database and its data. You can use these scripts if you prefer to put the bookbiz database on your own database management system or you need to recreate it on Adaptive Server Anywhere (perhaps after some experimentation that inadvertently removed tables). The complete structure of bookbiz and statements for entering all of its data are in Appendix D.

Whatever your situation, here's how you get started:

- If you will be using Adaptive Server Anywhere, just follow the directions in the *readPSH4* file to install the software and the bookbiz database. You don't need to type CREATE statements you see in the book, but if you want to follow along or try variants, modify the object name (from create titles to create titlestest, for example). SQL does not allow multiple objects with the same name.
- To run the database on your own relational database management system, check the *creates inserts* and *creates* directories on the CD. They contain the CREATE and INSERT statements for the bookbiz database on Sybase Adaptive Server Enterprise, Microsoft SQL Server, Oracle, and Informix. If you are using a different version of one of these systems or a different front end, you may need to edit the file you choose.
- For RDBMSs not among those included, choose the file that seems closest to your system, and then make changes. For example, you may need to modify datatype names. You may also need to substitute a different command terminator (GO or semicolon are used in most of the files).

Distinguishing SQL Examples and Syntax

This is the first chapter for which you'll actually be sitting at a terminal and typing commands, so now is the time to get familiar with this book's

- SQL example conventions
- SQL syntax conventions

An *example* is a SQL command that you might actually type, just as it appears (see Figure 3.1).

```
select pub_id, pub_name, address, city, state
    from publishers
    where pub_id = '0736'
```
All words are in
lowercase letters.

Figure 3.1 An Example of an Example

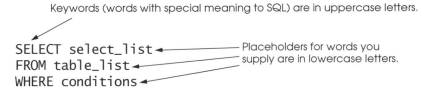

Keywords (words with special meaning to SQL) are in uppercase letters.

SELECT select_list ⟵——————— Placeholders for words you
FROM table_list ⟵ supply are in lowercase letters.
WHERE conditions ⟵

Figure 3.2 An Example of a Syntax Statement

A *syntax* statement is more like a template that tells you exactly what is required (and what's permitted) for the command in question (Figure 3.2).

Because a lot of information is packed into each syntax statement, it often helps to compare syntax statements to associated SQL examples.

Here are the conventions we use in this book for SQL syntax:

- Although SQL is a **free-form language**, meaning that there are no requirements for how many words you put on a line or where you break a line, the examples and syntax in this book are usually formatted so that each clause of a statement begins on a new line. Long or complex clauses extend to additional lines; these lines are indented.
- Words or phrases the user should supply are always in lowercase letters. In Figure 3.2, `select_list`, `table_list`, and `conditions` are place-holders for values you supply when you submit a command to SQL. These values can be constants, expressions, or **identifiers**—names of databases, tables, or other database objects. Check your system documentation for rules on identifiers: minimum and maximum length, characters that cannot be used (often blanks and periods), and the significance of case. The `AUTHORS` table may or may not be the same as the `authors` table—see "Character Sets and Sort Orders" in Chapter 5.
- SQL **keywords** in syntax statements are always shown in uppercase letters, although in most versions of SQL you may type them (unlike identifiers) in any case. The keywords in the syntax example (Figure 3.2) are SELECT, FROM, and WHERE; the ability to type them in any case means that "SELECT" is the same as "select" is the same as "SeLeCt."
- Curly braces ({ }) around words or phrases mean that you *must* choose at least one of the enclosed options. If the options are separated by vertical bars (|), you must pick only one. If they are separated by commas (,), you must pick one, but you may pick more.
- Square brackets ([]) mean using an option is . . . optional. If the options are separated by vertical bars (|), you can pick none or one, but if they are separated by commas (,), you can pick none, one, or more.

```
{early_lunch | no_lunch}          You must choose one

{soup , salad , sandwich}         You must choose one or more

[dessert]                         You don't have to choose it

[coffee | soda | wine]            You may choose none or one

[tomato , pickle , onion]         You may choose none, one, or more
```

Figure 3.3 Brackets, Braces, Vertical Bars, and Commas in Syntax

Figure 3.3 shows how braces, brackets, bars, and commas work together.

The braces and brackets are not part of the statement, so don't type them when you enter a SQL command. If you choose more than one option, separate your choices with commas. Ellipses (...) mean that you can repeat the last unit as many times as you like.

Here's a (non-SQL!) example of how these elements might be used in syntax:

```
BUY thing_name = price AS {cash | check | credit}
   [, thing_name = price AS {cash | check | credit}  ]...
```

SYNTAX

In the invented syntax statement you just saw, "BUY" and "AS" are required keywords. The items inside braces and separated by vertical bars indicate that you must choose one (and only one) of the methods of payment. You may also choose to buy additional things—as many of them as you like. For each thing you buy, give its name, its price, and a method of payment. Here's how you'd translate the syntax into a real-life example involving lunch and a book:

```
buy lunch = 4.95 as cash, book = 34.95 as check
```

When you see parentheses (( )) in syntax, they are actually part of what you type (unlike brackets and braces). Don't forget them.

A SQL statement generally requires a **terminator**, which sends the SQL command to the database management system for processing. Different SQL dialects use different terminators; common terminators include the semicolon (;) and the word "go." Database systems with graphical user interfaces (or GUIs, pronounced "gooeys") allow you to click a button or choose a menu option. Since the possibilities vary, we generally have not included terminators in the examples or syntax.

Coping with Failure

Errors in SQL statements occur for many reasons. Among the most common are

- Typing mistakes
- Syntax errors
- Failing to include character data in quotes
- Using an incorrect object name

Figure 3.4 illustrates these mistakes.

When you type a statement that your version of SQL does not understand, the command will not be executed. Instead, the system will display some sort of error message on your screen, the helpfulness of which varies a great deal from system to system (and even within systems). A good error message tells you as much as possible about where you went wrong, including the type of error that has been detected and the line on which the mistake is located.

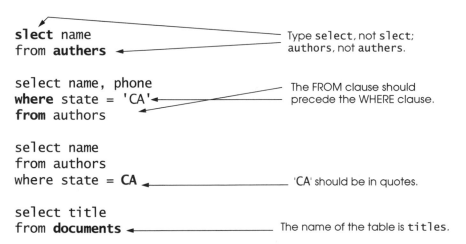

Figure 3.4 Common Errors in SQL Statements

Here are a couple of examples of error messages from Adaptive Server Anywhere:

```
SQL
select *
from pulbihsers
Table pulbihsers not found
slect *
from publishers
Syntax error near '*'
```

After looking at the message, you can correct the error and resubmit your SQL statement. (Error messages in other versions of SQL may look quite different.)

Working with Databases

A database is an organized collection of data—tables, views, indexes, and other objects. You begin by creating the database; then you create each of the objects in it. Some systems support multiple databases for each software installation, while others support a single database, often with internal partitions of some sort.

Getting Started

If you install the Adaptive Server Anywhere software on your personal computer, you won't need to ask for permission or create a database: `bookbiz` is already installed. However, you may prefer to use the RDBMS most favored at the office so that you can become familiar with it. In this case, you'll need to negotiate with the responsible parties.

Since a significant amount of storage space may have to be set aside for each new database (even if the database will never contain much data), permission to create databases is often jealously guarded in multiuser environments. If this is the case in your situation, you can go on to the sections that discuss creating database objects. However, you will have to ask your system administrator either to issue the command to create a database for you or to give you permission to work in a "scratch area" available for casual use.

Recognizing Roles

In multiuser RDBMSs, each database is controlled or owned by a specified user, charged with certain responsibilities, and bestowed with certain rights. These rights and responsibilities vary widely among database management systems, but they often include

- Setting up permissions for other users within the database
- Making backup copies of the database on a regular basis and running the recovery procedures in case of system failure
- Enlarging the database if more space becomes necessary
- Owning most of the production database objects
- Understanding the kind of data that is in the database and how it is used

In most database system installations, only the system administrator worries about physical storage. Users who issue the SQL commands to create databases or the objects in them (tables and views, for example) may do so according to instructions from the system administrator.

Depending on both the database software and the hardware you're using, databases may be physically stored on disks, on disk partitions, or in operating system files. We use the generic term **database device** for all of these possibilities.

Reserving Space for Database Objects

The process of setting up databases varies a great deal from vendor to vendor. In some cases, a single RDBMS server supports multiple databases, each dedicated to a particular kind of data or application. In others, a server and a database are pretty much the same thing, but space within the single database is clearly divided among different uses by permissions, ownership, and space allocations. You create a database with a vendor utility or GUI tool or a CREATE DATABASE command.

The 1992 SQL ANSI standard (often called SQL-92) does not include a CREATE DATABASE command. Instead, it provides a CREATE SCHEMA command for defining the part of a database that a specific user owns. Typically, a database consists of more than one **schema**.

Most commercial versions of SQL, however, have a CREATE DATABASE   **SQL**
command. The full syntax for the Adaptive Server Anywhere CREATE DATA-   **VARIANTS**
BASE command, for example, looks like this:

```
Adaptive Server Anywhere
CREATE    DATABASE    db-file-name
[
[ [ TRANSACTION  ] LOG  OFF
    | [ TRANSACTION  ] LOG  ON  [ log-file-name-string  ]
        [ MIRROR  mirror-file-name-string  ]]...
    [ CASE  { RESPECT  | IGNORE  } ]
[ PAGE SIZE  page-size  ]
[ COLLATION  collation-label  ]
[ ENCRYPTED  { ON  | OFF  } ]
[ BLANK  PADDING  { ON  | OFF  } ]
[ ASE  [ COMPATIBLE  ] ]
[ JAVA  { ON  | OFF  } ]
[ JCONNECT  { ON  | OFF  } ]
                                    ]
```

Choosing Databases

Creating a database does not necessarily imply using it. In a multidatabase
system, you may have to type a USE, DATABASE, or CONNECT command in
order to access a database—or even to create its objects. Nowadays, you're
likely to have a graphical user interface to make it easy to indicate which database you want. Check your system documentation for specifics.

Creating Simple Tables

Once you've created a database or otherwise reserved space for your work, you
can begin creating tables.

Tables are the basic building blocks of any database. They hold the rows and
columns of your data. With SQL's data definition commands, you can create
tables, drop tables, and alter them (add, remove, or rearrange columns or
change their characteristics).

In most SQL implementations, the user who creates a table is its owner and is responsible for granting permission for its use to other users. When you create a table with SQL, you do at least the following:

- Name the table
- Name the columns it contains
- Specify the datatype of each column
- Specify the null status of each column—whether that column permits or forbids null values

The bookbiz database, for maximum flexibility, uses only these basic elements in table definitions. However, almost all vendors have accepted additional possibilities for the CREATE TABLE statement supported in SQL-92, including

- **Defaults** (values assumed when you don't explicitly enter anything, such as today's date, on a sales order)
- Constraints that check (limit) the possible values you can enter for a column (for example, pub_ids can be 0736, 0877, or 1389 only)
- Constraints defining a column as a primary key, unique, or both
- Constraints setting up reference checks among primary and foreign keys

We'll start with simplified CREATE TABLE syntax (column name, datatype, and null status) and discuss the constraints later in this chapter.

The SQL command for setting up a table is called CREATE TABLE. (Make sure you're using the correct database before you enter a CREATE TABLE statement.) A simplified form of the CREATE TABLE syntax is

```
CREATE TABLE table_name
(column_name datatype [NULL | NOT NULL]
[, column_name datatype [NULL| NOT NULL] ]...)
```

An example is the CREATE TABLE statement for the authors table:

SQL
```
create table authors
  (au_id     char(11)      not null,
   au_lname  varchar(40)   not null,
   au_fname  varchar(20)   not null,
```

```
phone       char(12)         null,
address     varchar(40)      null,
city        varchar(20)      null,
state       char(2)          null,
zip         char(5)          null)
```

Systems handle NULL differently. Informix, for example, does not allow the keyword NULL in CREATE TABLE statements. Instead, it assumes NULL in the absence of NOT NULL. The Informix code for authors looks like this:

SQL VARIANTS

```
Informix
create table authors
    (au_id      char(11)        not null,
    au_lname    varchar(40)     not null,
    au_fname    varchar(20)     not null,
    phone       char(12)                ,
    address     varchar(40)             ,
    city        varchar(20)             ,
    state       char(2)                 ,
    zip         char(5)                 )
```

Let's go back and examine the CREATE TABLE syntax (the general syntax "template" before the specific create table authors example) because it's more complicated than any syntax introduced so far.

- The first clause, the CREATE TABLE clause, is straightforward—just make sure the table names you choose follow your system's rules for identifiers.
- The second line of the syntax begins with an opening parenthesis, which you must be sure to type.
- Then give the name of the first column, followed by a space and the name of its datatype. (For some datatypes, you must specify additional information: a length for character data types or a scale and precision for decimal datatypes. This is usually done by putting one or two integers in parentheses immediately following the datatype.)
- The keywords NULL and NOT NULL inside square brackets indicate that they are optional. The vertical bar between them means you can use only one or the other, not both. The system makes the choice if the

user doesn't. The SQL-92 default is to permit nulls, but not all commercial systems follow it. Get in the habit of explicitly spelling out the options you choose, even if you are accepting defaults. It'll make your work much easier to follow.

- The third line of the syntax, also enclosed in square brackets, repeats the definition of a column and is followed by an ellipsis. The brackets mean that defining a second column is optional; the ellipsis means that you can define as many columns as you like (within the limitations of your system—check your reference guide). Note that each column definition is separated from the next by a comma. Don't forget the parenthesis at the end of the list of columns.

TIP In addition to system-specific limits on the number of columns that you may include in a single table, check restrictions on row length (the total bytes that all the columns use). Usually, the limit is large enough so that you won't have to think about it. But if you're defining a table with lots of columns or with very large columns, you may have to compute exactly how long each row will be. To figure this out, add together the lengths of the longest data value each column can hold—determined by the column's assigned length (if it has one) or by the length that applies to its datatype.

Choosing Datatypes

The datatype of a column specifies what kind of information the column will hold (characters, numbers, dates, and so on) so that the system will know how the data is to be physically stored and how it can be manipulated. For example, a character datatype holds letters, numbers, and special characters, while an integer datatype holds whole numbers only. Data in integer columns can be manipulated with arithmetic operators, while character data cannot.

Relational systems can handle a wide variety of datatypes, but be careful in making assumptions—even when two systems use the same datatype name, their meanings may be different. You'll want to check your system's reference manuals to find out what datatypes are available to you and when and how to use them.

Choosing the proper datatypes is more binding than many other design decisions. In many versions of SQL it is difficult to change a column's datatype identity. However, most SQLs provide datatype conversion functions (see "Converting from One Datatype to Another" in Chapter 11) so that data stored as one type can be treated as if it were another type. For example, even if you have stored only numbers in a character column, it may be difficult or impossible to change the datatype of the column. However, you may be able, with the help of a data conversion function, to perform arithmetic operations on those numbers, even though those operations are incompatible with character columns.

Following is a summary of some possible datatypes, along with hints on the kind of data for which each is typically used. You'll find more information on datatypes in Appendix B.

- **Character datatypes** hold letters, numbers, and special characters. The two general types are fixed-length character (CHARACTER or CHAR) and variable-length character (VARIABLE CHARACTER or VARCHAR). Fixed- or variable-length national character (NATIONAL CHARACTER, NCHAR, NATIONAL CHARACTER VARYING, NVARCHAR) is also available for specific character sets. Some systems make special character datatypes available for storing large pieces of text; they are often called LONG or TEXT. Most character datatypes require that you give a length parameter specifying the maximum size of the column (a number in parentheses after the datatype).

   That character datatypes are the best choice in some situations—such as zip codes and phone numbers—may seem surprising at first. Zip codes are best stored in character columns because they often need to be sorted, and codes that begin with zero may not sort properly if they are stored as numbers. Some systems, in fact, simply strip leading zeroes off all numbers. (Sort order varies from implementation to implementation.)

   Special characters often used in phone numbers (hyphens and parentheses) are rejected unless a column is stored as characters.
- **Whole-number datatypes** hold integers only (no fractions or decimals). They are often known by such names as NUMBER, INTEGER, INT, SMALLINT, and TINYINT. All commercial versions of SQL provide arithmetic operations for use with whole numbers and aggregate functions that allow you to find the maximum, minimum, average, total, and count of the values in a column of whole numbers. Some SQLs provide other functions, such as statistical operations.
- **Decimal datatypes** hold numbers with fractions. Exact decimal numbers are known as DECIMAL or NUMERIC. You can usually define their precision (the total number of digits on both sides of the decimal point) and scale (the number of digits after the decimal point). Approximate decimal numbers have names like REAL, DOUBLE, DOUBLE

PRECISION, FLOAT, and SMALLFLOAT. Their precision and number of significant digits vary among database management systems, sometimes depending on the particular hardware you're using.

- **Money datatypes** hold currency values. If your system does not have a specific MONEY datatype, use an exact decimal type.
- **Date datatypes** and **time datatypes** record date, time, and combinations of date and time. Special date functions for determining the interval between two dates and for adding or subtracting a given amount of time to a date are sometimes provided.
- **Binary datatypes** hold code, images, and hexadecimal data. Like character data, they come in fixed and variable lengths and may have long versions.
- **Bit datatypes** can be 0 or 1.
- **Serial datatypes** maintain a sequentially increasing number. In some cases this feature is treated as a distinct datatype. In others, it may be available as a property, default, or function you apply to one of the basic datatypes (usually integer) or as a separate database object you associate with a table.

Become familiar with the characteristics of your system's datatypes so that you can use them effectively.

Figuring Datatype Lengths   Be sure to check on how your system handles the physical storage of datatypes. Find out which datatypes are **fixed length**—in other words, those for which the amount of storage space specified in the CREATE TABLE statement is allocated for each value in the column, no matter how much data is actually entered. For example, a column defined as CHAR(10) is allocated ten bytes or characters of storage space, no matter what value you enter in the column. Longer values may be truncated; values shorter than ten characters may be padded with blanks at the end, like this:

```
name
----------
Greenjeans
Kangaroo__
Ho_____
Rumpelstil
```

Datatypes that don't take length specifications are often fixed length. If your implementation allocates eight bytes of storage for integer columns, for example, all eight bytes will be used whether the value you enter in the column is "3" or "300000".

The data in variable-length datatypes is stored as its actual length, not as its defined length. Suppose your system supplies a variable-length character datatype, and you've defined a column like the one shown earlier as VARCHAR(10) instead of CHAR(10). The "10" still represents the maximum length, but shorter values are not blank padded. The first value (Greenjeans) would take ten bytes of storage, but the second (Kangaroo) would take only eight, the third (Ho) would take two, and so on.

> Using fixed-length datatypes when much of the actual data is a great deal shorter than the length specified can waste storage space.

TIP

Specifying Precision and Scale   Exact decimal datatypes may allow you to choose precision and scale. For example, if you expect an exact decimal number to have a total of six places, including three to the right of the decimal point, you'd describe it as something like DECIMAL (6, 3).

Assigning NULL and NOT NULL

Most systems allow you to assign NULL or NOT NULL to each column when you create a table. A few systems do not support null values at all—they always insert some default value other than NULL (such as zero or blank) when a column has no entered value.

Assigning NULL to a column instructs the system to insert NULL in that column if the user does not enter a value. As we've explained, NULL represents some unknown, unavailable, or inapplicable value—it's not the same as blank or zero.

Assigning NOT NULL to a column means that nonentries in that column are not allowed. If you don't specify a value for that column, the system will reject the entry and display an error message. (In systems that provide the capability of specifying default values for a column, the default is automatically entered if you don't specify a value for a not null column.) In many systems, null is the default. But don't rely on the default: Spell out what you want so that others will know what you had in mind.

How do you decide the null status of columns when you're designing a table? You should not permit NULLs in columns in which known values are essential to the utility of the database. Primary key columns should never allow NULLs, because the primary keys uniquely identify the row. For example, without the `au_id` column, you'd have no way to find a book's author(s) in the `bookbiz` database. The database was designed so that the `authors` table can be linked to `titles` by joins on the `au_id` and `title_id` columns.

You may decide that other columns should forbid null entries, too: Perhaps you should disallow NULLs in the `au_lname` and `au_fname` columns on the grounds that it doesn't make sense to enter an author's address or phone number without entering his or her name.

However, when you know or suspect that a column will contain some unknown or inapplicable data, it should permit NULLs. Missing addresses and phone numbers are common, so these columns should allow NULLs. And the first name column in an authors table might permit nulls because an author's *nom de plume* could consist of a single name (such as Colette).

In the `titles` table, the `title_id` and `title` columns do not allow NULLs. They are forbidden because `title_id` is the primary key—each title identification number indicates a unique book. On the other hand, the `advance` column does permit null values. While an advance with a NULL title ID would make no sense at all, a title ID with a NULL advance might simply mean that the publisher and the author haven't agreed on the exact amount yet or that the clerk hasn't entered it yet.

While NULL would mean "not yet known" in the case of an advance not yet decided, it can have slightly different meanings in other situations. NULL can mean that the value will never be known. For example, if you added a `phone` column to the `authors` table and some authors' telephone numbers were unlisted, you'd have to reconcile yourself to a permanent NULL. Then again, NULL might mean something like "not applicable"—for example, if the author didn't have a telephone.

Unlike primary keys, foreign keys sometimes can have null values. In the case of books and publishers, the `titles.pub_id` column allows NULL. This is because, in the `bookbiz` business model, books are sometimes acquired by the mother publishing company and assigned to one of the subsidiary lines later on. For a short time, a book might lack a publisher.

TIP

Note that the decision about whether to allow NULLs in a foreign key depends not on theoretical considerations, but on the logical meaning of the relationship between the information in the primary and foreign key columns—and that depends on the real-world situation: a company policy, an organization's rule, and so on.

Planning Tables

Creating a table involves a series of steps that begins with design and ends with issuing a SQL command. Following is an outline of the process for creating tables without any SQL-92 constraints. It assumes you've already designed and normalized your database and therefore know which columns will be in each table.

1. Decide on the datatype (and length, precision, and scale, if required) of each column.

2. Decide which columns should accept null values and which should not.

3. Decide which columns need to be unique, that is, cannot allow duplicate values. (In a system that doesn't use constraints, you'll enforce uniqueness with indexes, discussed in this chapter and in Chapter 10. Information on PRIMARY KEY and UNIQUE constraints is covered later in this chapter.)

4. Make a note of primary key/foreign key pairings. The simple syntax used in the CREATE TABLE statements for bookbiz doesn't allow you to do anything with the pairs, except to make sure that they have compatible datatypes, sizes, and null status. In the more complex syntax we'll explore later on, you'll be able to use REFERENCES constraints to enforce some referential integrity.

5. If you're in a multiuser environment, make sure you have permission to create tables and indexes. If not, see your system administrator or the owner of the database in which you're working.

6. Create the table (and any indexes it needs) with the CREATE TABLE and CREATE INDEX statements.

Figure 3.5 shows the structure of the titles table: column names, datatypes, NULL status, columns that must be unique, and primary and foreign keys.

Defining the Tables in bookbiz

Now you are ready to apply these syntax rules to real tables. Following is a CREATE TABLE command for the titles table. If you are using the software on the CD, you don't need to create this table—it's already built. To create a

Column	Datatype	Null?	Unique?	Keys
title_id	char(6)	not null	yes—unique titleidind index	primary
title	varchar(80)	not null	no—titleind index not unique	
type	char(12)	null		
pub_id	char(4)	null		foreign (publishers table)
price	money	null		
advance	money	null		
ytd_sale	int	null		
contract	bit	not null		
notes	varchar(200)	null		

Figure 3.5 Charting the titles **Table Structure**

table just like it for practice, use a different table name (make it titles2, for example). Relational databases don't allow multiple tables with the same name and owner.

SQL
```
create table titles
(title_id char(6) not null,
title varchar(80) not null,
type char(12) null,
pub_id char(4) null,
price numeric(8,2)  null,
advance numeric(10,2) null,
ytd_sales int null,
```

```
contract bit not null,
notes varchar(200) null,
pubdate date null)
[table created]
```

The CREATE TABLE statements for the eight remaining tables in the bookbiz database are contained in Appendix D and on the CD.

You'll see some variation in datatype names, so be sure to check your documents. Oracle, for example, uses VARCHAR2 rather than VARCHAR. There is a datatype comparison chart in "Datatype Comparison" in Appendix B.

SQL VARIANTS

Creating Indexes

In a relational database management system, an index is a mechanism for boosting performance. Just as an index in a book helps you quickly find the pages you want to read, an index on a column helps the system find data. When you're looking for a particular subject in a book, you don't want to read every page to find the topic of interest. Similarly, when you're searching for a given piece of data, an index can serve as a logical pointer to its physical location.

There are several important differences, however, between an index in a book and an index in a relational database management system. The reader of a book decides whether to consult the index. The user of a relational database management system decides whether to create an index, and the system itself determines if and how the index is used for each query the user submits. Indexes, once they are set up, are transparent to database users (except where vendors have added SQL extensions to give expert users or database administrators some control over system use of indexes—a topic beyond the scope of this book).

While each edition of a book and its index are printed once, the data in a relational system and its indexes may change frequently. Each time the data in a table is modified, one or more of the table's indexes may have to change to reflect those modifications. Again, users have nothing to do with keeping the indexes up to date; the system handles this task on its own.

A characteristic shared by indexes on database tables and book indexes is that it's very common for a table to have more than one index (just as some books are indexed by subject and by author). It's also possible for a table (and for a book) to have no index at all.

This section explains the syntax of the CREATE INDEX and DROP INDEX statements, describes the varieties of indexes typically available in relational systems, and gives some pointers about how to decide which columns to index. Chapter 10 discusses in more detail how indexes affect performance.

The CREATE INDEX Statement

Most systems have a command with syntax similar to this:

SYNTAX

```
CREATE [UNIQUE] INDEX index_name
ON table_name (column_name)
```

The column and table names specify the column you want indexed and the table that contains it. To create an index on the au_id column of the authors table, the command is

```
SQL
create index auidind
on authors (au_id)
[index created]
```

TIP

It's a good idea to plan and create your indexes when you create your table, particularly if you need the indexes to guarantee uniqueness. However, SQL allows you to create indexes after there's data in a table, and this may be more efficient for some situations.

Most systems allow **composite indexes** (indexes involving more than one column) and **unique indexes** (indexes that prevent duplication of data). Another indexing option provided in some systems is a **clustered index** (one that sorts the table rows in the same physical order as the index). Check your system's reference manuals to see which types of indexes are allowed.

Composite Indexes   Composite indexes are used when two or more columns are best searched as a unit because of their logical relationship. For example, the authors table has a composite index on au_lname and au_fname.

The syntax for creating a composite index must specify all the columns in it. A command to create a composite index on the `authors` table might look something like this:

SQL

```
create index aunameind
on authors (au_lname, au_fname)
```

The composite index columns don't have to be in the same order as the columns in the CREATE TABLE statement. For example, the order of `au_lname` and `au_fname` could be reversed in the preceding index creation statement. For performance reasons, it's important to start with the name of the column you use most often in searches.

Unique Indexes   A unique index is one in which no two rows are permitted to have the same index value. The system checks for duplicate values when the index is created (if data already exists) and each time data is added. Unique indexes are usually created on the primary key column(s) in order to enforce their function as unique identifiers of the row.

Specifying a unique index makes sense only when uniqueness is a characteristic of the data itself. For example, you would not want a unique index on a `last_name` column because there is likely to be more than one *Smith* or *Wong* in tables of even a few hundred rows. On the other hand, a unique index on a column holding Social Security numbers would be a good idea. Uniqueness is a characteristic of the data: Each person has a different Social Security number. Furthermore, a unique index serves as an integrity check. A duplicate Social Security number reflects some kind of error in data entry or an error on the part of the government.

SQL implementations that support unique indexes must have some way of enforcing that uniqueness. Usually the system guarantees uniqueness by rejecting commands that would

- Create a unique index on existing data that includes duplicate values
- Change data on which there is a unique index in such a way that duplicates would be introduced

You can use the UNIQUE keyword on composite indexes as well as on single-column indexes.

How, What, and Why to Index

Indexes speed the retrieval of data. An index on a column can often make the difference between a nearly immediate response to a query and a long wait.

So why not index every column? The most significant reason is that building and maintaining an index takes time and storage space on the database device.

A second reason is that inserting, deleting, or updating data in indexed columns takes a little longer than in unindexed columns because of the time it takes the system to maintain the index when key values are changed. However, this cost is usually outweighed by the extent to which indexes improve retrieval performance.

In general, it's usually appropriate to put indexes on columns you use frequently in retrievals, especially primary key columns and columns used in joins and sorts. Here are some more precise guidelines:

- A unique index on the column or columns that store the table's primary key prevents duplicates and guarantees that every value in the primary key column will in fact *uniquely* identify the row. The primary key is frequently joined to columns in other tables, so the index is useful for that, in addition to guaranteeing uniqueness.
- A column that is often accessed in sorted order probably should be indexed so that the system can take advantage of the indexed order.
- Columns that are regularly used in joins should be indexed because the system can perform the join faster.
- A column that is often searched for ranges of values might be a good choice for indexing if your system provides clustered indexes. Once the row with the first value in the range is found, rows with subsequent values are guaranteed to be physically adjacent. A clustered index does not offer as much of an advantage for searches on single values.

These are some cases in which indexes are not useful:

- Columns that are rarely referenced in queries don't benefit from indexes in terms of performance because the system seldom or never has to search for rows on the basis of values in these columns. However, you may still want to use an index to enforce uniqueness.
- Columns that can have only two or three values (for example, male, female, unknown) gain no real advantage from being indexed.

- Small tables with few rows don't get a performance boost from indexes: The system will generally choose a **table scan** (examining the table rows one by one) instead of using an index. The length of time it takes to perform a scan is related to the number of rows in the table.

Indexes are a very complex issue. To use them well, you need to understand how your system optimizes queries and what performance issues your application has—topics not covered in this book. Generally speaking, you should start by picking what seem to be reasonable indexes and then look for performance problems during your prototyping, benchmarking, and testing phases. When you have a clear idea of your needs, you can adjust the indexes to meet them.

Creating Tables With SQL-92 Constraints

Most commercial systems have adopted the SQL-92 CREATE TABLE options for PRIMARY KEY, UNIQUE, DEFAULT, CHECK, REFERENCES, and FOREIGN KEY. These elements provide important data integrity protections. A column-level constraint applies to a single column (for example, `au_id`). A table-level constraint applies to multiple columns (perhaps the combination of `au_lname` and `au_fname`)—not to the whole table.

- PRIMARY KEY marks the column (which cannot allow NULLs) as the primary key of the table. Every value entered must be unique, or the input is rejected. The handling of this constraint internally varies from system to system, but it is often equivalent to a unique index.
- UNIQUE also guarantees the distinctness of every value in the column, but it allows the column to be defined as NULL. In some systems, only *one* null entry is allowed per UNIQUE column. UNIQUE is also often implemented as an index.
- DEFAULT defines a value that the system automatically supplies when the user entering data doesn't give one explicitly. For example, you might define a default for the `type` column of the `titles` table. If a book hasn't yet been categorized and the data entry clerk can't make an entry in the `type` column, the system would automatically insert whatever default value you've chosen—perhaps the word "unclassified." Be sure to test defaults with any applications or GUI tools you use; sometimes they insert NULL when no value is provided and override the default. (If no default is defined and the `type` column permits null values, the system will automatically insert the value "NULL.")

- CHECK specifies what data may be entered in a particular column: It is a way of defining the domain of the column. For example, you might want to make sure that a `title_id` is always two letters followed by four numerals, or a `type` is one of a list of six acceptable terms. If a user attempts to make an entry that violates a check constraint, the system rejects the data modification command. Check constraints are sometimes called **rules** or **validation rules** because they allow the system to check whether a value being entered in a column falls within the column's domain. Check constraints that involve more than one column are defined as table-level constraints.
- REFERENCES and FOREIGN KEY tie primary and foreign keys together. When you enter a value in a foreign key column defined with REFERENCES (for example, `titles.pub_id`), that value must exist in the table and column referenced (`publishers.pub_id`), or else the entry is rejected.

Sketching Constraints

Before you create a table with defaults and constraints, sketch your requirements. Figure 3.6 shows defaults and constraints you might use for the `titles` table.

The sketch includes the name, datatype, and NULL status of each column. In addition, it notes places where constraints might protect the data.

- Instead of creating indexes on `title_id` and `title`, you specify PRIMARY KEY and UNIQUE constraints. The `title_id` column is the unique identifier for the row and hence a perfect candidate for a PRIMARY KEY constraint. The UNIQUE constraint on `title` is parallel to the `titleind` index.
- The foreign key `titles.pub_id` benefits from a REFERENCES constraint against the master table/column combination (`publishers.pub_id`). This means no one will be able to enter `titles.pub_id` values that do not exist in `publishers.pub_id`.
- Both `type` and `pubdate` are good canidates for DEFAULTs ("unclassified" or some such and today's date). These values will be added by the SQL engine when you do not specify another value.
- Two columns have clear rules or definitions of the kind of data they can hold: `title_id` and `type`. A CHECK constraint can enforce the rules and prevent dirty data from entering the table.

Column	Datatype	Null?	Key	Default	Check	References
title_id	char(6)	not null	primary, unique		2 letters followed by 4 digits	
title	varchar(80)	not null	unique			
type	char(12)	null		unclassified	business, mod_cook, trad_cook, psychology, popular_comp, unclassified	
pub_id	char(4)	null	foreign key			publishers.pub_id
price	numeric(8,2)	null				
advance	numeric(10,2)	null				
ytd_sale	integer	null				
contract	bit	not null				
notes	varchar(200)	null				
pubdate	date	null		today		

Figure 3.6 Using Constraints in Creating the titles Table

Syntax for constraints varies from vendor to vendor, so check your system manuals for specifics. Usually it looks something like the following syntax summary with column-level constraints optionally following each column definition. The constraint clauses always include the constraint keyword (DEFAULT, CHECK, PRIMARY KEY, UNIQUE, FOREIGN KEY, REFERENCES) and optionally the word CONSTRAINT and a name for the constraint. (Naming constraints may simplify the process of dropping or changing them. Although most systems generate constraint labels you can use, they are often cumbersome.) We've put table-level (multicolumn) constraints at the end of the list of elements, but that's not required. Notice that a column can have more than one constraint and that constraints are *not* separated with commas, although columns are.

SYNTAX
```
CREATE TABLE table_name
(column_name datatype [NULL | NOT NULL] [DEFAULT default_value]
 [column_constraint_clause]...
 [, column_name datatype [NULL | NOT NULL][DEFAULT default_value]
 [column_constraint_clause]...]...
 [table_constraint_clause]...)
```

Implementing Constraints on Individual Columns

Following is the code for creating an Adaptive Server Anywhere version of the `titles` table with SQL-92 constraints. The table name is `titlescnstr` to avoid conflict with the `titles` table, which already exists in the `bookbiz` database. The `titlescnstr` definition uses the defaults and constraints shown in Figure 3.6. All of the constraints in this case apply to single columns.

SQL
```
alter table publishers
add primary key(pub_id)
[command completed]

create table titlescnstr
(title_id char(6) not null
primary key  check (title_id like '[A-Z][A-Z][0-9] [0-9] [0-9][0-9]'),
title varchar(80) not null
  unique,
type char(12)
 default 'unclassified' null
  check (type in ('business', 'mod_cook', 'trad_cook',
    'psychology',  'popular_comp', 'unclassified')),
pub_id char(4) null
  references publishers (pub_id),
price money null,
advance money null,
ytd_sales int null,
contract bit not null,
notes varchar(200) null,
pubdate datetime null
  default current date)
```

A few points need some explanation:

- Adaptive Server Anywhere requires outside-table columns noted in REFERENCE clauses to be PRIMARY KEY columns, not just columns with a unique index of some sort, hence the ALTER TABLE publishers statement (more on this later).
- You'll find an explanation of LIKE and IN in the next chapter.
- For pubdate, CURRENT DATE is an Adaptive Server Anywhere DEFAULT option that supplies today's date. Other systems provide similar functions.

The Sybase Adaptive Server Enterprise code for the same table differs in a few areas:

SQL VARIANTS

```
Adaptive Server Enterprise
create table titlescnstr
(title_id char(6) not null
 constraint tididx primary key
 constraint tidcheck check
 (title_id like '[A-Z] [A-Z] [0-9] [0-9] [0-9] [0-9]'),
title varchar(80) not null
 constraint titleidx unique,
type char(12)
 default 'unclassified' null
constraint typecheck check
 (type in ('business', 'mod_cook', 'trad_cook',
  'psychology', 'popular_comp', 'unclassified')),
   pub_id char(4) null
     references publishers (pub_id),
   price money null,
   advance money null,
   ytd_sales int null,
   contract bit not null,
   notes varchar(200) null,
   pubdate datetime
     default getdate() null)
```

Check your system manuals for details on the implementation you use.

Column	Datatype	Null?	Key	Default	Check	References
au_id	char(11)	not null	primary key			authors.au_id
title_id	char(6)	not null				titles.title_id
au_ord	tinyint	null				
royaltyshare	float	null				

Figure 3.7 Using Constraints in Creating titleauthors

If your system does not support the LIKE syntax shown in this example for the title_id CHECK constraint, try a BETWEEN clause with CAST datatype conversion for the number part—there is information on CAST in "Converting from One Datatype to Another" in Chapter 11.

SQL
```
create table titlescnstr
(title_id char(6) not null
  primary key
  check ((substring( title_id, 1, 2) between 'AA' and 'ZZ' ) and
      cast (substring( title_id, 3, 6) as int) between 0 and 9999), ....
[code fragment]
```

Implementing Multicolumn Constraints

Multicolumn (or table-level) constraints involve more than one column. Figure 3.7 shows constraints you could use for the titleauthors table.

The following example shows how you'd use Adaptive Server Anywhere to implement the references and primary key requirements in the constraint version of the titleauthors table (called titleauthorscnstr to avoid confusion). The primary key constraint is a table-level constraint because it includes more than one column.

SQL

```
create table titleauthorscnstr
(au_id char(11) not null references authors (au_id),
title_id char(6) not null references titles (title_id),
au_ord tinyint null,
royaltyshare float null,
primary key (au_id, title_id))
```

For Adaptive Server Anywhere, you'd have to make sure to have a PRIMARY KEY constraint on `authors.au_id` and `titles.title_id` before running this statement. You could specify this in an ALTER TABLE statement, as shown earlier.

CHECK constraints can also be table level, when they involve more than one column (but they must be from the same table). In the `salesdetails` table, there are columns for the quantity ordered and the quantity shipped. You could use a table-level CHECK constraint to make sure the quantity shipped is never larger than the quantity ordered.

Figure 3.8 charts the table requirements, including two REFERENCEs, the CHECK on quantity, and a table-level (multicolumn) PRIMARY KEY. The following CREATE TABLE code implements these requirements:

SQL

```
create table salesdetailscnstr
  (sonum int not null references sales (sonum),
  qty_ordered smallint not null,
  qty_shipped smallint null,
  title_id char(6) not null references titles (title_id),
  date_shipped datetime null,
  check (qty_shipped <= qty_ordered),
  primary key (sonum, title_id))
```

Several systems provide commands outside the CREATE TABLE context to handle defaults, rules, and integrity constraints. Early systems sometimes considered defaults and integrity constraints an application-by-application decision and did not support them through SQL.

Column	Datatype	Null?	Key	Default	Check	References
sonum	int	not null	primary key			authors.au_id
title_id	char(6)	not null				titles.title_id
qty_shipped	smallint	null			qty_shipped not > qty_ordered	
qty_ordered	smallint	not null				
date_shipped	datetime	null				

Figure 3.8 Using Constraints in salesdetails

Changing and Deleting Databases and Objects

By now you've noticed a pattern: You build database objects with a CREATE command of some sort. Most systems have corresponding DROP commands to remove database objects. (Strangely enough, not until its 1988 draft did the ANSI standard include such a command.) ALTER commands arc also common for changing objects.

Changing Databases

Some SQL versions include a command that allows you to change the size of a database (usually to make it bigger). The ability to add database device space for a database is extremely important for any application that will grow over time. Also important (and less frequently implemented) is the ability to shrink a database in order to reclaim unused database device space.

Changing Table Definitions

After you've designed and created your database and worked with it for a while, you may find that it isn't quite right or that the application requirements have changed.

- Most systems allow you to change the structure of a table (even after it has data in it) with the ALTER TABLE command. Syntax may include keywords to add and drop columns and to change a column's name, datatype, length, null status, and constraints.
- You can also change table definitions by defining a view of the table or by creating a new table, loading the existing data into it, and then dropping the old. Some systems provide a single command that allows you to create and load a new table based on an old one.

Using ALTER TABLE   For example, to add a column to the `authors` table, most SQLs allow you to type something like this:

SQL

```
alter table authors
add birth_date datetime null
[column added]
```

Usually columns added with the ALTER TABLE statement must allow NULLs. That's because when the new column is added to all the existing rows, it must contain some value, and "NULL" (unknown) is the obvious choice.

Many relational systems provide commands for making structural changes besides the addition of columns—for changing a column's datatype or null status, removing columns, or renaming columns with MODIFY (sometimes ALTER) or DELETE (DROP) clauses in ALTER TABLE. Two examples follow: The first changes the datatype of the new `birth_date` column; the second removes the column.

```
Adaptive Server Anywhere
alter table authors
modify birth_date char(10)
[datatype modified]
alter table authors
delete birth_date
[column removed]
```

SQL VARIANTS

Because they reflect space use and other architectural issues, the ALTER TABLE clauses vary from system to system and are often associated with limiting conditions. Microsoft ALTER COLUMN syntax is similar to ASA's

MODIFY syntax, as shown in the example following, but the two RDBMSs have different rules for when you can use the various clauses.

```
SQL Server
alter table authors
alter column birth_date char(10)
23 rows affected.
alter table authors
drop column birth_date
The command(s) completed successfully.
```

Creating Views and Tables   If your system doesn't provide the ALTER TABLE options you want, there are several other ways to approach the problem.

If you can't physically drop a column, for example, you can create a view that excludes it and do all your data retrieval and modification commands through that view. (See Chapter 9 for information on views.) You can also use a view to create the illusion of a permanent change in

- The name of a column, simply by giving the column a new heading in the SELECT clause of the CREATE VIEW statement, or
- The datatype of a column, assuming your system has some sort of data conversion function

Another possible work-around for a not-quite-right table is to create a new table with the structure you want and then transfer data from the old to the new with an INSERT INTO...SELECT command, described later in this chapter.

In some systems, a single command allows you to create the table and load data from an existing table. See "Creating Copies of Data" in Chapter 9 for details.

Removing Databases

Removing a database or a database object deletes both the structure and any data associated with it. For that reason, most systems allow you to issue a DROP command only if you own the object or have special permission to delete it.

The syntax of the DROP DATABASE command is usually something like this:

    DROP DATABASE database_name

The DROP DATABASE command is very dangerous because removing a database obliterates all of its contents.

Removing Tables

The command to remove a table from a database is DROP TABLE:

    DROP TABLE table_name

When you issue this command, you remove the specified table from the database, together with its contents.

If you want to keep the table structure but remove all of its data, use the DELETE command (more about it later in this chapter).

Removing Indexes

There are two situations in which you might want to drop an index:

- You or someone else has created an index on a column, but the index is not used for most or all queries.
- You are about to issue a large number of data modification statements that will change key values. Because the system may have to do a lot of work to keep the index up-to-date, it might be more efficient to drop the index and then re-create it (with the CREATE INDEX statement) after changing the data.

It may still take some time to rebuild the index later, but you may prefer to postpone the lag time rather than endure a degradation in the system's performance during the data modifications. If one of the purposes of the index is to guarantee uniqueness, find another way to prevent duplicates before dropping the index.

In most systems, the command to remove an index has syntax something like this:

SYNTAX

```
DROP INDEX [qualifier]index_name
```

The qualifier may be a table or owner name, depending on your system. When you issue this command, the system removes the specified index from the database.

SQL VARIANTS   To drop the index `auidind` in the `authors` table, Transact-SQL uses the table name as qualifier, while Oracle uses the owner name.

Transact-SQL
```
drop index authors.auidind
```

Oracle
```
SQL> drop index scott.auidind;
Index dropped.
```

Adding, Changing, and Removing Data

Once you've designed and created a database, its tables, and (optionally) its indexes, you'll want to put data into the tables and start to work—adding, changing, and removing data as necessary. You've got the structure; now you need some contents.

SQL provides three basic commands for changing data, collectively called data modification statements.

- The INSERT statement adds new rows to the database.
- The UPDATE statement changes existing rows in the database.
- The DELETE statement removes rows from the database.

This section discusses the SQL data modification commands. The next section gives samples of the INSERT statements that load the sample data from the `bookbiz` database.

Another method of adding data to a table is to load it from an operating system file with some kind of bulk copy or bulk insert command. This method is especially appropriate when you are transferring data that was used with one database management system to another system.

Many relational database systems also have a graphical user interface **form** (like a paper form with blanks where you can type data) for data modification. A form is often more convenient than a data modification statement because it gives you a context in which to work. However, all data modification actions in a relational database system are based on SQL commands, so it's a good idea to look at their syntax even if you don't plan to use them.

Data modification statements are not necessarily available to everyone. The database owner and the owners of database objects can use the GRANT and REVOKE commands to decide which users are allowed to issue which data modification statements.

With INSERT, UPDATE, or DELETE, you modify data in only one table per statement. However, in some systems, the modifications you make can be based on data in other tables, even data in other databases. You can actually pull values from one table into another, using a SQL SELECT statement within a data modification command. Instructions on this variation on data modification are given later in this chapter.

The data modification statements work on views as well as on tables, with some restrictions. See Chapter 9 for details.

Adding New Rows: INSERT

The INSERT statement allows you to add rows to the database in two ways:

- With the VALUES keyword
- With a SELECT statement

Inserting Data into All Columns with VALUES   The VALUES keyword specifies data values for some or all of the columns in a new row. A generalized version of the syntax for the INSERT command using the VALUES keyword is the following:

```
INSERT INTO table_name [(column1 [, column2]...)]
VALUES (constant1 [, constant2]...)
```

SYNTAX

This INSERT statement adds a new row to the `publishers` table, giving a value for every column in the row:

SQL
```
insert into publishers
values ('1622', 'Jardin, Inc.', '5 5th Ave.', 'Camden', 'NJ')
```

Notice that you have to type the data values in the same order as the column names in the original CREATE TABLE statement (that is, first the ID number and then the name, the address, the city, and finally the state), separated by commas. The VALUES data is surrounded by parentheses, and SQL requires single quotes around character and date data.

Use a separate INSERT statement for each row you add.

Inserting Data into Some Columns with VALUES When you add data in some, but not all, of the columns in a row, you need to specify those columns. The columns that you don't put data into need to have defaults or be defined as null to prevent failure. For example, adding data in only two columns (say, `pub_id` and `pub_name`) requires a command like this:

SQL
```
insert into publishers (pub_id, pub_name)
values ('1756', 'HealthText')
```

The order in which you list the column names has no effect on the INSERT statement as long as the order in which you list the data values matches it. The following example (which reverses the order of `pub_name` and `pub_id`) has exactly the same effect as the previous example. (SQL won't allow the second command if you have already issued the first insert because the two inserts have the same `pub_id` and `pub_id` is defined as unique. Change the `pub_id` to 1757, and the command will work fine.)

SQL
```
insert into publishers (pub_name, pub_id)
values ('HealthText', '1756')
```

The INSERT statement, in either form, puts "1756" in the identification number column and "HealthText" in the publisher name column. What happened in the `address`, `city`, and `state` columns? The following SELECT statement shows the row that was added to `publishers`:

SQL
```
select pub_id, pub_name, address, city, state
from publishers
where pub_name = 'HealthText'
```

pub_id	pub_name	address	city	state
1756	HealthText	(NULL)	(NULL)	(NULL)

[1 row]

The system enters null values in the `address`, `city`, and `state` columns because there were no values for these columns in the INSERT statement, and the `publishers` table allows null values in these columns.

If you had defined `city` and `state` as NOT NULL in the CREATE TABLE statement, the insert wouldn't have worked because columns that don't permit null values won't accept a nonentry. Here's what happens with Transact-SQL when you try an INSERT statement that doesn't specify a value for the `pub_id` column, which was assigned not null status when the `publishers` table was created:

SQL
```
insert into publishers (pub_name, address, city, state)
values ('Tweedledum Books', '1 23rd St.', 'New York', 'NY')
column 'pub_id' in table 'publishers' cannot be NULL
```

Inserting Data into All Columns with SELECT   You can use a SELECT statement in an INSERT statement to get values from one or more other tables. A simple version of the syntax for the INSERT command using a SELECT statement is this:

```
INSERT INTO table_name [(insert_column_list)]
SELECT column_list
  FROM table_list
  WHERE search_conditions
```

SYNTAX

SELECT in an INSERT statement lets you pull data from all or some of the columns from one table into another. If you insert values for a subset of the columns, you can use UPDATE at another time to add the values for the other columns.

When you insert rows from one table into another, the two tables must have compatible structures—that is, the matching columns must be the same datatypes or datatypes between which the system automatically converts.

If all the columns of the two tables are compatible in the same order that they appeared in their CREATE TABLE statements, you don't need to specify column names in either table. Suppose a table called newauthors contains some rows of author information in the same format as authors. To add all the rows in authors to newauthors, type a command like either of the following:

SQL
```
insert into newauthors
select au_id, au_lname, au_fname, phone, address, city, state, zip
from authors
```

or

```
insert into newauthors
select *
from authors
```

If the columns in the two tables (the one you're inserting into and the one you're getting data from) are not in the same order in their respective CREATE TABLE statements, you can use either the INSERT or the SELECT clause to reorder the columns so that they match.

Without a match, the system cannot complete the INSERT operation, or it will complete it incorrectly, putting data in the wrong columns. For example, you might get truncated address data in the au_lname column, if those two columns were positionally switched in their respective CREATE TABLE statements.

Using Expressions One of the beneficial side effects of using a SELECT statement inside an INSERT statement is that it allows you to include **expressions** (strings of characters, mathematical calculations, and functions, alone or in combination with columns or with each other) to change the data that you're pulling in. (See Chapters 4, 5, 6, 7, and 8 for a full range of possibilities.)

Here's an example of a SELECT clause with an expression involving a column and a mathematical computation: Imagine that one of the publishing subsidiaries has purchased a series of books from another publishing company that conveniently uses a table with exactly the same structure as the `titles` table. The newly purchased books are in a table named `Books`, and you want to load this data into `titles`. However, the company from which the books were purchased underpriced its wares, and you want to increase the price of all the new books by 50 percent. A statement to increase the prices and insert the rows from `Books` into `titles` looks like this:

SQL
```
insert into titles
select title_id, title, type, pub_id, price * 1.5,
   advance, royalty, ytd_sales, contract, notes, pubdate
   from Books
```

Inserting Data into Some Columns with SELECT   You can use the SELECT statement to add data to some, but not all, of the columns in a row, just as you do with the VALUES clause. Simply specify the columns to which you want to add data in the INSERT clause.

For example, if there are books in the `titles` table that do not yet have contracts and hence do not have entries in the `titleauthors` table, you might try to use this statement to pull their `title_id` numbers out of the `titles` table and insert them into the `titleauthors` table as placeholders:

SQL
```
insert into titleauthors (title_id)
select title_id
   from titles
   where contract = 0
```

However, this statement is not legal because a value is required for the `au_id` column of `titleauthors` (the table definition doesn't permit nulls, and there is no default value). You can put in *xxxxxx* as a **dummy value** for `au_id` like this, using it as a constant:

SQL
```
insert into titleauthors (title_id, au_id)
select title_id, 'xxxxxx'
   from titles
   where contract = 0
```

The `titleauthors` table now contains two new rows with entries for the `title_id` column, dummy entries for the `au_id` column, and null values for the other two columns. If you have a unique index or UNIQUE or PRIMARY KEY constraint on the column, however, this maneuver won't work.

Changing Existing Data: UPDATE

While the INSERT statement adds new rows to a table, the UPDATE statement changes existing rows. Use it to change values in single rows, groups of rows, or all the rows in a table.

The UPDATE statement specifies the row or rows you want to change and the new data. The new data can be a constant or expression that you specify, or it can be data pulled from other tables.

Here's a simplified version of the UPDATE syntax for updating specified rows with an expression:

SYNTAX

```
UPDATE table_name
SET column_name = expression
[WHERE search_conditions]
```

Specifying the Table: UPDATE Clause   The UPDATE keyword is followed by the name of a table or view. As in all the data modification statements, you can change the data in only one table or view at a time.

If an UPDATE statement violates an integrity constraint (one of the values being added is the wrong datatype, for example), the system does not perform the update and usually displays an error message. See Chapter 9 for restrictions on updating views.

Specifying Columns: SET Clause   The SET clause specifies the column(s) and the changed value(s). The WHERE clause determines which row or rows will be updated. Note that if you don't have a WHERE clause, you'll update the specified columns of *all* the rows with the values in the SET clause.

For example, here's what the `publishers` table looks like after adding two rows (see Adding New Rows: INSERT):

SQL
```
select *
from publishers
pub_id pub_name              address         city                  state
====== ==================== =============== ==================== =====
0736   New Age Books         1 1st St.       Boston                MA
0877   Binnet & Hardley      2 2nd Ave.      Washington            DC
1389   Algodata Infosystems  3 3rd Dr.       Berkeley              CA
1622   Jardin, Inc.          5 5th Ave.      Camden                NJ
1756   HealthText            (NULL)          (NULL)                (NULL
[5 rows]
```

If all the publishing houses in the `publishers` table move their head offices to Atlanta, Georgia, this is how you would update the city and state entries in the table:

SQL
```
update publishers
set city = 'Atlanta', state = 'GA'
```

Here's what the table looks like now:

SQL
```
select *
from publishers
pub_id pub_name              address         city                  state
====== ==================== =============== ==================== =====
0736   New Age Books         1 1st St.       Atlanta               GA
0877   Binnet & Hardley      2 2nd Ave.      Atlanta               GA
1389   Algodata Infosystems  3rd Dr.         Atlanta               GA
1622   Jardin, Inc.          5 5th Ave.      Atlanta               GA
1756   HealthText            (NULL)          Atlanta               GA
[5 rows]
```

To restore the city and state values, try variations on the following UPDATE statement, supplying the correct location and `pub_id` for each of the three original rows. (You'll delete Jardin and HealthText later, so don't bother to update those rows.)

```
SQL
update publishers
set city = 'Boston', state = 'MA'
where pub_id = '0736'
```

You can also use computed column values in an update. To double all the prices in the titles table, use this statement:

```
SQL
update titles
set price = price * 2
```

Because there is no WHERE clause, the change in prices is applied to every row in the table. To restore the original prices, just cut them in half.

```
SQL
update titles
set price = price / 2
```

Specifying Rows: WHERE Clause The WHERE clause in an UPDATE statement specifies which rows to change. (It is similar to the WHERE clause in a SELECT statement, which is discussed in Chapters 4, 5, 6, 7, and 8.) For example, in the unlikely event that northern California becomes a new state called Pacifica (abbreviated PC) and the people of Oakland vote to change the name of their city (to Big Bay City, for example), here is how you can update the authors table for only the residents of the city formerly known as Oakland:

```
SQL
update authors
set state = 'PC', city = 'Big Bay City'
where state = 'CA' and city = 'Oakland'
```

Here's the new look of the authors table:

SQL

```
select au_fname, au_lname, city, state
from authors
```

au_fname	au_lname	city	state
===================	========================	===================	=====
Abraham	Bennet	Berkeley	CA
Marjorie	Green	**Big Bay City**	**PC**
Cheryl	Carson	Berkeley	CA
Albert	Ringer	Salt Lake City	UT
Anne	Ringer	Salt Lake City	UT
Michel	DeFrance	Gary	IN
Sylvia	Panteley	Rockville	MD
Heather	McBadden	Vacaville	CA
Dirk	Stringer	**Big Bay City**	**PC**
Dick	Straight	**Big Bay City**	**PC**
Livia	Karsen	**Big Bay City**	**PC**
Stearns	MacFeather	**Big Bay City**	**PC**
Ann	Dull	Palo Alto	CA
Akiko	Yokomoto	Walnut Creek	CA
Michael	O'Leary	San Jose	CA
Burt	Gringlesby	Covelo	CA
Morningstar	Greene	Nashville	TN
Johnson	White	Menlo Park	CA
Innes	del Castillo	Ann Arbor	MI
Sheryl	Hunter	Palo Alto	CA
Chastity	Locksley	San Francisco	CA
Reginald	Blotchet-Halls	Corvallis	OR
Meander	Smith	Lawrence	KS

[23 rows]

To restore the data, use an UPDATE like this:

SQL

```
update authors
set state = 'CA', city = 'Oakland'
where state = 'PC' and city = 'Big Bay City'
```

The WHERE clause of an UPDATE statement can also contain a subquery that refers to one or more other tables. For information on subqueries, see Chapter 8.

Removing Data: DELETE

It's just as important to be able to remove rows as it is to be able to add or change them. Like INSERT and UPDATE, DELETE works for single-row operations as well as for multiple-row operations, and like the other data modification statements, you can delete rows based on data in other tables.

The DELETE syntax looks like this:

SYNTAX

```
DELETE FROM table_name
WHERE search_conditions
```

The WHERE clause specifies which rows to remove. If you decide to remove two rows from `publishers`—the rows added for publisher identification number 1622 and 1756—type this:

SQL
```
delete from publishers
where pub_id = '1622' or pub_id = '1756'
```

Note that once you delete the row that describes this publisher, you can no longer find the books the company publishes by joining the `publishers` and `titles` tables on publisher identification numbers.

To clean up the `titleauthors` table, use the following DELETE:

SQL
```
delete from titleauthors
where au_id = 'xxxxxx'
```

If there is no WHERE clause in a DELETE statement, *all* rows in the table are removed.

Summary

This chapter goes over the process of creating a database and adding data. It covers

- Creating a database
- Planning and creating simple tables, including choosing datatypes and deciding on null/not null status
- Creating indexes with the CREATE INDEX command
- Planning and creating more complex tables with constraints, such as PRIMARY KEY, UNIQUE, REFERENCES, and CHECK
- Changing and deleting database objects
- Inserting, updating, and deleting rows

Now that you understand how to create a database and insert sample data, it's time to retrieve this data using the SELECT command. Chapter 4 covers SELECT in detail.

Chapter 4

Selecting Data from the Database

In This Chapter

- SELECT Overview and Syntax
- Choosing Columns: The SELECT Clause
- Specifying Tables: The FROM Clause
- Selecting Rows: The WHERE Clause

SELECT Overview and Syntax

In many ways, the SELECT statement is the real heart of SQL. It lets you find
and view your data in a variety of ways. You use it to answer questions based
on your data: how many, where, what kind of, even what if. Once you become
comfortable with its sometimes dauntingly complex syntax, you'll be amazed
at what the SELECT statement can do.

Because SELECT is so important, five chapters focus on it:

- This chapter begins with the bare bones: the SELECT, FROM, and
  WHERE clauses, search conditions, and expressions.
- Chapter 5 delves into some SELECT refinements: ORDER BY, the DIS-
  TINCT keyword, and aggregates.
- Chapter 6 covers the GROUP BY clause, the HAVING clause, and mak-
  ing reports from grouped data. Chapter 6 also summarizes the issues
  regarding null values in database management.
- Chapter 7 introduces multiple-table queries with a comprehensive dis-
  cussion of joining tables.
- Chapter 8 moves on to **nested queries**, also known as **subqueries**.

Queries in this chapter use single tables so that you can focus on manipulating the syntax in a simple environment. Following is an example of a SELECT query—don't worry about the syntax yet:

```
SQL
select address
from publishers
where pub_id = '0877'

address
==========================================
2 2nd Ave.
[1 row]
```

Basic SELECT Syntax

Discovering the structure of the SELECT statement begins with this skeleton:

- The SELECT clause identifies the *columns* you want to retrieve.
- The FROM clause specifies the *tables* those columns are in.
- The WHERE clause qualifies the *rows*—it chooses the ones you want to see.

```
SELECT select_list
FROM table_list
WHERE search_conditions
```

SYNTAX

Select_list and Search_condition Expressions   Both the SELECT and WHERE clauses (in the select_list or search_conditions) can include

- Plain column names (`price`)
- Column names combined with other elements, such as calculations (`price * 1.085`)
- Constants (character strings or display headings)

Collectively, these are expressions. Because the column name expression is the simplest case, examples often start there and then go on to a more complex expression. This does not mean that a column name is not an expression—it's just the place to start looking at expressions. Syntax that includes "expression" or "expr" or "char_expr" means that you can use a column name or a more complex expression.

pub_id	name	address	city	state
0736	New Age Books	1 1st St.	Boston	MA
0877	Binnet & Hardley	2 2nd Ave.	Washington	DC
1389	Algodata Infosystems	3 3rd Dr.	Berkeley	CA

Figure 4.1 Locating a Specific Piece of Data in a Table

Combining SELECT, FROM, and WHERE Artful combinations of the SELECT, FROM, and WHERE clauses produce meaningful answers to your questions and keep you from drowning in a sea of data. Think of the SELECT and WHERE clauses as horizontal and vertical axes on a matrix. (Figure 4.1 illustrates the query you saw at the beginning of the chapter.) The data you get from the SELECT statement is at the intersection of the SELECT (column) and WHERE (row) clauses.

Let's look at a SELECT statement with another `bookbiz` table, `authors`. The `authors` table stores information about authors: ID numbers, names, addresses, and phone numbers. If you want to know just the names of authors who live in California (not their addresses and phone numbers), use the SELECT clause and the WHERE clause to limit the data that the SELECT statement returns.

Here's a query that uses the SELECT clause's select_list to limit the *columns* you see. It lists just the names for the authors, ignoring their ID numbers, addresses, and phone numbers.

```
SQL
select au_lname, au_fname
from authors
au_lname                              au_fname
================================      ====================
Bennet                                Abraham
Green                                 Marjorie
Carson                                Cheryl
Ringer                                Albert
Ringer                                Anne
DeFrance                              Michel
Panteley                              Sylvia
```

McBadden	Heather
Stringer	Dirk
Straight	Dick
Karsen	Livia
MacFeather	Stearns
Dull	Ann
Yokomoto	Akiko
O'Leary	Michael
Gringlesby	Burt
Greene	Morningstar
White	Johnson
del Castillo	Innes
Hunter	Sheryl
Locksley	Chastity
Blotchet-Halls	Reginald
Smith	Meander

[23 rows]

This display still doesn't provide exactly what you want because it lists all authors regardless of the state they live in. You need to refine the data retrieval statement further with the WHERE clause.

SQL
```
select au_lname, au_fname
from authors
where state = 'CA'
```

au_lname	au_fname
===================================	====================
Bennet	Abraham
Green	Marjorie
Carson	Cheryl
McBadden	Heather
Stringer	Dirk
Straight	Dick
Karsen	Livia
MacFeather	Stearns
Dull	Ann
Yokomoto	Akiko
O'Leary	Michael
Gringlesby	Burt

```
White                              Johnson
Hunter                             Sheryl
Locksley                           Chastity
[15 rows]
```

Now you're looking at just the names of the 15 authors having a California address. The rows for the eight authors living elsewhere are not included in the display.

Full SELECT Syntax

In practice, SELECT syntax can be either simpler or more complex than the example just shown. It can be simpler in that the SELECT and (in most systems) FROM clauses are the only required ones in a SELECT statement. The WHERE clause (and all other clauses) are optional. On the other hand, the full syntax of the SELECT statement includes all of the following phrases and keywords:

SYNTAX

```
SELECT [ALL | DISTINCT] select_list
   FROM table/view_list
   [WHERE search_conditions]
   [GROUP BY group_by_list ]
    [HAVING search_conditions]
   [ORDER BY order_by_list ]
```

SELECT Statement Clause Order Although SQL is a free-form language, you do have to keep the clauses in a SELECT statement in syntactical order (for example, a GROUP BY clause must come before an ORDER BY clause). Otherwise, you'll get syntax errors.

Naming Conventions You may need to qualify the names of database objects (according to the customs of your SQL dialect) if there is any ambiguity about which object you mean. In this database, there are several columns called `title_id` (in the `titles` table, the `titleauthors` table, and the `titleview` view, among others—see Figure 2.13). When you are working with multiple tables, you may have to specify which `title_id` column you're talking about by including the table or view name, usually separated from the column name by a period (`titles.title_id`). If the system allows multiple tables with the same name, add the owner name (`mary.titles.title_id` or `dba.titles.title_id`)—some possible combinations appear in Figure 4.2.

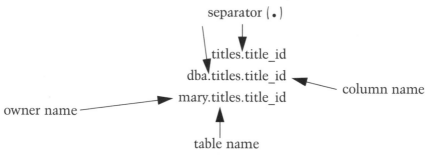

Figure 4.2 Qualifying Columns

You may also see larger elements, such as database and server names, used this way, but that is less common.

The examples in this chapter involve queries on a single table, so qualification is not an important issue here. Qualifiers are also omitted in most books, articles, and reference manuals on SQL because the short forms make SELECT statements more readable. However, it's never wrong to include them.

Choosing Columns: The SELECT Clause

The first clause of the SELECT statement—the one that begins with the keyword SELECT—is required in all SELECT statements. The keywords ALL and DISTINCT, which specify whether duplicate rows are to be included in the results, are optional. DISTINCT and ALL are discussed in the next chapter.

The select_list specifies the columns you want to see in the results. It can consist of these items individually or together:

- An asterisk, shorthand for all the columns in the table, displayed in CREATE TABLE order
- One or more column names, in any order
- One or more character constants (such as "Total") used as display headings or text embedded in the results
- One or more SQL functions (AVG) and arithmetic operators, generally used with columns (`price * 1.085`)

You can mix these elements freely. As mentioned earlier, columns, constants, functions, and combinations of these elements, with or without arithmetic operators, are collectively called expressions. Separate with a comma each element in a SELECT list from the following element.

Choosing All Columns: SELECT *

The asterisk (*) has a special meaning in the select_list. It stands for *all the column names* in *all the tables* in the table list. The columns are displayed in the order in which they appeared in the CREATE TABLE statement(s). Most people read a SELECT * statement as "select star." Use it when you want to see all the columns in a table.

The general syntax for selecting all the columns in a table is this:

```
SELECT *
FROM table/view_list
```

Because SELECT * finds all the columns currently in a table, changes in the structure of a table (adding, removing, or renaming columns) automatically modify the results of a SELECT *. Listing the columns individually gives you more precise control over the results, but SELECT * saves typing (and the frustration of typographical errors). SELECT * is most useful for tables with few columns because displays of many columns can be confusing. It also comes in handy when you want to get a quick look at a table's structure (what columns it has and in what order they appear).

The following statement retrieves all columns in the publishers table and displays them in the order in which they were defined when the publishers table was created. Because no WHERE clause is included, this statement retrieves every row.

SQL
```
select *
from publishers
```

pub_id	pub_name	address	city	state
0736	New Age Books	1 1st St.	Boston	MA
0877	Binnet & Hardley	2 2nd Ave.	Washington	DC
1389	Algodata Infosystems	3 3rd Dr.	Berkeley	CA

[3 rows]

You get exactly the same results by listing all the column names in the table in CREATE TABLE order after the SELECT keyword:

SQL
```
select pub_id, pub_name, address, city, state
from publishers
pub_id pub_name                  address           city          state
====== ======================    ================= ============  =====
0736   New Age Books             1 1st St.         Boston        MA
0877   Binnet & Hardley          2 2nd Ave.        Washington    DC
1389   Algodata Infosystems      3 3rd Dr.         Berkeley      CA
[3 rows]
```

Choosing Specific Columns

To select a subset of the columns in a table, as some of the previous examples have demonstrated, simply list the columns you want to see in the SELECT list:

```
SELECT column_name[, column_name]...
FROM table_list
```

SYNTAX

Separate each column name from the following column name with a comma.

Rearranging Result Columns The order in which columns appear in a display is completely up to you: Use the SELECT list to order them in any way that makes sense.

Following are two examples. Both of them find and display the publisher names and identification numbers from all three of the rows in the `publishers` table. The first one prints `pub_id` first, followed by `pub_name`. The second reverses that order. The information is exactly the same; only the display format changes.

SQL
```
select pub_id, pub_name
from publishers
```

```
pub_id pub_name
====== =======================================
0736   New Age Books
0877   Binnet & Hardley
1389   Algodata Infosystems
[3 rows]


select pub_name, pub_id
from publishers
pub_name                                      pub_id
====================================== ======
New Age Books                                 0736
Binnet & Hardley                              0877
Algodata Infosystems                          1389
[3 rows]
```

More Than Column Names

The SELECT statements you've seen so far show exactly what's stored in a table. This is useful, but often not useful enough. SQL lets you add to and manipulate these results to make them easier to read or to do "what if" queries. This means you can use strings of characters, mathematical calculations, and functions provided by your system in the SELECT list, with or without column names.

Display Label Conventions   When the results of a query are displayed, each column has a default heading—its name as defined in the database. Column names in databases are often cryptic (so they'll be easy to type) or have no meaning to users unfamiliar with departmental acronyms, nicknames, or project jargon.

You can solve this problem by specifying **display labels** (sometimes called **column aliases** or **headings**) to make query results easier to read and understand. To get the heading you want, simply type `column_name column_heading`, or `column_name as column_heading` in the SELECT clause in place of the column name. For example, to change the `pub_name` column heading to `Publisher`, try one of the following statements:

SQL
```
select pub_name Publisher, pub_id
from publishers
```

SQL
```
select pub_name as Publisher, pub_id
from publishers
```

Some systems also allow this syntax:

Adaptive Server Anywhere
```
select Publisher = pub_name, pub_id
from publishers
```

The results of all three methods show a new column heading:

Results

Publisher	pub_id
New Age Books	0736
Binnet & Hardley	0877
Algodata Infosystems	1389
[3 rows]	

For consistency, pick one of these formats and stick with it. Many users prefer the AS convention—it has the advantage of being simple and unambiguous.

TIP

SQL VARIANTS

Check to see how your system handles column headings that are longer than defined column size. For example, what happens when you change the pub_id column heading to a string such as "Identification #"? Does your system increase the display size of the column or shorten the new column heading to the size of the column data? The following queries show two possibilities:

```
Adaptive Server Anywhere
select pub_name as Publisher, pub_id as Identification#
from publishers
Publisher                                Identification#
======================================== ================
New Age Books                            0736
Binnet & Hardley                         0877
Algodata Infosystems                     1389
[3 rows]


Oracle
PUBLISHER                                IDEN
---------------------------------------- ----
New Age Books                            0736
Binnet + Hardley                         0877
Algodata Infosystems                     1389
```

(Oracle SQL Plus shows display headings as uppercase by default. Enclose the heading text in double quotes to preserve case.) If you use a smaller heading, however, SQL doesn't shrink the display size to less than its datatype-defined size.

Display Label Limitations Most SQL dialects that allow you to add display labels have some restrictions. Check your reference guide for details on

- Quotes (single and double)
- Embedded spaces
- Special characters

For example, Adaptive Server Anywhere allows single and double quotes around column headings. The quotes are not needed unless there is an embedded space in the column heading.

```
Adaptive Server Anywhere
select pub_name as 'Publisher #', pub_id as "Identification #"
from publishers;
Publisher #                              Identification #
======================================== ================
New Age Books                            0736
Binnet & Hardley                         0877
Algodata Infosystems                     1389
```

However, other systems are not as forgiving.

Oracle SQL Plus rejects single quotes around column headings.

```
Oracle
SQL> select pub_name as Publisher, pub_id as 'Identification #'
  2    from publishers;
ERROR at line 1:
ORA-00923: FROM keyword not found where expected
```

Change the single quotes to double, and the query works fine. In addition, the original case of the heading is preserved.

```
Oracle
SQL> select pub_name as "Publisher #", pub_id as "Identification #"
  2  from publishers;
Publisher #                               Iden
---------------------------------------- ----
New Age Books                             0736
Binnet & Hardley                          0877
Algodata Infosystems                      1389
```

Other implementations object to spaces or special characters.

```
Informix
select pub_name as Publisher, pub_id as Identification#
from publishers
SQL Error. An illegal character has been found.
```

The illegal character is the pound sign (#). Quotation marks don't help in this case.

Character Strings in Query Results   Sometimes a little text can make query results easier to understand. That's where **strings** (of characters) come in handy.

Let's say you want a listing of publishers with something like "The publisher's name is" in front of each item. All you have to do is insert the string in the correct position in the SELECT list. Be sure to enclose the entire string in quotes (single quotes are standard, but some dialects allow both single and double quotes) so your system can tell it's not a column name and separate it with commas from other elements in the select_list .

Follow your system's rules for protecting embedded apostrophes and quotes, if any appear in the string. In most cases, double single quotes do the trick and prevent the apostrophe from being interpreted as a close quote.

```
SQL
select 'The publisher''s name is', pub_name as Publisher
from publishers


'The publisher''s name is' Publisher
========================= =============================
The publisher's name is    New Age Books
The publisher's name is    Binnet & Hardley
The publisher's name is    Algodata Infosystems
[3 rows]
```

The constants create a new column in the display only—what you see doesn't affect anything that's physically in the database.

Combining Columns, Display Headings, and Text   You can combine columns, display headings, and text in a SELECT list.

Remember to put quotes around the text but not around the column names. You need quotes around display headings only if they contain spaces (or other special characters). Figure 4.3 illustrates mixing several techniques.

Computations with Constants   The SELECT list is the place where you indicate computations you want to perform on numeric data or constants.

Here are the available **arithmetic operators**:

Symbol	Operation
+	addition
−	subtraction
/	division
*	multiplication

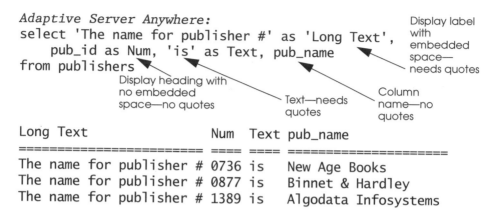

```
Adaptive Server Anywhere:
select 'The name for publisher #' as 'Long Text',
    pub_id as Num, 'is' as Text, pub_name
from publishers
```

Display label with embedded space—needs quotes

Display heading with no embedded space—no quotes

Text—needs quotes

Column name—no quotes

```
Long Text                        Num  Text  pub_name
===========================      ====  ====  ======================
The name for publisher # 0736 is       New Age Books
The name for publisher # 0877 is       Binnet & Hardley
The name for publisher # 1389 is       Algodata Infosystems
```

Figure 4.3 Column Names, Text, and Display Headings

The arithmetic operators—addition, subtraction, division, and multiplication—can be used on any numeric column.

Certain arithmetic operations can also be performed on date columns, if your system provides date functions.

You can use all of these operators in the SELECT list with column names and numeric constants in any combination. For example, to see what a projected sales increase of 100 percent for all the books in the `titles` table looks like, type this:

SQL

```
select title_id, ytd_sales, ytd_sales * 2
from titles
```

```
title_id    ytd_sales  titles.ytd_sales*2
========    =========  ==================
PC8888           4095                8190
BU1032           4095                8190
PS7777           3336                6672
PS3333           4072                8144
BU1111           3876                7752
MC2222           2032                4064
TC7777           4095                8190
TC4203          15096               30192
PC1035           8780               17560
BU2075          18722               37444
PS2091           2045                4090
```

PS2106	111	222
MC3021	22246	44492
TC3218	375	750
MC3026	(NULL)	(NULL)
BU7832	4095	8190
PS1372	375	750
PC9999	(NULL)	(NULL)

[18 rows]

Notice the null values in the ytd_sales column and the computed column. When you perform any arithmetic operation on a null value, the result is NULL.

SQL VARIANTS   The null value may show up as a blank, as the word NULL, or as some other symbol determined by the system. Check your vendor's documentation: You may have a way to change the default NULL display.

```
Oracle
SQL> select title_id, ytd_sales, ytd_sales * 2
  2  from titles
  3  where title_id > 'M' and title_id < 'PS';
TITLE_ YTD_SALES YTD_SALES*2
------ --------- -----------
MC2222      2032        4064
MC3021     22246       44492
MC3026
PC1035      8780       17560
PC8888      4095        8190
PC9999
6 rows selected.
```

Computed Column Display Headings   You can give the computed column a heading (for example, Projected_Sales):

SQL
```
select title_id, ytd_sales, ytd_sales * 2 as Projected_Sales
from titles
```

For a fancier display, try adding character strings such as "Current sales =" and "Projected sales are" to the SELECT statement.

Sometimes, as in the previous example, you'll want both the original data and the computed data in your results. But you don't have to include the column on which the computation takes place in the SELECT list. To see just the computed values, type this:

SQL

```
select title_id, ytd_sales * 2
from titles
```

title_id	titles.ytd_sales*2
========	==================
PC8888	8190
BU1032	8190
PS7777	6672
PS3333	8144
BU1111	7752
MC2222	4064
TC7777	8190
TC4203	30192
PC1035	17560
BU2075	37444
PS2091	4090
PS2106	222
MC3021	44492
TC3218	750
MC3026	(NULL)
BU7832	8190
PS1372	750
PC9999	(NULL)

[18 rows]

Computations with Column Names   You can also use arithmetic operators for computations on the data in two or more columns, with no constants involved. Here's an example:

```
SQL
select title_id, ytd_sales * price
from titles
title_id    titles.ytd_sales*titles.price
========  =================================
PC8888                          81900.00
BU1032                          81859.05
PS7777                          26654.64
PS3333                          81399.28
BU1111                          46318.20
MC2222                          40619.68
TC7777                          61384.05
TC4203                         180397.20
PC1035                         201501.00
BU2075                          55978.78
PS2091                          22392.75
PS2106                            777.00
MC3021                          66515.54
TC3218                           7856.25
MC3026                            (NULL)
BU7832                          81859.05
PS1372                           8096.25
PC9999                            (NULL)
[18 rows]
```

Finally, you can compute new values on the basis of columns from more than one table. (Chapter 7, on joining, and Chapter 8, on subqueries, give information on how to work with multiple-table queries, so check them for details.)

Arithmetic Operator Precedence   When there is more than one arithmetic operator in an expression, the system follows rules that determine the order in which the operations are carried out (Figure 4.4). According to commonly used precedence rules, multiplication and division are calculated first, followed by subtraction and addition. When more than one arithmetic operator in an expression has the same level of precedence, the order of execution is left to right. Expressions within parentheses take precedence over all other operations.

Here's an example: The following SELECT statement subtracts the advance on each book from the gross revenues realized on its sales (price multiplied by

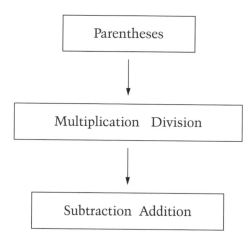

Figure 4.4 Precedence Hierarchy for Arithmetic Operators

ytd_sales). The product of ytd_sales and price is calculated first because the operator is multiplication.

SQL
```
select title_id, ytd_sales * price - advance
from titles
```

To avoid misunderstandings, use parentheses. The following query has the same meaning and gives the same results as the previous one, but it is easier to understand:

SQL
```
select title_id, (ytd_sales * price) - advance
from titles

title_id titles.ytd_sales*titles.price
======== =============================
PC8888                        155800.00
BU1032                        117809.05
PS7777                         56014.64
PS3333                        120119.28
BU1111                         80078.20
MC2222                         60939.68
```

TC7777	114809.05
TC4203	327357.20
PC1035	370101.00
BU2075	233073.78
PS2091	42612.75
PS2106	-4113.00
MC3021	273975.54
TC3218	8356.25
MC3026	(NULL)
BU7832	117809.05
PS1372	8596.25
PC9999	(NULL)

[18 rows]

Another important use of parentheses is changing the order of execution: Calculations inside parentheses are handled first. If parentheses are nested (one set of parentheses inside another), the most deeply nested calculation has precedence. For example, the result and meaning of the query just shown can be changed if you use parentheses to force evaluation of the subtraction before the multiplication:

SQL

```
select title_id, ytd_sales * (price - advance)
from titles
```

title_id	titles.ytd_sales*(titles.pric
PC8888	-32596200.00
BU1032	-20352190.95
PS7777	-13283985.36
PS3333	-8021880.72
BU1111	-19294921.80
MC2222	60939.68
TC7777	-32637190.95
TC4203	-60052642.80
PC1035	-61082899.00
BU2075	-189317051.22
PS2091	-4607487.25
PS2106	-664113.00
MC3021	-333401024.46
TC3218	-2609643.75

```
MC3026                         (NULL)
BU7832                   -20352190.95
PS1372                    -2609403.75
PC9999                         (NULL)
[18 rows]
```

Specifying Tables: The FROM Clause

The **table list** names the table(s), the view(s), or both, that contain columns included in the SELECT list and in the WHERE clause. (Views are covered in Chapter 9—for now, just consider them a kind of table.) Separate table names in the table list with commas. The FROM syntax looks like this:

SYNTAX

```
SELECT select_list
FROM [qualifier.]{table_name | view_name} [alias]
  [, [qualifier.]{table_name | view_name} [alias] ]...
```

The full naming syntax for tables and views, with qualifying database and owner names, is always permitted in the table list. It's necessary, however, only when there might be some confusion about the name.

Using Table Aliases

In many SQL dialects, you can give table names **aliases** to save typing. Assign an alias in the table list by giving the alias after the table name, like this:

SQL

```
select p.pub_id, p.pub_name
from publishers p
```

The **p** in front of each of the column names in the SELECT list acts as a substitute for the full table name (publishers). This query is equivalent to

SQL

```
select publishers.pub_id, publishers.pub_name
from publishers
```

You can't combine the two naming conventions. Once you assign an alias, you must use the alias or no qualifier—alternately using the alias and the full table name in a given query isn't allowed because the alias actually substitutes for the table or view name during the query. In effect, the table name does not exist. Here's an example of assigning an alias but also using the full name:

> *SQL*
> select **publishers**.pub_id, **p**.pub_name
> from publishers p
> **Correlation name 'publishers' not found.**

Since only one table is involved in these queries, there is no ambiguity about which pub_id column you're referencing, so using the table name—either its alias or its full name—as a qualifier is optional. Aliases are really useful only in multiple-table queries where you need to qualify columns from different tables. You'll see examples of their use in Chapters 7 and 8.

Skipping FROM

Some systems allow you to write queries *without* a FROM clause. For example, a query for the current date and time (information not stored in a table) may work fine, like this:

> *Adaptive Server Anywhere*
> select current date
> current date
> ============
> Mar 01 2000 12:00am
> [1 row]

SQL
VARIANTS   Other systems don't allow you to skip FROM. When you retrieve nontable information, you must use FROM with a dummy table that you create or the system supplies (for Oracle, dual).

```
Oracle
SQL> select sysdate
  2  from dual;
SYSDATE
--------------------
Mar 01 2000 12:00 AM
```

Selecting Rows: The WHERE Clause

The WHERE clause is the part of the SELECT statement that specifies the search conditions. These conditions determine exactly which rows are retrieved. The general format is this:

SYNTAX

```
SELECT select_list
FROM table_list
WHERE search_conditions
```

When you run a SELECT statement with a WHERE clause, your system searches for the rows in the table that meet your conditions (also called **qualifications**).

SQL provides a variety of operators and keywords for expressing the search conditions, including these:

- **Comparison operators** (=, <, >, and so on)
  ```
  select title
  from titles
  where advance * 2 > ytd_sales * price
  ```

- Combinations or logical negations of conditions (AND, OR, NOT)
  ```
  select title
  from titles
  where advance < 5000 or ytd_sales > 2000
  ```

- Ranges (BETWEEN and NOT BETWEEN)
  ```
  select title
  from titles
  where ytd_sales between 4095 and 12000
  ```

- Lists (IN, NOT IN)
  ```
  select pub_name
  from publishers
  where state in ('CA', 'IN', 'MD')
  ```

- Unknown values (IS NULL and IS NOT NULL)
  ```
  select title
  from titles
  where advance is null
  ```

- Character matches (LIKE and NOT LIKE)
  ```
  select au_lname
  from authors
  where phone not like '415%'
  ```

Each of these keywords and operators is explained and illustrated in this chapter. In addition, the WHERE clause can include join conditions (see Chapter 7) and subqueries (see Chapter 8).

Comparison Operators

You often want to look at values in relation to one another to find out which is "larger" or "smaller" or "lower" in the alphabet sort or "equal" to some other database value or to a constant. SQL provides a set of comparison operators for these purposes. In most dialects, the comparison operators are these:

Operator	Meaning
=	equal to
>	greater than
<	less than
>=	greater than or equal to
<=	less than or equal to
< >	not equal to

The operators are used in the syntax:

SYNTAX

```
WHERE expression comparison_operator expression
```

An expression can be a plain column name or something more complex—a character string, a function or calculation (usually involving a column name), or any combination of these elements connected by arithmetic operators. When evaluated, an expression produces a single value per row.

In contexts other than SQL, the comparison operators are usually used with numeric values. In SQL, they are also used with *char* and *varchar* data (< means earlier in the dictionary order and > means later) and with dates (< means earlier in chronological order and > means later). When you use character and date values in a SQL statement, be sure to put quotes around them.

TIP

The order in which uppercase and lowercase characters and special characters are evaluated depends on the character-sorting sequence you are using, imposed by your database system or by the machine you are using. (There are more details on sort order in "Character Sets and Sort Orders"). Check your system to see how it handles trailing blanks in comparisons. Is "Dirk" considered the same as "Dirk "?

Comparing Numbers   The following SELECT statements and their results should give you a good sense of how the comparison operators are used. The first query finds the books that cost more than $25.00.

SQL
```
select title, price
from titles
where price > $25.00
```

title	price
Secrets of Silicon Valley	40.00
The Busy Executive's Database Guide	29.99
Prolonged Data Deprivation: Four Case Studies	29.99
Silicon Valley Gastronomic Treats	29.99
Sushi, Anyone?	29.99
But Is It User Friendly?	42.95
Onions, Leeks, and Garlic: Cooking Secrets of the Mediterranean	40.95
Straight Talk About Computers	29.99
Computer Phobic and Non-Phobic Individuals: Behavior Variations	41.59

[9 rows]

SQL VARIANTS   Check your system to see if it allows dollar signs with money values. Most do not. Transact-SQL is an exception, and so is Adaptive Server Anywhere.

Comparing Character Values   The next SELECT statement finds the authors whose last names follow McBadden in the alphabet. Notice the name is in single quotes. (Some systems allow both single and double quotes around character and date constants in the WHERE clause, but most allow single quotes only.)

```
SQL
select au_lname, au_fname
from authors
where au_lname >'McBadden'
au_lname                                  au_fname
====================================== ================
O'Leary                                   Michael
Panteley                                  Sylvia
Ringer                                    Albert
Ringer                                    Anne
Smith                                     Meander
Straight                                  Dick
Stringer                                  Dirk
White                                     Johnson
Yokomoto                                  Akiko
[9 rows]
```

(Your results may differ, depending on the sort order your system uses. See Chapter 5 for more on this issue.)

Comparing Imaginary Values   The next query displays hypothetical information—it calculates double the price of all books for which advances over $10,000 were paid and displays the title identification numbers and calculated prices:

```
SQL
select title_id, price * 2
from titles
where advance > 10000
```

title_id	titles.price*2
==========	================
BU2075	25.98
MC3021	25.98
[2 rows]	

Finding Values Not Equal to Some Value   Following is a query that finds the telephone numbers of authors who don't live in California, using the not equal comparison operator (in some SQL dialects, you can use != as the not equal operator).

```
SQL
select au_id, phone
from authors
where state <> 'CA'
```

au_id	phone
=============	==============
998-72-3567	801 826-0752
899-46-2035	801 826-0752
722-51-5454	219 547-9982
807-91-6654	301 946-8853
527-72-3246	615 297-2723
712-45-1867	615 996-8275
648-92-1872	503 745-6402
341-22-1782	913 843-0462
[8 rows]	

Connecting Conditions with Logical Operators

Use the **logical operators** AND, OR, and NOT when you're dealing with more than one condition in a WHERE clause. The logical operators are also called **Boolean operators**.

AND   AND joins two or more conditions and returns results only when all of the conditions are true. For example, the following query will find only the rows in which the author's last name is Ringer and the author's first name is Anne. It will not find the row for Albert Ringer.

SQL
```
select au_id, au_lname, au_fname
from authors
where au_lname = 'Ringer'
  and au_fname = 'Anne'
```

au_id	au_lname	au_fname
899-46-2035	Ringer	Anne

[1 row]

The next example finds business books with a price higher than $20.00 and for which an advance of less than $20,000 was paid:

SQL
```
select title, type, price, advance
from titles
where type = 'business'
  and price > 20.00
  and advance < 20000
```

title	type	price	advance
The Busy Executive's Database Guide	business	29.99	5000.00
Cooking with Computers: Surreptitious Balance Sheets	business	21.95	5000.00
Straight Talk About Computers	business	29.99	5000.00

[3 rows]

OR   OR also connects two or more conditions, but it returns results when any of the conditions is true. The following query searches for rows containing Anne or Ann in the au_fname column:

SQL

```
select au_id, au_lname, au_fname
from authors
where au_fname = 'Anne'
  or au_fname = 'Ann'
```

au_id	au_lname	au_fname
899-46-2035	Ringer	Anne
427-17-2319	Dull	Ann

[2 rows]

The following query searches for books with a price higher than $20.00 *or* an advance less than $5,000:

SQL

```
select title, type, price, advance
from titles
where price > $30.00
  or advance < $5000
```

title	type	price	advance
Secrets of Silicon Valley	popular_comp	40.00	8000.00
Emotional Security: A New Algorithm	psychology	17.99	4000.00
Prolonged Data Deprivation: Four Case Studies	psychology	29.99	2000.00
Silicon Valley Gastronomic Treats	mod_cook	29.99	0.00
Fifty Years in Buckingham Palace Kitchens	trad_cook	21.95	4000.00
But Is It User Friendly?	popular_comp	42.95	7000.00
Is Anger the Enemy?	psychology	21.95	2275.00
Onions, Leeks, and Garlic: Cooking Secrets of the Mediterranean	trad_cook	40.95	7000.00
Computer Phobic and Non-Phobic Individuals: Behavior Variations	psychology	41.59	7000.00

[9 rows]

Semantic Issues with OR and AND   One more example using OR will demonstrate a potential for confusion. Let's say you want to find all the business books, as well as any books with a price higher than $10 and any books with an advance less than $20,000. The English phrasing of this problem suggests the use of the operator AND, but the logical meaning dictates the use of OR because you want to find all the books in all three categories, not just books that meet all three characteristics at once. Here's the SQL statement that finds what you're looking for:

SQL
```
select title, type, price, advance
from titles
where type - 'business'
  or price > $20.00
  or advance < $20000
```

title	type	price	advance
Secrets of Silicon Valley	popular_comp	40.00	8000.00
The Busy Executive's Database Guide	business	29.99	5000.00
Emotional Security: A New Algorithm	psychology	17.99	4000.00
Prolonged Data Deprivation:			
Four Case Studies	psychology	29.99	2000.00
Cooking with Computers:			
Surreptitious Balance Sheets	business	21.95	5000.00
Silicon Valley Gastronomic Treats	mod_cook	29.99	0.00
Sushi, Anyone?	trad_cook	29.99	8000.00
Fifty Years in Buckingham Palace Kitchens	trad_cook	21.95	4000.00
But Is It User Friendly?	popular_comp	42.95	7000.00
You Can Combat Computer Stress!	business	12.99	10125.00
Is Anger the Enemy?	psychology	21.95	2275.00
Life Without Fear	psychology	17.00	6000.00
The Gourmet Microwave	mod_cook	12.99	15000.00
Onions, Leeks, and Garlic:			
Cooking Secrets of the Mediterranean	trad_cook	40.95	7000.00
Straight Talk About Computers	business	29.99	5000.00
Computer Phobic and Non-Phobic			
Individuals: Behavior Variations	psychology	41.59	7000.00

[16 rows]

Compare this query and its results to the earlier example that is identical except for the use of AND instead of OR.

NOT   The logical operator NOT negates an expression. When you use it with comparison operators, put it before the expression rather than before the comparison operator. The following two queries are equivalent:

SQL

```
select au_lname, au_fname, state
from authors
where state <> 'CA'
```

SQL

```
select au_lname, au_fname, state
from authors
where not state = 'CA'
```

Here are the results:

```
Results
au_lname                              au_fname          state
================================ ================ =====
Ringer                                Albert            UT
Ringer                                Anne              UT
DeFrance                              Michel            IN
Panteley                              Sylvia            MD
Greene                                Morningstar       TN
del Castillo                          Innes             MI
Blotchet-Halls                        Reginald          OR
Smith                                 Meander           KS
[8 rows]
```

Logical Operator Precedence   Like the arithmetic operators, logical operators are handled according to precedence rules. When both kinds of operators occur in the same statement, arithmetic operators are handled before logical operators. When more than one logical operator is used in a statement, NOT is evaluated first, then AND, and finally OR. Figure 4.5 shows the hierarchy.

Some examples will clarify the situation. The following query finds all the business books in the `titles` table, no matter what their advances are, as well as all psychology books that have an advance greater than $5,500. The advance condition pertains to psychology books and not to business books because the AND is handled before the OR.

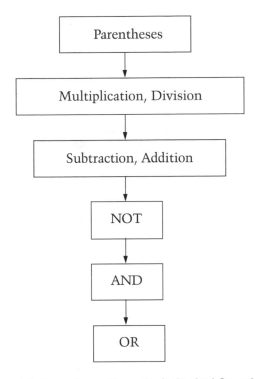

Figure 4.5 Precedence Hierarchy for Logical Operators

SQL
```
select title_id, type, advance
from titles
where type = 'business'
  or type = 'psychology'
  and advance > 5500
```

title_id	type	advance
BU1032	business	5000.00
BU1111	business	5000.00
BU2075	business	10125.00
PS2106	psychology	6000.00
BU7832	business	5000.00
PS1372	psychology	7000.00

[6 rows]

The results include three business books with advances less than $5,500 because the query was evaluated according to the following precedence rules:

1. Find all psychology books with advances greater than $5,500.
2. Find all business books (never mind about advances).
3. Display both sets of rows in the results.

You can change the meaning of the previous query by adding parentheses to force evaluation of the OR first. With parentheses added, the query executes differently:

1. Find all business and psychology books.
2. Locate those that have advances over $5,500.
3. Display only the final subset.

SQL
```
select title_id, type, advance
from titles
where (type = 'business' or type = 'psychology')
  and advance > 5500
title_id type                 advance
======== ============ ============
BU2075   business        10125.00
PS2106   psychology       6000.00
PS1372   psychology       7000.00
[3 rows]
```

The parentheses cause SQL to find all business and psychology books and, from among those, to find those with advances greater than $5,500.

Here's a query that includes arithmetic operators, comparison operators, and logical operators. It searches for books that are not bringing in enough money to offset their advances. Specifically, the query searches for any books with gross revenues (that is, `ytd_sales` times `price`) less than twice the advance paid to the author(s). The user who constructed this query has tacked on another condition: She wants to include in the results only books published before October 15, 2000, because those books have had long enough to establish a sales pattern. The last condition is connected with the logical operator

AND; according to the rules of precedence, it is evaluated after the arithmetic operations.

```
SQL
select title_id, type, price, advance, ytd_sales
from titles
where price * ytd_sales <  2 * advance
  and pubdate < '10/15/2000'
title_id type           price     advance     ytd_sales
======== =========== ========= =========== ===========
PS2106   psychology  17.00     6000.00     111
[1 row]
```

SQL VARIANTS   If you run this query on a system with a different date format, you may need to change the pubdate value to correspond to that format. For example, if your SQL engine expects dates to look like DD-MON-YYYY, you could write the query like this:

```
Oracle
SQL> select title_id, type, price, advance, ytd_sales
  2    from titles
  3    where price * ytd_sales <  2 * advance
  4    and pubdate < '21 OCT 2000';
TITLE_ TYPE            PRICE   ADVANCE YTD_SALES
------ ------------ --------- --------- ---------
PS2106 psychology         17      6000       111
```

Ranges (BETWEEN and NOT BETWEEN)

Another common search condition is a range. There are two different ways to specify ranges:

- With the comparison operators > and <
- With the keyword BETWEEN

Use BETWEEN to specify an **inclusive range**, in which you search for the lower value and the upper value as well as the values they bracket. For example, to find all the books with sales between (and including) 4,095 and 12,000, you could write this query:

SQL
```
select title_id, ytd_sales
from titles
where ytd_sales between 4095 and 12000
title_id    ytd_sales
========   ===========
PC8888           4095
BU1032           4095
TC7777           4095
PC1035           8780
BU7832           4095
[5 rows]
```

Notice that books with sales of 4,095 are included in the results. If there were any with sales of 12,000, they would be included too. In this way, the BETWEEN range is different from the greater-than/less-than (> <) range. The same query using the greater-than and less-than operators returns different results because the range is not inclusive:

SQL
```
select title_id, ytd_sales
from titles
where ytd_sales > 4095 and ytd_sales < 12000
title_id    ytd_sales
========   ===========
PC1035           8780
[1 row]
```

NOT BETWEEN   The phrase NOT BETWEEN finds all the rows that are not inside the range. To find all the books with sales outside the range of 4,095 to 12,000, type this:

SQL
```
select title_id, ytd_sales
from titles
where ytd_sales not between 4095 and 12000
title_id   ytd_sales
========  ============
PS7777          3336
PS3333          4072
BU1111          3876
MC2222          2032
TC4203         15096
BU2075         18722
PS2091          2045
PS2106           111
MC3021         22246
TC3218           375
PS1372           375
[11 rows]
```

You can get the same results with comparison operators, but notice in this query that you use OR between the two `ytd_sales` comparisons rather than AND.

SQL
```
select title_id, ytd_sales
from titles
where ytd_sales < 4095 or ytd_sales > 12000
title_id   ytd_sales
========  ============
PS7777          3336
PS3333          4072
BU1111          3876
MC2222          2032
TC4203         15096
BU2075         18722
PS2091          2045
PS2106           111
MC3021         22246
TC3218           375
PS1372           375
[11 rows]
```

This is another case where it's easy to get confused because of the way the question can be phrased in English. You might ask to see all books whose sales are less than 4,095 *and* all books whose sales are greater than 12,000. The logical meaning, however, calls for the use of the Boolean operator OR. If you substitute AND, you'll get no results at all because no book can have sales that are simultaneously less than 4,095 and greater than 12,000.

Lists (IN and NOT IN)

The IN keyword allows you to select values that match any one of a list of values. For example, without IN, if you want a list of the names and states of all the authors who live in California, Indiana, or Maryland, you can type this query:

```
SQL
select au_lname, state
from authors
where state = 'CA' or state = 'IN' or state = 'MD'
```

However, you get the same results with less typing if you use IN. The items following the IN keyword must be

- inside parentheses
- separated by commas
- enclosed in quotes, if they are character or date values

```
SQL
select au_lname, state
from authors
where state in ('CA', 'IN', 'MD')
```

Following is what results from either query:

```
Results
au_lname                                      state
=========================================== =====
Bennet                                        CA
Green                                         CA
Carson                                        CA
DeFrance                                      IN
Panteley                                      MD
```

```
McBadden                                          CA
Stringer                                          CA
Straight                                          CA
Karsen                                            CA
MacFeather                                        CA
Dull                                              CA
Yokomoto                                          CA
O'Leary                                           CA
Gringlesby                                        CA
White                                             CA
Hunter                                            CA
Locksley                                          CA
[17 rows]
```

The more items in the list, the greater the savings in typing by using IN rather than specifying each condition separately.

An important use for the IN keyword is in nested queries, also referred to as subqueries. For a full discussion of subqueries, see Chapter 8.

Selecting Null Values

From earlier chapters ("NULLs" in Chapter 1), you may recall that NULL is a placeholder for unknown information. It does not mean zero or blank.

To clarify this NULL–zero difference, take a look at the following listing showing title and advance amount for books belonging to one particular publisher.

SQL
```
select title, advance
from titles
where pub_id = '0877'
```

title	advance
===	========
Silicon Valley Gastronomic Treats	0.00
Sushi, Anyone?	8000.00
Fifty Years in Buckingham Palace Kitchens	4000.00
The Gourmet Microwave	15000.00
Onions, Leeks, and Garlic: Cooking Secrets of the Mediterranean	7000.00
The Psychology of Computer Cooking	(NULL)

[6 rows]

A cursory perusal shows that one book (*Silicon Valley Gastronomic Treats*) has an advance of $0.00, probably due to extremely poor negotiating skills on the author's part. This author will receive no money until the royalties start coming in. Another book (*The Psychology of Computer Cooking*) has a NULL advance: Perhaps the author and the publisher are still working out the details of their deal, or perhaps the data entry clerk hasn't made the entry yet. Eventually, in this case, an amount will be known and recorded. Maybe it will be zero, maybe millions, maybe a couple of thousand dollars. The point is that right now the data does not disclose what the advance for this book is, so the advance value in the table is NULL.

What happens in the case of comparisons involving NULLs? Since a NULL represents the unknown, it doesn't match anything, even another NULL. For example, a query that finds all the title identification numbers and advances for books with moderate advances (under $5,000) will not find the row for MC3026, *The Psychology of Computer Cooking*.

SQL

```
select title_id, advance
from titles
where advance < $5000
title_id      advance
========  =============
PS7777        4000.00
PS3333        2000.00
MC2222           0.00
TC4203        4000.00
PS2091        2275.00
[5 rows]
```

Neither will a query for all books with an advance over $5,000:

SQL

```
select title_id, advance
from titles
where advance > $5000
title_id      advance
========  =============
PC8888        8000.00
TC7777        8000.00
PC1035        7000.00
```

```
BU2075       10125.00
PS2106        6000.00
MC3021       15000.00
TC3218        7000.00
PS1372        7000.00
[8 rows]
```

TIP

NULL is neither above nor below (nor equal to) $5,000 because NULL is unknown.

IS NULL   But don't despair! You can retrieve rows on the basis of their NULL/NOT NULL status with the following special pattern:

SYNTAX

```
WHERE column_name IS [NOT] NULL
```

Use it to find the row for books with null advances like this:

SQL
```
select title_id, advance
from titles
where advance is null
title_id        advance
========  =============
MC3026          (NULL)
PC9999          (NULL)
[2 rows]
```

SQL VARIANTS

Some systems allow the equal sign, in addition to "is".

```
Adaptive Server Enterprise
select title_id, advance
from titles
where advance = null
```

Since IS NULL is specified in the ANSI standard, it makes sense to use it, rather than use the less common = NULL.

IS NULL and Other Comparison Operators   You can use the IS NULL pattern in combination with other comparison operators. Here's how a query for books with an advance under $5,000 *or* a null advance would look:

SQL

```
select title_id, advance
from titles
where advance < $5000
  or advance is null
```

title_id	advance
========	=============
PS7777	4000.00
PS3333	2000.00
MC2222	0.00
TC4203	4000.00
PS2091	2275.00
MC3026	**(NULL)**
PC9999	**(NULL)**
[7rows]	

Matching Character Strings: LIKE

Some problems can't be solved with comparisons. Here are a few examples:

- "His name begins with 'Mc' or 'Mac'—I can't remember the rest."
- "We need a list of all the 415 area code phone numbers."
- "I forget the name of the book, but it has a mention of exercise in the notes."
- "Well, it's Carson, or maybe Karsen—something like that."
- "His first name is 'Dirk' or 'Dick.' Four letters, starts with a *D* and ends with a *k*."

In each of these cases, you know a pattern embedded somewhere in a column, and you need to use the pattern to retrieve all or part of the row. The LIKE keyword is designed to solve this problem. You can use it with character fields (and on some systems, with date fields). It doesn't work with numeric fields defined as integer, money, and decimal or float. The syntax is this:

SYNTAX
```
WHERE column_name [NOT] LIKE 'pattern'
    [ESCAPE escape_char]
```

The pattern must be enclosed in quotes and must include one or more **wildcards** (symbols that take the place of missing letters or strings in the pattern). You use the ESCAPE keyword when your pattern includes one of the wildcards and you need to treat it as a literal.

ANSI SQL provides two wildcard characters for use with LIKE, the percent sign (%) and the underscore or underbar (_).

Wildcard	Meaning
%	any string of zero or more characters
_	any single character

SQL VARIANTS   Many systems offer variations (notations for single characters that fall within a range or set, for example). Check your system's reference guide to see what's available.

LIKE Examples   Following are answers to the questions just posed and the queries that generated them. First, the search for Scottish or Irish surnames:

```
SQL
select au_lname, city
from authors
where au_lname like 'Mc%' or au_lname like 'Mac%'
```

au_lname	city
McBadden	Vacaville
MacFeather	Oakland
[2 rows]	

The LIKE pattern instructs the system to search for a name that begins with "Mc" and is followed by a string of any number of characters (%) or that begins with "Mac" and is followed by any number of characters. Notice that the wildcard is inside the quotes.

Now the 415 area code list:

SQL

```
select au_lname, phone
from authors
where phone like '415%'
```

au_lname	phone
==========	=======
Bennet	415 658-9932
Green	415 986-7020
Carson	415 548-7723
Stringer	415 843-2991
Straight	415 834-2919
Karsen	415 534-9219
MacFeather	415 354-7128
Dull	415 836-7128
Yokomoto	415 935-4228
Hunter	415 836-7128
Locksley	415 585-4620

(11 rows affected)

Here again, you're looking for some known initial characters followed by a string of unknown characters.

The book with "exercise" somewhere in its notes is a little trickier. You don't know if it's at the beginning or end of the column, and you don't know whether the first letter of the word is capitalized. You can cover all these possibilities by leaving the first letter out of the pattern and using the same "string of zero or more characters" wildcard at the beginning and end of the pattern.

SQL

```
select title_id, notes
from titles
where notes like '%xercise%'
```

title_id	notes
==========	=======
PS2106	New **exercise**, meditation, and nutritional techniques that can reduce the shock of daily interactions. Popular audience. Sample menus included, exercise video available separately.

[1 row]

When you know the number of characters missing, you can use the single-character wildcard, (_). In the next example, the first letter is either *K* or *C* and the next to the last is either *e* or *o*. If the authors table contained the last name Karson, it would also be included in the results. Starson or Karstin would not.

SQL
```
select au_lname, city
from authors
where au_lname like '_ars_n'
```

au_lname	city
==	======================
Carson	Berkeley
Karsen	Oakland

(2 rows affected)

The next example is similar to the previous one. It looks for four-letter first names starting with *D* and ending with *k*.

SQL
```
select au_lname, au_fname, city
from authors
where au_fname like 'D__k'
```

au_lname	au_fname	city
==================================	==================	==============
Stringer	**Dirk**	Oakland
Straight	**Dick**	Oakland

[2 rows]

NOT LIKE You can also use NOT LIKE with wildcards. To find all the phone numbers in the authors table that do *not* have 415 as the area code, you could use either of these queries (they are equivalent):

SQL
```
select phone
from authors
where phone not like '415%'

select phone
from authors
where not phone like '415%'
```

Escaping   Wildcard characters are almost always used together with the LIKE keyword. Without LIKE, the wildcard characters are interpreted literally and represent exactly their own values. The query that follows finds any phone numbers that consist of the four characters "415%" only. It will not find phone numbers that start with 415:

SQL
```
select phone
from authors
where phone = '415%'
```

   What if you want to search for a value that contains one of the wildcard characters? For example, in one row in the `titles` table, the `notes` column contains a claim to increase readers' friends by some percentage. You can search for the percent mark by using ESCAPE to appoint a character to strip the percent sign of its magic meaning and convert it to an ordinary character. A wildcard directly after the **escape character** has only its literal meaning. Other wildcards continue to have their special significance. In the following LIKE expression, you are looking for a literal percent sign somewhere in the `notes` column. Since it's probably not the first or last character, you use wildcard percent signs at the beginning and end of the expression and a percent sign preceded by the escape character in the middle.

SQL
```
select title_id, notes
from titles
where notes like '%@%%' escape '@'
```

title_id	notes
======	===
TC7777	Detailed instructions on improving your position in life by learning how to make authentic Japanese sushi in your spare time. 5-10% increase in number of friends per recipe reported from beta test.

[1 row]

   Following are some examples of LIKE with escaped and unescaped wildcard character searches (the @ sign is the designated escape character):

Symbol	Meaning
LIKE '27%'	27 followed by any string of 0 or more characters
LIKE '27@%'	27%
LIKE '_n'	an, in, on, etc.
LIKE '@_n'	_n

Like, Is IN LIKE Equals . . . ?

Don't get confused by the similarities of equal, IN, and LIKE.

Equals   Use the equal comparison operator when you want all data that exactly matches a single value—you know just what you are looking for. You can use the equal comparison operator with any kind of data—character, date, or numeric. Put quotes around character and date data. In this query, you are looking for authors named "Meander."

```
SQL
select au_lname, au_fname,  phone
from authors
where au_fname = 'Meander'
```

au_lname	au_fname	phone
Smith	**Meander**	913 843-0462

[1 row]

IN   Use IN when you have two or more values and are looking for data that exactly matches any one of these values. IN works with any kind of data—character, date, or numeric. Put quotes around character and date data. Here, you are trying to find any writers called "Meander," "Malcolm," or "Stearns."

```
SQL
select au_lname, au_fname,  phone
from authors
where au_fname in ( 'Meander', 'Malcolm', 'Stearns')
```

au_lname	au_fname	phone
MacFeather	**Stearns**	415 354-7128
Smith	**Meander**	913 843-0462

[2 rows]

LIKE　Use LIKE when you want to find data that matches a pattern. For example, if you are trying to locate all the people with the letters "ea" in their names, you could write code like this:

```
SQL
select au_lname, au_fname,  phone
from authors
where au_fname like '%ea%'
```

au_lname	au_fname	phone
McBadden	Heather	707 448-4982
MacFeather	Stearns	415 354-7128
Smith	Meander	913 843-0462
[3 rows]		

In most cases, LIKE works with character and date data only.

Some systems support autoconvert capabilities that allow you to use LIKE with numeric data. Notice that you have to put quotes around the pattern, just as if it were character:

SQL VARIANTS

```
Oracle
SQL> select title_id, price
  2  from titles
  3  where price like '%.99'
```

TITLE_	PRICE
BU1032	29.99
PS7777	17.99
PS3333	29.99
MC2222	29.99
TC7777	24.99
BU2075	12.99
MC3021	12.99
BU7832	29.99
8 rows selected.	

Other systems give an error for the same code:

SQL Server
```
select title_id, price
from titles
```
where price like '%.99'
Server: Msg 257, Level 16, State 3, Line 1
Implicit conversion from data type money to varchar is not allowed.
Use the CONVERT function to run this query.

Comparing the Three The guidelines for differentiating among equal, IN, and LIKE are compared and summarized in Figure 4.6.

Keyword	Use	Example	Notes
=	Exact matches to a single value	where fname = **'Meander'**	All datatypes. Use quotes around character and date data.
IN	Exact matches to one or more values in a set of values—another way of specifying a series of OR clauses	where au_fname in (**'Meander'**, **'Malcolm'**, **'Stearns'**)	All datatypes. Use quotes around character and date data. Separate elements with commas.
LIKE	Matches to a pattern, always used with wildcards (%, _)	where au_fname like **'%ea%'**	Character and date datatypes—others if the system does some autoconversion. ESCAPE neutralizes the wildcards.

Figure 4.6 Equal, IN, LIKE

Summary

This chapter concentrates on the basic clauses of the SELECT statement. Now you are familiar with the SELECT statement basics. These include:

- Using the asterisk for all columns in CREATE TABLE order, or listing individual column names, in any order, for a tailored report. You've also learned how to modify display labels, add text, and perform calculations in the SELECT clause.
- Specifying tables in the FROM clause, and assigning aliases as needed.
- Selecting rows in the WHERE clause, using comparison operators, logical operators, IN, IS NULL, and BETWEEN to zero in on just the values you want.

The next chapter covers some refinements on selection: ordering results with ORDER BY, eliminating duplicates in results with DISTINCT, and using aggregate functions for creating summary values.

Chapter 5

Sorting Data and Other Selection Techniques

In This Chapter

- A New Batch Of SELECT Statement Clauses
- Sorting Query Results: ORDER BY
- Eliminating Duplicate Rows: DISTINCT and ALL
- Aggregate Functions

A New Batch of SELECT Statement Clauses

Now that you're familiar with the fundamentals of the SELECT statement—SELECT, FROM, and WHERE—it's time to go on to some additional features. These include ORDER BY (for sorting query results), DISTINCT (for eliminating duplicate rows), and **aggregate functions** (for calculating totals, sums, minimums, maximums, and counts).

ORDER BY is an optional clause, after the WHERE clause. DISTINCT and aggregate functions are part of the SELECT clause.

SYNTAX

```
SELECT [ALL | DISTINCT ] select_list
FROM table/view_list
[WHERE search_conditions]
[ORDER BY order_by_list ]
```

Chapter 6 covers GROUP BY (for creating groups), aggregate functions with groups, and HAVING (for putting conditions on groups).

Sorting Query Results: ORDER BY

The ORDER BY clause can make your results more readable. It allows you to sort by any expression or mixture of expressions in the SELECT list—from simple columns to more complex combinations of column names, functions, mathematical computations, strings, or display labels. Each sort can be in ascending or descending order. (See "Sort Up, Sort Down" later in this chapter for details.)

ORDER BY Syntax

The general syntax for the SELECT statement ORDER BY clause looks like this:

```
SELECT select_list
FROM table_list
[WHERE conditions]
[ORDER BY order_by_list]
```

SYNTAX

Like the SELECT list, the ORDER BY list can have one element or multiple elements. If there are multiple elements, they must be separated by commas. Each ORDER BY expression can be ascending (the default) or descending (DESC).

Here's a query that finds some information on business and psychology books:

```
SQL
select title_id, pub_id, price * ytd_sales as Income, price
from titles
where type in ('business', 'psychology')
```

title_id	pub_id	Income	price
BU1032	1389	122809.05	29.99
PS7777	0736	60014.64	17.99
PS3333	0736	122119.28	29.99
BU1111	1389	85078.20	21.95
BU2075	0736	243198.78	12.99
PS2091	0736	44887.75	21.95

```
PS2106    0736           1887.00    17.00
BU7832    1389         122809.05    29.99
PS1372    0736          15596.25    41.59
[9 rows]
```

To order the result rows by price, in descending order, add this ORDER BY clause:

SQL
```
select title_id, pub_id, price * ytd_sales as Income, price
from titles
where type in ('business', 'psychology')
order by price desc
```

title_id	pub_id	Income	price
==========	========	================	===========
PS1372	0736	15596.25	**41.59**
BU1032	1389	122809.05	**29.99**
PS3333	0736	122119.28	**29.99**
BU7832	1389	122809.05	**29.99**
BU1111	1389	85078.20	**21.95**
PS2091	0736	44887.75	**21.95**
PS7777	0736	60014.64	**17.99**
PS2106	0736	1887.00	**17.00**
BU2075	0736	243198.78	**12.99**

```
[9 rows]
```

Most (but not all) systems require that each item in the ORDER BY list also appear in the SELECT list. The ORDER BY list can include four kinds of expressions, ranging from simple to complex:

- A column name (`price` or `pub_id`)
- A column name and arithmetic operators or functions (`price * 1.0825`)
- A display label assigned to a column or expression in the SELECT clause (`Income`)
- A position number (the number of this column or expression in the SELECT list—in the example just given, `price` is the fourth entry in the SELECT list)

But before looking at more complex ORDER BY examples, take a minute to consider the basis of order.

Character Sets and Sort Orders

"A" comes before " B," right? How about "A" and "a"? Or "A" and "À"? The answer depends on the **character set** and **sort order**.

- A character set is a list of letters and special characters ($, #, @, and the like). Character sets may include non-English characters and may use various combinations of these characters. Consider the tilde in Spanish, accents in French, and the non-Roman symbols of Hebrew and Chinese.
- The sort order (also called the **collating sequence** or the **collation**) determines the order of the characters in the character set. A sort order may handle uppercase letters before lowercase letters or may consider them equivalent, for example.

Character set and sort order are not defined in terms of SQL commands, but most database systems allow you to load or choose which character set you want to use and decide among possible sort orders for that character set. However, neither of these is an on-the-fly decision. You generally specify character set and sort order when you set up the database system. SQL-92 provides some commands relevant to picking among available character sets and sort orders (CREATE CHARACTER SET, DROP CHARACTER SET, CREATE COLLATION, DROP COLLATION, COLLATE, and COLLATION FROM), but they are not widely implemented. Check your system manuals for specifics.

The examples in this book use the default sort order for the demo database system included on the CD, Adaptive Server Anywhere. The sort order is Latin1, sometimes called "code page 1252." If you are using a different system or installed a different character set on this one, your ORDER BY results for alphabetic data may look different.

Checking Sort Order   Most of the time, all you'll care about in terms of your system's default character set and sort order is how it handles uppercase and lowercase letters, and you can find this out with some simple tests. However, if you are curious, you can check your system documentation for information on these issues.

Character set and sort order are decided on a system level. You won't want to change them lightly.

SQL VARIANTS   Your vendor may provide a tool or command or system table that will show you what collation sequence or character set you have. These commands vary from system to system.

Microsoft SQL Server and Adaptive Server Enterprise offer the SP_HELP-SORT system procedure. The output from the two systems is not the same. In this case, MS SQL Server is using a case insensitive sort order.

```
MS SQL Server
exec sp_helpsort

Unicode data sorting
--------------------
Locale ID = 1033  case insensitive, kana type insensitive, width
insensitive

Sort Order Description
----------------------------------------------------------------
Character Set = 1, iso_1
ISO 8859-1 (Latin-1) - Western European 8-bit character set.
Sort Order = 52, nocase_iso
Case-insensitive dictionary sort order for use with several Western-
European languages including English, French, and German.
Uses the ISO 8859-1 character set.

Characters, in Order
----------------------------------------------------------------
    ! " # $ % & ' ( ) * + , - . / : ; < = > ? @ [ \ ] ^ _ ` { | }
  ~   ¡ ¢ £ ¤ ¥ ¦ § ¨ © ª « ¬ - ® ¯ ° ± ² ³ ´ µ ¶ · ¸ ¹ º » ¼ ½ ¾
  ¿ × ÷ 0 1 2 3 4 5 6 7 8 9 A=a À=à Á=á Â=â Ã=ã Ä=ä Å=å Æ=æ B=b C
=c Ç=ç D=d E=e È=è É=é Ê=ê Ë=ë F=f G=g H=h I=i Ì=ì Í=í Î=î Ï=ï J
=j K=k L=l M=m N=n Ñ=ñ O=o Ò=ò Ó=ó Ô=ô Õ=õ Ö=ö Ø=ø P=p Q=q R=r S
=s ß T=t U=u Ù=ù Ú=ú Û=û Ü=ü V=v W=w X=x Y=y Ý=ý ÿ Z=z Ð=ð Þ=þ
```

Adaptive Server Anywhere stores information about the character set and sort order in a system catalogue, syscollation. This query tells you the collation name, and so on.

Adaptive Server Anywhere
```
select collation_id, collation_label, collation_name
from syscollation
```

```
collation_id collation_label collation_name
============ =============== ========================================
          46 1252LATIN1      Code Page 1252, Windows Latin 1, Western
```

Your system may also support GUI tools that can give you this information.

Sorts Within Sorts

In the first ORDER BY query, you sorted the result rows by descending `price` (more about ascending and descending sorts in the next section). What if you also want to make sure books within each price category by the same publisher are listed together? Adding `pub_id` to the ORDER BY list is the way to do it. Separate `price` and `pub_id` with a comma.

SQL
```
select title_id, pub_id, price * ytd_sales as Income, price
from titles
where type in ('business', 'psychology')
order by price desc, pub_id
```
```
title_id pub_id         Income       price
======== ======  =============== ===========
PS1372   0736           15596.25     41.59
PS3333   0736          122119.28     29.99
BU1032   1389          122809.05     29.99
BU7832   1389          122809.05     29.99
PS2091   0736           44887.75     21.95
BU1111   1389           85078.20     21.95
PS7777   0736           60014.64     17.99
PS2106   0736            1887.00     17.00
BU2075   0736          243198.78     12.99
[9 rows]
```

When you use more than one column in the ORDER BY clause, sorts are nested (that is, ordered by `price` first and then by `pub_id` within each price category).

You can have as many levels of sorts as you like. Many systems require that each sort element appears in the SELECT list, but they don't insist on ORDER BY columns and expressions being in the same sequence as SELECT columns and expressions. If you changed the example so that it sorts first by `pub_id` and then by `price`, here's what you'd see:

SQL
```
select title_id, pub_id, price * ytd_sales as Income, price
from titles
where type in ('business', 'psychology')
order by pub_id,  price desc
```

title_id	pub_id	Income	price
==========	========	================	==========
PS1372	0736	15596.25	41.59
PS3333	0736	122119.28	29.99
PS2091	0736	44887.75	21.95
PS7777	0736	60014.64	17.99
PS2106	0736	1887.00	17.00
BU2075	0736	243198.78	12.99
BU1032	1389	122809.05	29.99
BU7832	1389	122809.05	29.99
BU1111	1389	85078.20	21.95

[9 rows]

The columns are listed in the same order as in the previous results: `title_id` first, then `pub_id`, followed by `Income`, with `price` last. But the rows are arranged differently: First you see all the rows with `pub_id` 0736 and then all those with 1389 (no `pub_id` 0877 rows qualify).

Sort Up, Sort Down

You can specify a direction—low to high or high to low—for each sort by using the ascending (ASC) or descending (DESC) keyword immediately after the sort item. Ascending is the default, assumed to be in effect unless you type DESC, which means you don't really need to use ASC except to make the direction of the sort unavoidably explicit to others who read the query.

Here's how you'd get `pub_ids` to display in descending order:

```
SQL
select title_id, pub_id, price * ytd_sales as Income, price
from titles
where type in ('business', 'psychology')
order by pub_id desc,  price desc
title_id pub_id          Income        price
======== ======  ==============   ===========
BU1032   1389        122809.05        29.99
BU7832   1389        122809.05        29.99
BU1111   1389         85078.20        21.95
PS1372   0736         15596.25        41.59
PS3333   0736        122119.28        29.99
PS2091   0736         44887.75        21.95
PS7777   0736         60014.64        17.99
PS2106   0736          1887.00        17.00
BU2075   0736        243198.78        12.99
[9 rows]
```

Now the `pub_id` order is descending (1389 before 0736).

What About More Complex Expressions?

What if you want to sort by an expression in the SELECT list—something more complicated than a simple column name? SQL allows you to sort by

- The expression's *position* in the SELECT list (represented with a number)
- The expression's *display label* (also called alias or heading—see "Display Label Conventions" in Chapter 4)

Some systems also allow you to use the *full expression* in the ORDER BY clause.

Here's an example of a query with a SELECT list expression (`price * ytd_sales`) on which you might want to sort:

SQL
```
select title_id, pub_id, price * ytd_sales, price
from titles
where type in ('business', 'psychology')
```

title_id	pub_id	titles.price*titles.ytd_sales	price
==========	========	===============================	=======
BU1032	1389	122809.05	29.99
PS7777	0736	60014.64	17.99
PS3333	0736	122119.28	29.99
BU1111	1389	85078.20	21.95
BU2075	0736	243198.78	12.99
PS2091	0736	44887.75	21.95
PS2106	0736	1887.00	17.00
BU7832	1389	122809.05	29.99
PS1372	0736	15596.25	41.59

[9 rows]

Sorting by Position   Let's say you want to see these results sorted by publisher and then by income (price * ytd_sales). Because income is a complex expression, you can't use a simple column name as the argument to order by. Instead, use the number "3" because the expression is the third element in the SELECT list. When counting SELECT list items, start with "1" and move from left to right. Signed numbers (–2, +4, etc.) are not allowed and don't make sense anyway.

SQL
```
select title_id, pub_id, price * ytd_sales, price
from titles
where type in ('business', 'psychology')
order by pub_id, 3
```

title_id	pub_id	titles.price*titles.ytd_sales	price
==========	========	===============================	=======
PS2106	0736	1887.00	17.00
PS1372	0736	15596.25	41.59
PS2091	0736	44887.75	21.95
PS7777	0736	60014.64	17.99
PS3333	0736	122119.28	29.99
BU2075	0736	243198.78	12.99
BU1111	1389	85078.20	21.95
BU1032	1389	122809.05	29.99
BU7832	1389	122809.05	29.99

[9 rows]

Position numbers work just like column names in ORDER BY. You can

- Use position numbers to represent simple columns as well as more complex expressions
- Freely mix position numbers and columns or expressions
- Specify a direction with ASC and DESC for position numbers just as with column names

Here's an example showing sorting on the pub_id column by name in ascending order and then the price column by number in descending order:

```
SQL
select title_id, pub_id, price * ytd_sales, price
from titles
where type in ('business', 'psychology')
order by pub_id , 3 desc
title_id pub_id titles.price*titles.ytd_sales        price
======== ====== ================================ ===========
BU2075   0736                         243198.78       12.99
PS3333   0736                         122119.28       29.99
PS7777   0736                          60014.64       17.99
PS2091   0736                          44887.75       21.95
PS1372   0736                          15596.25       41.59
PS2106   0736                           1887.00       17.00
BU1032   1389                         122809.05       29.99
BU7832   1389                         122809.05       29.99
BU1111   1389                          85078.20       21.95
[9 rows]
```

One thing to watch out for with numbered ORDER BY items is modifications to the SELECT list. The order of your results may well change dramatically when you add columns to or subtract columns from the SELECT list.

TIP

Sorting by Display Label If you assign display labels (or headings) to expressions in the SELECT list, you can sort by the labels. In fact, ANSI experts indicate sorting by position will probably be phased out in favor of this method. In this example, which returns the same results as the previous one (except for the changed heading), `price * ytd_sales` is named income, and the ORDER BY clause makes use of the heading, rather than the SELECT list number.

SQL
```
select title_id, pub_id, price * ytd_sales as income, price
from titles
where type in ('business', 'psychology')
order by pub_id, income desc
```

title_id	pub_id	income	price
==========	========	================	==========
BU2075	0736	243198.78	12.99
PS3333	0736	122119.28	20.99
PS7777	0736	60014.64	17.99
PS2091	0736	44887.75	21.95
PS1372	0736	15596.25	41.59
PS2106	0736	1887.00	17.00
BU1032	1389	122809.05	29.99
BU7832	1389	122809.05	29.99
BU1111	1389	85078.20	21.95

[9 rows]

Sorting by Complex Expression   Some systems allow you to sort by SELECT list expressions—you don't need positions or headings.

SQL VARIANTS

Check your system to see if this query is legal:

SQL
```
select pub_id, price * ytd_sales, price, title_id
from titles
order by pub_id, price * ytd_sales desc
```

Some systems give an error. To run the query, use a position number or assign a display label in the SELECT list and use it.

Informix
```
select pub_id, price * ytd_sales, price, title_id
from titles
order by pub_id, price * ytd_sales desc

SQL Error -201. A syntax error has occurred.
```

How Do You Sort Nulls?

Not all systems order nulls the same way. SQL-92 specifies that when nulls are sorted, they should be either greater than or less than all non-null values. Which you get depends on your implementation.

In Microsoft SQL Server, NULL is less than all non-null values, but in Sybase SQL Anywhere, NULLs are grouped together at the beginning of the display, whether the sort is ascending or descending. Oracle sorts NULL last. Here's one query, with different displays from each of these three systems:

SQL
VARIANTS

```
SQL
select title_id, pub_id, price * ytd_sales as income, price
from titles
where type = 'business' or price is null
order by price
```

```
MS SQL Server
title_id pub_id income                  price
-------- ------ --------------------    --------------------
MC3026   0877   NULL                    NULL
PC9999   1389   NULL                    NULL
BU2075   0736   243198.7800             12.9900
BU1111   1389   85078.2000              21.9500
BU1032   1389   122809.0500             29.9900
BU7832   1389   122809.0500             29.9900
(6 row(s) affected)
```

```
Adaptive Server Anywhere
title_id pub_id          income     price
======== ====== =============== ===========
MC3026   0877            (NULL)    (NULL)
PC9999   1389            (NULL)    (NULL)
BU2075   0736         243198.78     12.99
BU1111   1389          85078.20     21.95
BU1032   1389         122809.05     29.99
BU7832   1389         122809.05     29.99
[6 rows]
```

```
Oracle
TITLE_ PUB_    INCOME     PRICE
------ ----  ---------  ---------
BU2075 0736 243198.78     12.99
BU1111 1389   85078.2     21.95
BU1032 1389 122809.05     29.99
BU7832 1389 122809.05     29.99
MC3026 0877
PC9999 1389
6 rows selected.
```

Eliminating Duplicate Rows: DISTINCT and ALL

The DISTINCT and ALL keywords in the SELECT list let you specify what to
do with duplicate rows in your results.

- ALL returns all qualified rows and is the default. If you don't specify
  ALL or DISTINCT, ALL is assumed.
- DISTINCT returns only unique rows.

For example, if you search for all the author identification codes in the
titleauthors table, you'll find these rows:

```
SQL
select au_id
from titleauthors
order by au_id
au_id
===========
172-32-1176
213-46-8915
213-46-8915
238-95-7766
267-41-2394
267-41-2394
274-80-9391
409-56-7008
```

```
427-17-2319
472-27-2349
486-29-1786
486-29-1786
648-92-1872
672-71-3249
712-45-1867
722-51-5454
724-80-9391
724-80-9391
756-30-7391
807-91-6654
846-92-7186
899-46-2035
899-46-2035
998-72-3567
998-72-3567
[25 rows]
```

Looking at the results, you'll see that there are some duplicate listings because some authors have written more than one book. You can eliminate the duplicates, and see only the unique au_ids, with DISTINCT.

SQL
```
select distinct au_id
from titleauthors
order by au_id
au_id
===========
172-32-1176
213-46-8915
238-95-7766
267-41-2394
274-80-9391
409-56-7008
427-17-2319
472-27-2349
486-29-1786
648-92-1872
672-71-3249
```

```
712-45-1867
722-51-5454
724-80-9391
756-30-7391
807-91-6654
846-92-7186
899-46-2035
998-72-3567
[19 rows]
```

Six rows that are included in the first display are not in the second—they are duplicates.

DISTINCT Syntax

ALL is the default unless you explicitly specify DISTINCT. Because of this, you don't see ALL very often. It is indicated by the absence of DISTINCT. Here's what the basic syntax looks like:

SYNTAX

```
SELECT [DISTINCT | ALL] select_list
```

DISTINCT (or ALL) has some stringent requirements:

* Use it only *once* in a SELECT list.
* Make it the *first* word in the SELECT list.
* Do *not* put a comma after it.

The following example gives you a syntax error:

SQL
```
select state, distinct city
from authors
```

Error at line 1. Syntax error near 'distinct'

In other words, you can't display all the states and only the distinct cities in the same rows—you'd get impossible results for cities that appear in multiple states (Portland, Maine, and Portland, Oregon, for example).

DISTINCT with Multiple SELECT List Items

When there is more than one item in the SELECT list, DISTINCT finds the rows where the combination of items is unique.

Here's an example. First, take a look at the listing of pub_ids and types in the titles table.

SQL

```
select pub_id, type
from titles
order by pub_id
```

pub_id	type
======	=============
0736	**psychology**
0736	**psychology**
0736	business
0736	**psychology**
0736	**psychology**
0736	**psychology**
0877	mod_cook
0877	**trad_cook**
0877	**trad_cook**
0877	mod_cook
0877	trad_cook
0877	(NULL)
1389	**popular_comp**
1389	business
1389	business
1389	popular_comp
1389	business
1389	**popular_comp**

[18 rows]

There are eighteen rows. Notice that there is some repetition. (The ORDER BY is there only to make the display easy to read.) If you query for distinct publisher numbers, you'll get just three rows:

```
SQL
select distinct pub_id
from titles
order by pub_id

pub_id
======
0736
0877
1389
[3 rows]
```

If you query for distinct types, you'll get six rows:

```
SQL
select distinct type
from titles
order by type

type
============
(NULL)
business
mod_cook
popular_comp
psychology
trad_cook
[6 rows]
```

However, if you query for distinct combinations of publisher and type, you'll get seven rows:

```
SQL
select distinct pub_id, type
from titles
order by pub_id

pub_id type
====== ============
0736   business
0736   psychology
0877   (NULL)
```

```
0877    mod_cook
0877    trad_cook
1389    business
1389    popular_comp
[7 rows]
```

This result represents all the unique publisher-type combinations in the table. Publisher number 0736 has two types; publisher number 0877 has two types (and a NULL); and publisher number 1389 has two types, giving a total of seven rows. The DISTINCT applies to the SELECT list as a whole, not to individual columns.

Are NULLs Distinct?   Although null values are by definition unknown and are never equal to each other, DISTINCT treats each NULL in a particular column as a duplicate of all other null values in that column. If publisher number 0877 had more than one book with a NULL type and you ran a query with DISTINCT to retrieve the two columns, you'd still see the publisher/NULL combination listed only once.

Using DISTINCT *   If your system allows DISTINCT *, compare the results of two queries like these:

SQL
```
select distinct *
from titles
```

SQL
```
select *
from titles
```

If your database design is correct, both queries will return all columns and all rows. If the results are different, take another look at the database design. Why is there more than one row with a given set of values in a table? How can you retrieve a particular row if it is precisely the same as one or more other rows?

DISTINCT and Non-Select-List ORDER BY   In most SQL dialects, every element in the ORDER BY clause must appear in the SELECT list. If your system allows non-select-list elements in the ORDER BY clause, notice how they interact with DISTINCT in the SELECT list.

SQL VARIANTS With Adaptive Server Enterprise, sorting by a column not in the DISTINCT SELECT list has the same effect as including that column in the DISTINCT SELECT list: It increases the number of rows displayed. Take a look at this query (you'll get an error if you try to run it on Adaptive Server Anywhere):

```
Adaptive Server Enterprise
select distinct pub_id
from titles
order by type
```

Because there are only three publishers in the database, you'd probably expect three rows in the results. However, this is what you get:

```
Results
pub id
------
0877
0736
1389
0877
1389
0736
0877
(7 rows affected)
```

Why are there seven rows in the results? The clue is in the ORDER BY clause, where `type` stars: You get the same number of rows when you turn the query around, searching for distinct types but sorting by publishers. ASE handles the query as if it were a request for all possible unique combinations of the items in the DISTINCT SELECT list and the non-SELECT-list ORDER BY items. There are, in fact, seven unique combinations of `pub_id` and `type`.

If your system allows non-SELECT-list elements in the ORDER BY clause, run a few experimental queries to see how it handles this kind of situation. "Distinguishing DISTINCTs" in Chapter 11 includes more examples of DISTINCT use.

Aggregate Functions

Aggregates are functions you can use to get summary values. You apply aggregates to **sets** of rows: to all the rows in a table, to just those rows specified by a WHERE clause, or to groups of rows set up in the GROUP BY clause (discussed in the next chapter). No matter how you structure the sets, you get *a single value for each set of rows*.

Take a look at the difference in the results of the following two queries: The first finds each individual yearly sale value in the `titles` table (one sale listing per row); the second calculates the total yearly sales for all books in the `titles` table (one total sale listing per set, and the table is the set).

SQL
```
select ytd_sales
from titles
```

```
  ytd_sales
============
       4095
       4095
       3336
       4072
       3876
       2032
       4095
      15096
       8780
      18722
       2045
        111
      22246
        375
     (NULL)
       4095
        375
     (NULL)
[18 rows]
```

SQL
```
select sum(ytd_sales)
from titles
sum(titles.ytd_sales)
=====================
               97446
```
[1 row]

The first returns results for each qualified row in the table; the second summarizes all the qualified rows into one row.

Column headings for the aggregate column vary from system to system. You can use a display label to make the results easier to read:

SQL
```
select sum(ytd_sales) as Total
from titles
        Total
===========
        97446
```
[1 row]

The ANSI standard and most dialects of SQL do not allow you to mix row-by-row results and set results. The SELECT list must be pure, either all expressions (row values) or all aggregates (set values). The only exception is for grouping columns—columns on which you base groups when you use a GROUP BY clause. (GROUP BY and aggregates are covered in Chapter 6.)

SQL VARIANTS   Here's a query that's usually not allowed, because it mixes a row value (price) with a set value (sum(price)):

Adaptive Server Enterprise
```
select price, sum(price)
from titles
```

The problem is that price returns a value for each row, while sum(price) returns a value for each set (here, the table as a whole). Unless your system is designed to handle this kind of query, it will find the two results incompatible and will give you a syntax error.

To get summary and row results on most systems, you have to run two queries. To display the results simultaneously, use a report generator of some kind.

Aggregate Syntax

The general syntax of the aggregate functions is this:

```
aggregate_function([DISTINCT] expression)
```

SYNTAX

Since aggregates are functions, they always take an **argument**. The argument is an expression, and it is enclosed in parentheses. The expression is often a column name, but it can also be a constant, a function, or any combination of column names, constants, and functions connected by arithmetic operators. Figure 5.1 lists the aggregate functions.

Aggregate Function	Result
SUM([DISTINCT]expression)	The total of (distinct) values in the numeric expression
AVG([DISTINCT]expression)	The average of (distinct) values in the numeric expression
COUNT([DISTINCT]expression)	The number of (distinct) non-null values in the expression
COUNT(*)	The number of selected rows
MAX(expression)	The highest value in the expression
MIN(expression)	The lower value in the expression

Figure 5.1 Aggregate Functions

You can use DISTINCT with any aggregate except COUNT(*). However, note that DISTINCT gives you no advantage with MIN and MAX because the minimum distinct price is the same as the minimum price.

COUNT and COUNT(*) The apparent similarity of COUNT and COUNT(*) can lead to confusion. However, the two are really not the same.

- COUNT takes an expression (a simple column name or some more complex combination of elements) as an argument and discovers all non-null occurrences of that argument.
- COUNT(*) always takes an asterisk as the argument and tallies all rows, whether any particular column contains a null value.

The following example lets you compare the two:

```
SQL
select count(price), count(*)
from titles
count(titles.price)     count(*)
==================== ===========
                  16          18
[1 row]
```

The results produced by the two functions are different because two rows in the `titles` table have NULL in the `price` column. If you used a column with no nulls instead, you'd get the same results from COUNT() and COUNT(*):

```
SQL
select count(title_id), count(*)
from titles
count(titles.title_id)     count(*)
======================= ===========
                     18          18
[1 row]
```

The difference in function between the two counts can be useful for tracking null values in particular columns.

Aggregates and Datatypes You can use SUM and AVG with numeric columns only. MIN, MAX, COUNT, and COUNT(*) work with all types of data.

For example, you can use MIN (minimum) to find the lowest value—the one closest to the beginning of the alphabet—in a CHAR column:

```
SQL
select min(au_lname)
from authors
min(authors.au_lname)
=========================================
Bennet
[1 row]
```

Of course, there is no meaning in the sum or average of all author last names.

DISTINCT Aggregates   You can use DISTINCT with SUM, AVG, COUNT, MIN, and MAX (it goes inside the parentheses and before the argument). As noted earlier, DISTINCT doesn't change the results with MIN and MAX.

DISTINCT eliminates duplicate values before calculating the sum, average, or count. Here's an example:

```
SQL
select count(price)
from titles
count(titles.price)
===================
                 16
[1 row]

SQL
select count(distinct price)
from titles
count(distinct titles.price)
============================
                  9
[1 row]
```

The first query finds out how many non-null prices there are in the `titles` table; the second calculates the number of different non-null prices. Apparently there is some overlap: five books have the same price.

Some systems specify that when you use DISTINCT, the argument can't be an arithmetic expression; it must be a column name only. However, other systems are more lenient. Check your reference manual to find out what you can do. You might want to see if you can run this query:

SQL
```
select count(distinct price * ytd_sales)
from titles
count(distinct titles.price*t

==============================
                            15
[1 row]
```

Systems that do not allow calculated columns with DISTINCT will rule the query illegal.

DISTINCT Limitations   DISTINCT does not work at all with COUNT(*). This is because COUNT(*) always returns one and only one row. DISTINCT has no meaning here.

Generally speaking, you can use DISTINCT no more than once in a SELECT list. This is because, when no aggregates are involved, DISTINCT applies to the SELECT list as a whole and not to individual columns in the SELECT list. But limiting DISTINCT to once per SELECT list can cause some special problems when you use aggregates. For example, consider comparing the results of two aggregate operations. If you take the count and the sum of the price column, you'll get these results:

SQL
```
select count(price), sum(price)
from titles
count(titles.price) sum(titles.price)

=================== =================
                 16            442.26
  [1 row]
```

It's easy to see that the average price is $442.26 divided by 16.

If you use DISTINCT with one of the two columns, the results may not be so useful:

SQL

```
select count(price), sum(distinct price)
from titles
count(titles.price) sum(distinct titles.price)
=================== ==========================
                 16                     265.41
[1 row]
```

The difference between this and the previous sum value indicates that there are duplicate prices and that they have not been included in this sum calculation. However, they still show up in the count column. Dividing the distinct sum by the count will not give an accurate value for average price.

Putting DISTINCT on the count rather than the sum also gives incorrect data for calculating an average price.

SQL

```
select count(distinct price), sum(price)
from titles
count(distinct titles.price) sum(titles.price)
============================ =================
                           9           442.26
[1 row]
```

It's clear that what you need here is either no DISTINCT or two DISTINCTs. Because of this requirement, SQL-92 supports multiple DISTINCTs when you have multiple aggregates. Following is an example:

SQL

```
select count(distinct price), sum(distinct price)
from titles
count(distinct titles.price) sum(distinct titles.price)
============================ ==========================
                           9                     265.41
[1 row]
```

Note that DISTINCT in the SELECT list and DISTINCT as part of an aggregate do not give the same results:

```
SQL
select count(au_id)
from titleauthors
count(titleauthors.au_id)
=========================
                      25
[1 row]
```

```
SQL
select count(distinct au_id)
from titleauthors
count(distinct titleauthors.a
=============================
                      19
[1 row]
```

```
SQL
select distinct count(au_id)
from titleauthors
count(titleauthors.au_id)
=========================
                      25
[1 row]
```

The first query finds all the author identification numbers in the table. The second counts the unique numbers only. Applying a DISTINCT to the SELECT list as a whole in the third query rather than in the aggregate, gives the same result as the first query. This is because the aggregate does its work first, returning one row; then DISTINCT cheerfully eliminates any duplicates of this row. Since there is only one row of results, there are, by definition, no duplicates.

Aggregates and WHERE   You can use aggregate functions in a SELECT list, as in the previous examples, or in the HAVING clause of a SELECT statement (more about this in Chapter 6).

You can't use aggregate functions in a WHERE clause. If you do, you'll get a syntax error. However, you can use a WHERE clause to restrict the rows used in the aggregate calculation.

Following is a statement that finds the average advance and total year-to-date sales for all the rows in the `titles` table:

```
SQL
select avg(advance), sum(ytd_sales)
from titles

avg(titles.advance) sum(titles.ytd_sales)
=================== =====================
            5962.50                 97446
[1 row]
```

To see the same figures for business books only, you could write this query:

```
SQL
select avg(advance), sum(ytd_sales)
from titles
where type = 'business'

avg(titles.advance) sum(titles.ytd_sales)
=================== =====================
            6281.25                 30788
[1 row]
```

Apparently, business writers do a little better than the average writer.

How do the aggregates and the WHERE clause interact? The WHERE clause does its job first, finding all business books. Then the functions perform their calculations on the retrieved rows.

Null Values and the Aggregate Functions If there are any null values in the column on which the aggregate function is operating, they are ignored for the purposes of the function.

For example, if you ask for the COUNT of advances in the `titles` table, your answer is not the same as if you ask for the COUNT of title names because of the null values in the `advance` column:

```
SQL
select count(advance)
from titles
count(titles.advance)
======================
                    16
[1 row]
```

```
SQL
select count(title)
from titles
count(titles.title)
===================
                 18
[1 row]
```

The exception to this rule is COUNT(*), which counts each row, whether a column value is NULL. If no rows meet the query conditions, COUNT returns zero. The other functions all return NULL. Here are examples (there is no "poetry" type in the `titles` table):

```
SQL
select count(distinct title)
from titles
where type = 'poetry'
count(distinct titles.title)
============================
                          0
[1 row]
```

```
SQL
select avg(advance)
from titles
where type = 'poetry'
avg(titles.advance)
===================
               NULL
[1 row]
```

Some systems provide additional aggregate functions. Following are some examples. **SQL VARIANTS**

Adaptive Server Anywhere adds the LIST function to the standard set. This query displays `types` associated with a `pub_id`.

```
Adaptive Server Anywhere
select list (distinct type)
from titles
where pub_id = '1389'

list (distinct type)
===========================
popular_comp, business
[1 row]
```

Oracle has functions for calculating STDDEV and VARIANCE.

```
Oracle
SQL> select avg (price), stddev (price), variance (price)
  2  from titles;
AVG(PRICE) STDDEV(PRICE) VARIANCE(PRICE)
---------- ------------- ---------------
  14.76625     6.8429388      46.825812
```

Informix supports STDEV (same function, different spelling), VARIANCE, and RANGE.

```
Informix
select avg(price),  range(price)
from titles;

(avg)           (range)
------------- ----------
$14.76625     $19.96
```

Microsoft SQL Server also offers some nonstandard aggregates.

Summary

This chapter focuses on sorting. It covers the following topics:

- Sorting query results with ORDER BY. You can sort up or down, and you can sort by column, display label, or position in the SELECT list. Sorts can be nested.
- Eliminating duplicate result rows with DISTINCT. DISTINCT can be a little tricky because it must be the first element in the SELECT list, and it applies to all elements. DISTINCT looks for all unique combinations of the listed expressions.
- Finding summary values with aggregates (SUM, MIN, MAX, AVG, and COUNT). Just to keep you on your toes, the rules for DISTINCT with aggregates are different from the rules for DISTINCT with expressions.

The next chapter explores the GROUP BY clause and the use of aggregate functions with groups to return an array of values (one per group). The HAVING clause, closely bound to GROUP BY and vector aggregates, is also explored. Finally, NULL is taken apart and put back together one last time.

Chapter 6

Grouping Data and Reporting from It

In This Chapter

- Grouping and Aggregates
- The GROUP BY clause
- The HAVING clause
- All About NULLs

Grouping and Aggregates

Chapter 5, "Sorting Data and Other Selection Techniques," discussed some SELECT features: the DISTINCT keyword and the ORDER BY clause. It also introduced the aggregate functions. There, aggregates were used only with the table as a whole—but that's just a small part of the aggregate story. In real life, aggregate functions are most frequently used in combination with the GROUP BY clause.

This chapter focuses on GROUP BY, which returns groups of rows, and on the HAVING clause, which puts conditions on GROUP BY results much as WHERE qualifies individual rows. The chapter concludes with a recapitulation of everything you need to know about null values.

The GROUP BY Clause

The GROUP BY clause is intimately connected to aggregates. In fact, GROUP BY doesn't really have much use without aggregate functions: it divides a table into sets of rows, and aggregate functions produce summary values for each set. These values are called **vector aggregates**. (A **scalar aggregate** is a single

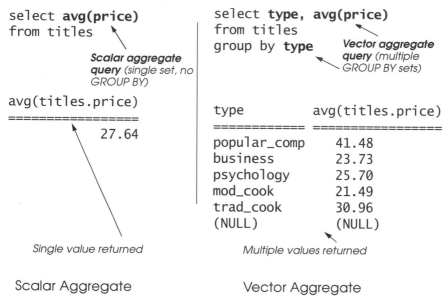

```
select avg(price)
from titles
```
Scalar aggregate query (single set, no GROUP BY)

```
avg(titles.price)
=================
           27.64
```

Single value returned

Scalar Aggregate

```
select type, avg(price)
from titles
group by type
```
Vector aggregate query (multiple GROUP BY sets)

```
type          avg(titles.price)
============  =================
popular_comp      41.48
business          23.73
psychology        25.70
mod_cook          21.49
trad_cook         30.96
(NULL)            (NULL)
```

Multiple values returned

Vector Aggregate

Figure 6.1 Scalar and Vector Aggregates

value produced by an aggregate function as discussed in the previous chapter.) Figure 6.1 shows examples of scalar and vector aggregate queries.

GROUP BY Syntax

Here's what GROUP BY looks like in the context of a SELECT statement:

```
SELECT select_list
FROM table_list
[ WHERE conditions ]
[ GROUP BY group_by_list ]
[ ORDER BY order_by_list ]
```

In most SQL dialects, every item in the GROUP BY list must appear in the SELECT list—you can make groups only out of things you select. Systems vary in what they allow in a GROUP BY list, in addition to column names: More complex expressions, display labels, and SELECT list position numbers are all possibilities. Following is an example with a single column in the GROUP BY clause. The query figures how many books each publisher has.

SQL

```
select pub_id, count(title_id)
from titles
group by pub_id
pub_id count(titles.title_id)
====== ======================
1389                        6
0736                        6
0877                        6
[3 rows]
```

You include the grouping column (pub_id) as well as the aggregate (COUNT) in the SELECT list. All the rows that make up the first group have 1389 in the pub_id column; all those in the second have 0736; and all those in the third have 0877. The COUNT generates a single value (the number of titles) for each group. Both items in the SELECT list (the publishers and the COUNT) are single valued per set—there is only one publisher and one title total for each group.

Groups Within Groups   Just as you can sort by multiple items, so can you form groups within groups. Separate the grouping elements with commas, and go from large groups to progressively smaller ones.

SQL

```
select pub_id, type, count(title)
from titles
group by pub_id, type
pub_id type            count(titles.title)
====== ============    ===================
1389   popular_comp                      3
1389   business                          3
0736   psychology                        5
0877   mod_cook                          2
0877   trad_cook                         3
0736   business                          1
0877   (NULL)                            1
[7 rows]
```

This example is much the same as the previous one, but it uses nested groups. Here are the steps your system goes through with nested groups.

1. Divide the rows in the table by publisher.

2. Separate the rows in each publisher group by type, ending up with seven publisher/type groups, or sets.

3. Apply the aggregate to each set, and come up with a number that reveals how many books belong to each type within each publisher.

Cautions and Restrictions

GROUP BY looks straightforward, but it's caused its share of headaches for SQL users. Here, for example, is a query that seems reasonable but won't work on most systems:

```
SQL (variant)
select pub_id, type, count(title)
from titles
group by pub_id
```

Since the table is divided into sets by publisher (`group by pub_id`) and there are three publishers, the query must return no more than three rows, and each SELECT list item must have a single value for the set. Unfortunately, there is more than one type per publisher, so most systems find the query impossible to answer. You could solve this problem by adding `type` to the GROUP BY clause, as shown in Groups Within Groups.

One system that handles this nonconforming GROUP BY query is Adaptive Server Enterprise. It returns results like the following, rather than an error:

SQL VARIANTS

```
Adaptive Server Enterprise
select pub_id, type, count(title)
from titles
group by pub_id
```

```
pub_id type
------ ----              ----------
1389   popular_comp          6
1389   business              6
0736   psychology            6
0736   psychology            6
1389   business              6
0877   mod_cook              6
0877   trad_cook             6
0877   trad_cook             6
1389   popular_comp          6
0736   business              6
0736   psychology            6
0736   psychology            6
0877   mod_cook              6
0877   trad_cook             6
0877   NULL                  6
1389   business              6
0736   psychology            6
1389   popular_comp          6
(18 rows affected)
```

In this case, ASE finds the number of books for each group (6 for 1389, 6 for 0877, 6 for 0736). It then combines these set results with row results for the whole table. The results erroneously imply that there are six books in each pub_id-type group or 18 * 6 (108) books.

Using Complex Expressions   Another limitation in some SQL implementations concerns expressions. You're always safe with vanilla column names in the GROUP BY clause. Aggregate expressions, display labels, and SELECT list position numbers may or may not be allowed, depending on the SQL dialect you're using.

Multiple Summary Values for Multiple Levels of Grouping   How about multiple summary values for multiple levels of grouping? Let's say you're grouping by pub_id and type. You want to see the total number of books for each publisher and the total number of books for each type of book the publisher carries. You might think something like the following query would do the trick, but the results show you're on the wrong track:

SQL
```
select pub_id, count(title_id), type, count(title_id)
from titles
group by pub_id, type
```

pub_id	count(titles.title_id)	type	count(titles.title_id)
1389	3	popular_comp	3
1389	3	business	3
0736	5	psychology	5
0877	2	mod_cook	2
0877	3	trad_cook	3
0736	1	business	1
0877	1	(NULL)	1

[7 rows]

The number of books is the same for publisher and for type, and the results don't make much sense in light of what you are trying to get. What you're seeing (in two columns) is the number of books for each publisher/type combination because that is the bottom level of the group. To get the results you want, you need to run *two* queries: the first one grouped by publisher (to give the publisher totals) and the second grouped by publisher and then by type within each publisher (to give the publisher/type totals).

SQL
```
select pub_id, count(title_id)
from titles
group by pub_id
```

pub_id	count(titles.title_id)
1389	6
0736	6
0877	6

[3 rows]

Each publisher has six books. The next query finds the total number of books for each publisher/type combination.

SQL
```
select pub_id, type, count(title_id)
from titles
group by pub_id, type
pub_id type           count(titles.title_id)
====== ============= ======================
1389   popular_comp                        3
1389   business                            3
0736   psychology                          5
0877   mod_cook                            2
0877   trad_cook                           3
0736   business                            1
0877   (NULL)                              1
[7 rows]
```

If you group by type alone, the query has a different meaning, and you'll get different results:

SQL
```
select type, count(title_id)
from titles
group by type
type           count(titles.title_id)
============= ======================
popular_comp                        3
business                            4
psychology                          5
mod_cook                            2
trad_cook                           3
(NULL)                              1
[6 rows]
```

This last set of results shows the number of books of each type, regardless of publisher. There are four books in the business category. However, two publishers sell this type of book: One has a single business book, and the other has three. The query results don't show how many are in each publisher/type combination.

Because the need to see multiple levels of summary values is so pervasive, many database vendors provide a report generator of some type. However, the report generator usually is an application program rather than a part of SQL because report results with multiple levels of summary values cannot be represented as relational tables.

Transact-SQL provides an extension that represents a SQL-based approach to the problem. Here's an example:

```
Transact-SQL
select pub_id, type, title_id
from titles
where type like '%cook%'
order by pub_id, type
compute count(title_id) by pub_id, type
compute count(title_id) by pub_id
pub_id type          title_id
------ ----          --------
0877   mod_cook      MC2222
0877   mod_cook      MC3021
                     count
                     --------
                            2
0877   trad_cook     TC3218
0877   trad_cook     TC4203
0877   trad_cook     TC7777
                     count
                     --------
                            3
                     count
                     --------
                            5
```

These results show row values, subgroup totals, and group totals in one set of results. Note that these results, unlike the results of other SQL queries, are not a relation and cannot be further manipulated by other SQL statements.

Oracle SQL Plus provides tools for creating similar reports.

NULLs and Groups

Because NULLs represent "the great unknown," there is no way to know whether one NULL is equal to any other NULL. Each unknown value may or may not be different from another.

However, if the grouping column contains more than one NULL, all of them are put into a single group.

COUNT(*) and COUNT()   The type column in the titles table contains a NULL. Here's an example that groups the rows by the type column and counts the number of rows in each group:

SQL
```
select type, count(*)
from titles
group by type
```

type	count(*)
============	============
popular_comp	3
business	4
psychology	5
mod_cook	2
trad_cook	3
(NULL)	1

[6 rows]

Notice that there is one row that has a NULL type. If you used count(type) instead of count(*) in the query, you'd get 0 instead of 1 in the second column:

SQL
```
select type, count(type)
from titles
group by type
```

type	count(titles.type)
============	==================
popular_comp	3
business	4
psychology	5
mod_cook	2
trad_cook	3
(NULL)	0

[6 rows]

Why is there a NULL group if it has zero rows? It's because of the difference in meaning between COUNT(*) and COUNT(expression):

- COUNT(*) finds *all rows* in a group, independent of the value in any particular column.
- COUNT() finds *all non-null values for the specified column.*

GROUP BY registers the existence of a type called NULL and forms a group for it. *COUNT(type)* duly calculates how many items are in the group. It finds only a NULL, which it doesn't include in the total, and hence records zero.

Multiple NULLs in a Group   What happens if there's more than one NULL in a grouping column (like advance)? Here's a query that answers the question:

SQL
```
select advance, count(*)
from titles
group by advance
```

advance	count(*)
========:	:========:
8000.00	2
5000.00	3
4000.00	2
2000.00	1
0.00	**1**
7000.00	3
10125.00	1
2275.00	1
6000.00	1
15000.00	1
(NULL)	**2**

[11 rows]

Two books have NULL advances; both of them are grouped under NULL advance. Note that, as expected, zero advance forms a separate group because zero is not the same as NULL. The group of two null values does not imply that these NULLs are equal to each other.

SQL
VARIANTS   If you're running these queries on a system other than the Adaptive Server Anywhere included on the CD, you may see your result rows in a different order. GROUP BY does some sorting as it creates groups, and this sometimes has the same effect as ordering by the GROUP BY column. Here are a couple of examples. Notice the position of NULL and zero in the advance column:

```
Microsoft SQL Server
select advance, count(*)
from titles
group by advance
advance
--------------------- -----------
NULL                      2
.0000                     1
2000.0000                 1
2275.0000                 1
4000.0000                 2
5000.0000                 3
6000.0000                 1
7000.0000                 3
8000.0000                 2
10125.0000                1
15000.0000                1
(11 row(s) affected)


Oracle
SQL> select advance, count(*)
  2  from titles
  3  group by advance;

  ADVANCE  COUNT(*)
--------- ---------
        0         1
     2000         1
     2275         1
     4000         2
     5000         3
     6000         1
```

```
     7000          3
     8000          2
    10125          1
    15000          1
                   2
  11 rows selected.
```

In Oracle SQL Plus, the default display for NULL is spaces. You can use SQL Plus features to change it.

GROUP BY: Aggregate Interactions

GROUP BY and aggregates work well together, but you can use them alone. The previous chapter examined aggregates without groups. Now let's look at GROUP BY alone and with aggregates.

GROUP BY Without Aggregates   Used without aggregates, GROUP BY is like DISTINCT. It divides a table into groups and returns one row for each group. Remember, whenever you use GROUP BY, each item in the SELECT list has to produce a single value per set. Following are some examples to make the relationship to DISTINCT clearer. First, a listing of all the publishers in the titles table:

```
SQL
select pub_id
from titles
pub_id
------
1389
1389
0736
1389
0877
0877
0877
1389
1389
```

```
1389
0877
0736
0736
0736
0736
0877
0877
0877
[18 rows]
```

Next, a listing of all the publishers grouped by publisher compared to a listing of all distinct publishers:

SQL
```
select pub_id          select distinct pub_id
from titles      or    from titles
group by type

            pub_id
            ======
            1389
            0736
            0877
            [3 rows]
```

GROUP BY with Aggregates   The last chapter discussed basic aggregate syntax without GROUP BY; so far this chapter has covered GROUP BY syntax. Now we can put the two together. The fact is, GROUP BY and aggregates were made for each other. GROUP BY creates the sets, and aggregates calculate per-set values. The two together can give you some very useful information.

Let's examine some typical queries. This statement finds the average advance and sum of year-to-date sales for *each type of book:*

SQL

```
select type, avg(advance), sum(ytd_sales)
from titles
group by type
```

type	avg(titles.advance)	sum(titles.ytd_sales)
======	======	======
popular_comp	7500.00	12875
business	6281.25	30788
psychology	4255.00	9939
mod_cook	7500.00	24278
trad_cook	6333.33	19566
(NULL)	(NULL)	(NULL)

[6 rows]

The summary values produced by SELECT statements with GROUP BY and aggregates appear as new columns in the results. (Your display for avg(advance) results may vary, depending on the datatype used for advance.)

Here's a query looking for relationships between price categories and average advance:

SQL
```
select price, avg(advance)
from titles
group by price
order by price
```

price	avg(titles.advance)
======	======
(NULL)	(NULL)
12.99	12562.50
17.00	6000.00
17.99	4000.00
21.95	3758.33
29.99	4000.00
40.00	8000.00
40.95	7000.00
41.59	7000.00
42.95	7000.00

[10 rows]

Check your system to see if you need the ORDER BY. In some systems, a GROUP BY implies an ORDER BY. In others, it does not.

GROUP BY with WHERE

You've seen that when there's no grouping and aggregates are working on the table as a whole, you can use the WHERE clause to specify which rows partici- pate in the aggregate calculations. The same is true when you have groups. Here are the steps when a query includes WHERE, GROUP BY, and aggregates:

1. The WHERE clause acts first to find the rows you want.

2. The GROUP BY clause divides these favored few (or many) rows into groups.

3. After the groups are formed, SQL calculates the group values.

Here's an example, first with and then without a limiting WHERE clause:

SQL
```
select type, avg(price)
from titles
where advance > 5000
group by type
type            avg(titles.price)
============ =================
popular_comp              41.48
trad_cook                 35.47
business                  12.99
psychology                29.30
mod_cook                  12.99
[5 rows]
```

Now here's the same query without the WHERE clause. Both the number of groups and summary values are different:

SQL
```
select type, avg(price)
from titles
group by type
```

```
type            avg(titles.price)
============    ==================
popular_comp                41.48
business                    23.73
psychology                  25.70
mod_cook                    21.49
trad_cook                   30.96
(NULL)                     (NULL)
[6 rows]
```

The second query returns an extra row (one with a NULL type and NULL average price) and different average price values for all but the popular computing type (business book average changes from 12.99 to 23.73; psychology from 29.30 to 25.70; etc.). The extra row is easy to explain: Because the WHERE clause looked for rows with advances greater than $5,000, it didn't include any rows with NULL advances.

If you look at results from a query for type, price, and advance and then apply the WHERE clause manually by marking with asterisks the rows in each group that have an advance greater than $5,000, you'll see how the results of the first query (the one with both WHERE and GROUP BY) were generated:

SQL
```
select type, price, advance
from titles
type            price        advance
============    ==========   ============
(NULL)          (NULL)        (NULL)

business        29.99        5000.00
business        21.95        5000.00
business        12.99        10125.00****
business        29.99        5000.00

mod_cook        29.99           0.00
mod_cook        12.99        15000.00****

popular_comp    40.00        8000.00****
popular_comp    42.95        7000.00****
popular_comp    (NULL)        (NULL)
```

```
psychology            17.99       4000.00
psychology            29.99       2000.00
psychology            21.95       2275.00
psychology            17.00       6000.00****
psychology            41.59       7000.00****

trad_cook             29.99       8000.00****
trad_cook             21.95       4000.00
trad_cook             40.95       7000.00****
[18 rows]
```

Only the rows with advances greater than $5,000 are included in the groups that give rise to the query results. Since there's just one row in the business group with a qualifying advance, the average price is the same as the price in that row. In the popular_comp group, on the other hand, two rows meet the WHERE conditions, and the average is halfway between the two.

The column in the WHERE clause doesn't have to have anything to do with the SELECT list or the grouping list.

GROUP BY and ORDER BY

GROUP BY divides tables into sets of rows, but it doesn't necessarily put those sets in any order. If you want your results sorted in some particular way, use ORDER BY (see "ORDER BY Syntax" in Chapter 5). Remember that the sequence of clauses in SELECT statements is fixed, and ORDER BY always goes after GROUP BY. For example, to find the average price for books of each type with advances over $5,000 and order the results by average price, the statement is this:

SQL
```
select type, avg(price)
from titles
where advance > 5000
group by type
order by 2
```

```
type           avg(titles.price)
============   =================
business                   12.99
mod_cook                   12.99
psychology                 29.30
trad_cook                  35.47
popular_comp               41.48
[5 rows]
```

The HAVING Clause

In its most common use, the HAVING clause is a WHERE clause for groups. Just as WHERE limits rows, HAVING limits groups. Most of the time, you use HAVING with GROUP BY.

```
SELECT select_list
FROM table_list
[WHERE conditions]
[GROUP BY group_by_list]
[HAVING conditions]
[ORDER BY order_by_list]
```

SYNTAX

When there are aggregates in the SELECT list of a query, WHERE clause conditions apply to the rows that are used to calculate the aggregates, while HAVING conditions apply to the final results after you've calculated the aggregates and set up the groups. One way to keep this difference in mind is to recall the order of the clauses in the SELECT statement. Remember that WHERE comes after FROM, and HAVING comes after GROUP BY. An example at the end of this section explores WHERE and HAVING interactions in some detail.

Here are the steps when a query includes WHERE, GROUP BY, aggregates, and HAVING:

1. The WHERE clause acts first to find the rows you want.

2. The GROUP BY clause divides these rows into groups.

3. After the groups are formed, SQL calculates the aggregate values (SUM, MIN, etc.) for each group.

4. HAVING checks the resulting group rows to see which ones qualify for the final display.

TIP   Any rows you can remove with WHERE, rather than HAVING, make your query more efficient because you have fewer rows to group and fewer to aggregate. Use HAVING to qualify groups, not rows.

Garden-Variety HAVING

Here's the standard use of HAVING: GROUP BY divides the rows into sets (by type), and HAVING puts a condition on the sets. In this example HAVING eliminates those sets that include only one book:

```
SQL
select type, count(*)
from titles
group by type
having count(*) > 1
type                count(*)
============ ===========
popular_comp            3
business                4
psychology              5
mod_cook                2
trad_cook               3
[5 rows]
```

HAVING Restrictions   You couldn't simply substitute WHERE for HAVING in the preceding query because WHERE does not allow aggregates. In addition, most systems require expressions in the HAVING clause to be either

- An aggregate expression; or
- A subset of SELECT list expressions.

In terms of allowed elements, HAVING search conditions are identical to WHERE search conditions, with the one exception already noted: WHERE search conditions cannot include aggregates, while HAVING search conditions often do. In most systems, each element in the HAVING clause must also appear in the SELECT list. WHERE, of course, does not have this limitation. You can put as many conditions as you want in a HAVING clause.

Every SQL system can run queries like this, where the HAVING clause condition is both an aggregate and an expression in the SELECT statement:

```
SQL
select type, count(*), avg(price)
from titles
group by type
having avg ( price) >25
type              count(*) avg(titles.price)
============= =========== ==================
popular_comp          3             41.48
psychology            5             25.70
trad_cook             3             30.96
[3 rows]
```

The query still works if you remove avg(price) from the SELECT list:

```
SQL
select type, count(*)
from titles
group by type
having avg ( price) >25
type              count(*)
============= ===========
popular_comp          3
psychology            5
trad_cook             3
[3 rows]
```

Here's an example of a HAVING clause without aggregates. It groups the titles table by type and eliminates those types that do not have "p" as the first letter: Note that type is in the SELECT clause:

```
SQL
select type
from titles
group by type
having type like 'p%'
```

```
type
============
popular_comp
psychology
[2 rows]
```

In this case, you would have been better off putting the type qualification in the WHERE clause. That way, you could eliminate all non-p types before grouping, rather than after, and save some work.

SQL
```
select type
from titles
where type like 'p%'
group by type
type
------------
popular_comp
psychology
[2 rows]
```

SQL
VARIANTS
In most systems, every element in the HAVING clause must appear in the SELECT list. Check your SQL engine to see how it handles this query—where the group value avg(price) is in the SELECT and GROUP BY list, but the row value price is in HAVING.

SQL
```
select type, count(*), avg(price)
from titles
group by type
having price > 35
```

The query runs on all systems if the HAVING clause uses a group value.

SQL
```
select type, count(*), avg(price)
from titles
group by type
having avg(price) > 35
```

```
type                 count(*) avg(titles.price)
============ =========== =================
popular_comp          3              41.48
[1 row]
```

Multiple HAVING Conditions When you want more than one condition included in the HAVING clause, you can combine conditions with AND, OR, or NOT. For example, to group the `titles` table by publisher and to include only those groups of publishers with identification numbers greater than 0800, and who have paid more than $15,000 total in advances and whose books average less than $20 in price, the statement is this:

SQL
```
select pub_id, sum(advance), avg(price)
from titles
group by pub_id
having sum(advance) > 15000
 and avg(price) > 20
 and pub_id > '0800'
```
```
pub_id sum(titles.advance) avg(titles.price)
====== =================== =================
1389             30000.00             32.98
0877             34000.00             27.17
[2 rows]
```

Here the last HAVING condition would be more efficient in the WHERE clause because it applies to row values, not to set values, and can disqualify rows before grouping:

SQL
```
select pub_id, sum(advance), avg(price)
from titles
where  pub_id > '0800'
group by pub_id
having sum(advance) > 15000
 and avg(price) > 20
```

The results are the same.

WHERE, GROUP BY, HAVING, ORDER BY

The following statement adds an ORDER BY and gives you all clauses in one SELECT statement. It produces the same groups and summary values as the previous example but orders the results by pub_id:

```
SQL
select pub_id, sum(advance), avg(price)
from titles
where   pub_id > '0800'
group by pub_id
having sum(advance) > 15000
  and avg(price) > 20
order by pub_id
pub_id sum(titles.advance) avg(titles.price)
====== =================== =================
0877                34000.00             27.17
1389                30000.00             32.98
[2 rows]
```

All About NULLs

NULLs and the quirks connected with them have come up several times in this chapter and in earlier chapters. In this section, we'll pull all those bits and pieces together and go into more detail about the conceptual problems of NULLs. Our goal is to help you avoid some of the mistakes that often result from misunderstandings about NULLs.

The first point to consider, although it is hardly reassuring, is that even the experts consider NULLs a pesky problem; some think they should be done away with altogether. Part of the difficulty with NULLs arises from the fact that they can represent a number of different kinds of incomplete information:

- Data that may never be known ("present whereabouts" for an escaped criminal)
- Data that isn't known now but will be determined later (the price and advance columns of the titles table)
- Characterizations that are inapplicable to the data ("assessed value of house" for a renter)

In today's database products, NULLs are used to represent both missing and inapplicable values.

There are other wrinkles, too. Sometimes you don't know precisely what a value is, but you know something about what it's not. You might not know a person's exact birth date, for example, but you know it was between 1910 and 1930. Or negotiations with an author might already be far enough along so that it's clear the advance is going to be larger than $10,000. These kinds of unknown pieces of information are called **distinguished nulls**—their values are not precisely known, but some things about them are clear.

Some types of computer programs—statistical packages, for example—support many kinds of distinguished nulls. In relational database management systems, however, distinguished nulls are problematic in terms of both definition and implementation. To date, no system we know of supports them.

Let's summarize what we've said about NULLs in earlier chapters.

NULLs and Database Design

As you recall, you specify whether a column allows NULL when you create a table. Setting up columns that can accept NULL means that the database system can gracefully handle these two situations:

- A user is adding a new row to a table but doesn't have the information to be entered in some of the fields. The database system automatically marks these positions as NULLs.
- You're restructuring a table by adding a new column to it. What gets entered in that new column in all the existing rows? Again, the database system automatically enters NULLs.

If a piece of information is required (a product name, an ID number), the column that contains it cannot be NULL. For more on this topic, see "Assigning Null Status" in Chapter 3.

Comparisons Involving NULLs

We pointed out in Chapter 3 that because NULLs represent the unknown, you cannot determine whether a NULL exactly matches any other value, even another NULL.

For example, the advance for the book called *Net Etiquette* is represented as NULL. Does this mean that it is larger than $5,000? Smaller than $5,000? Is it larger or smaller than the advance for *The Psychology of Computer Cooking*, also represented as NULL?

Based on the definition of NULL as unknown, of course, the answer to all these questions is unknown. You might also say that the answer is "maybe." That's what we mean when we say that NULL implies three-valued logic instead of the more intuitively understandable two-valued logic. With NULLs, the possibilities are never just true and false; they're true, false, and maybe.

The counterintuitive nature of three-valued logic often leads to confusion. Consider the unsuspecting user who asks for a listing of all titles with advances greater than $5,000 and gets a list of eight titles. The user then asks for the titles with advances less than $5,000 and gets five. Finally, he or she determines that there are three titles with advances of exactly $5,000. The user then concludes that there are sixteen titles in all, forgetting that the two titles with unknown advances are not reported by any of the queries. This is because, of course, the database system interpreted the first question as "Give me all titles *known* to have advances greater than $5,000."

Here are a few other likely sources of confusion. If you sort the books by advance, all those with NULL advances are shown at the beginning or the end of the report, depending on how your system sorts NULLs. This implies pretty strongly that these advances are less than (or more than) any of the others and that all the NULLs are the same because they are shown together.

Similarly (as far as confusion potential goes), when you select distinct values, all the NULLs are eliminated except one. This suggests that the NULLs in question are equal to each other!

One aspect of the problem of NULLs is simply remembering that they may exist. For example, suppose you want to notify all the authors whose royalty payments for the year totaled less than $600 that they need not report this amount to the IRS. Those whose payments are unknown wouldn't show up in your report unless you specifically searched for them with an operator such as IS NULL.

NULLs and Computations

The really sticky problems associated with NULLs become apparent when you try to figure out what to do with those unknown values when you operate on them.

It's easy enough to see that when you perform an arithmetic operation on an unknown value, the result can only be unknown. You can double all the advances, for example, and the advance for *Net Etiquette* is still NULL. You can subtract the NULL advance from the advance for *The Psychology of*

Computer Cooking, and you certainly can't say that the answer is zero: It is still NULL.

But what if you want to find the average of all advances? Here's what you'd do:

```
SQL
select avg(advance)
from titles
avg(titles.advance)
===================
            5962.50
[1 row]
```

Let's check up on SQL by querying it first for the sum of all the advances and then for the number of books:

```
SQL
select sum(advance)
from titles
sum(titles.advance)
===================
           95400.00
[1 row]

select count(*)
from titles
  count(*)
===========
        18
[1 row]
```

Don't reach for your calculator. What you'll find is that 95,400 divided by 18 does not give the answer that SQL did. The reason for the discrepancy is that SQL throws out the two NULL advances in the sum and in the count that it does for the purposes of calculating the average. However, COUNT(*) counts the number of *rows,* ignoring NULLs in any particular column.

The situation is very confusing. You asked for the average of all the advances and got a figure that looked very precise. But it cannot be precise because the data on which it was based is itself incomplete and imprecise. Your query actually found the average for all *known* advances.

SQL does the best it can, as the rules for NULLs and aggregates given earlier demonstrate.

Defaults as Alternatives to NULLs

One alternative to a NULL is a default, a value entered by the database management system when the user provides no explicit value. SQL allows you to specify defaults in the CREATE TABLE command (and the ALTER TABLE command).

> **TIP**
>
> One of the advantages of defaults over NULLs is that you can give a particular column an appropriate value, instead of having to rely on NULL everywhere. A good default for the `type` column might be "unknown," while a good default for the `date` column might be today's date. On the other hand, defaults of zero (for numeric columns) or blank (for character columns) or "01/01/0000" (for date columns) are likely to cause more trouble than NULLs because their meaning and implementation will vary (one space or a whole string?). NULLs have the advantage of being consistent across RDBMSs. In addition, defaults don't help with any of the computational dilemmas just discussed. NULLs, with all their complexities, will always be with us.

Functions That Work with NULLs

Most systems provide a function that allows you to substitute a display value for NULLs on the fly; the ANSI version is called COALESCE. In this example, the function has two arguments: the name of the column and the value to display for any NULLs found in that column.

SQL
```
select type, coalesce( type, 'Who knows?') as NewType, count(*) as Count
from titles
group by type
```

```
type            NewType              Count
===========   ============   ===========
popular_comp  popular_comp            3
business      business                4
psychology    psychology              5
mod_cook      mod_cook                2
trad_cook     trad_cook               3
(NULL)        Who knows?              1
[6 rows]
```

There is more on COALESCE in "Changing Null Displays" in Chapter 11.

On Oracle and Informix, the function is called NVL.   **SQL**
                                                                   VARIANTS

```
Oracle
SQL> select type, NVL(type, 'NO TYPE'), count(*)
  2  from titles
  3  group by type;
TYPE            NVL(TYPE,'NO  COUNT(*)
-----------   ------------   ---------
business      business                4
mod_cook      mod_cook                2
popular_comp  popular_comp            3
psychology    psychology              5
trad_cook     trad_cook               3
              NO TYPE                 1
6 rows selected.
```

On Microsoft SQL Server and Sybase systems, you can use ISNULL (which is not the same as IS NULL):

```
Microsoft SQL Server:
select isnull(type, 'What?'), count(*)
from titles
group by type

-----------   -----------
What?                   1
business                4
mod_cook                2
```

```
popular_comp          3
psychology            5
trad_cook             3
```

(6 rows affected)

NULL Functions and "What-If" Calculations

You can also use the function for doing "what if" math, substituting different display values for the original NULLs. Of course, the actual value in the database is not affected. Here's a query that shows type and average price for each type in the first two columns. The third column uses COALESCE to calculate the average price if each NULL were $50.00. Values change only in the groups that contain NULLs.

SQL
```
select type, avg(price), avg ( coalesce (price, 50.00) )
from titles
group by type
```

type	avg(titles.price)	avg(coalesce(titles.price,50.
popular_comp	41.48	44.32
business	23.73	23.73
psychology	25.70	25.70
mod_cook	21.49	21.49
trad_cook	30.96	30.96
(NULL)	(NULL)	50.00

[6 rows]

Summary

Now you know all about grouping, a very useful element in SQL.

- Divide data into groups with the GROUP BY clause. Like ORDER BY, GROUP BY allows nesting—that is, you can group within groups. However, GROUP BY is more restrictive than ORDER BY in the kinds of expressions it allows in the GROUP BY list. GROUP BY does some sorting as it builds groups, but don't make assumptions—the ordering tends to vary a great deal from system to system and even from release to release.

- Limit the group results with the HAVING clause. Don't think of HAVING as a later form of WHERE. The two are different in terms of when they are processed. Use WHERE to remove row results before grouping and HAVING to remove group results after grouping. WHERE does not allow aggregates (except in subqueries—more on that later), but HAVING thinks they are swell.

- Use groups with aggregates. You can get very useful results from this combination.

- Understand the role of NULL in groups, and do some experiments.

GROUP BY is a powerful tool. It's worth putting time into understanding it. ORDER BY is intuitive for most users, but GROUP BY takes more practice.

The next two chapters give more information about working with multiple tables. Chapter 7 focuses on joins, while Chapter 8 explores nested queries, or subqueries.

Chapter 7

Joining Tables for Comprehensive Data Analysis

In This Chapter

- Defining Joins
- Why Joins Are Necessary
- Getting a Good Join
- Improving the Readability of Join Results
- Specifying Join Conditions
- Exploring Exotic Joins
- Avoiding a Common Source of Errors
- Going Beyond Joins: UNION, INTERSECT, MINUS

Defining Joins

Joins complete the triad of operations that a relational query language must provide: selection, projection, and join. The join operation lets you retrieve and manipulate data from more than one table in a single SELECT statement. Joining two tables is a little like making a seam to join two pieces of material. Once you have made the seam, you can work with the whole cloth.

You specify each join (there can be more than one in a single SELECT statement) on two tables at a time, using a column from each table as a **connecting column** or **join column**. Connecting columns should have values that match or compare easily, representing the same or similar data in each of the tables participating in the join. For example, the `title_id` column in the `titles` table matches the `title_id` column in the `salesdetails` table.

Joining the `titles` and `salesdetails` tables allows you to retrieve, display, and operate on data in both tables with the same query. For example, you might want to know how sales have been doing over the past six months for books with advances greater than $10,000. The advance information is in `titles`; the sales ship date information is in `salesdetails`.

You can join columns with different names (`authors.au_id` and `editors.ed_id`) as long as the connecting columns are **join-compatible**: Their values come from the same general class of data. In fact, it's best if they have exactly the same datatype. Minor differences in datatypes (CHAR versus VARCHAR, or CHAR that allows NULL versus CHAR that does not allow NULL) can lead to performance problems.

Why Joins Are Necessary

In a database that has been designed according to the normalization rules, one table might not give you all the information you need about a particular entity. For comprehensive data analysis, you must assemble data from several tables. The relational model—having led you to partition your data into several single-subject tables following the rules of normalization and good, clean database design—relies on the join operation to enable you to perform ad hoc queries and produce comprehensible reports. In the same way, you are not limited in the kind of new tables you can add to the database. Thus the join operation is one of the key operations of the relational model. Joins are possible because of the relational model, and they are necessary because of the relational model.

Associating Data from Separate Tables

Joins are necessary in a relational database management system because the relational model's data independence permits you to bring data from separate tables into new and unanticipated relationships. Relationships among data values become explicit when the data is manipulated—when you *query* the database, not when you *create* it.

You need not know in advance that data will join. You can discover new relationships among data in different tables by joining them. For example, you could use a join to find out whether any editor is also an author. Figure 7.1 shows two versions of the join; they differ only in syntax—more on this later.

This query is a little tricky. Because an editor and an author can have the same last name but still be different people, you need to join on the ID column, which uniquely identifies the suspects. As a row's unique identifier, a primary key is often particularly useful in join queries.

```
SQL                             SQL
select ed_lname                 select ed_lname
from editors, authors           from editors join authors
where ed_id = au_id             on ed_id = au_id
```

```
         ed_lname
         ================================
         Greene
         del Castillo
         [2 rows]
```

Figure 7.1 Comparing Join Queries

Joins are necessary because during the process of analysis that distributes data over the relational database landscape, you cleanly separate information on independent entities. You can get a comprehensive view of your data only if you can reconnect the tables. That's the whole point of joins.

Providing Flexibility

A corollary of the join capability is that it gives you unlimited flexibility in adding new kinds of data to your database. Joins are always possible. You can create a new table that contains data about a different subject. If the new table has an eligible field, you can link it to existing tables by joining.

That's how relational databases grow: If tables need to split, you can always reconstruct the rows by joining. If new, related information appears, you can design tables with appropriate join columns, so the new data can be linked to the existing data.

For example, our bookbiz database might need an invoices table for billing stores. Such a table could link to the sales and salesdetails tables by sonum (sales order number) and (presumably) to a new stores table on the stor_id column.

Your database design should anticipate likely joins and build in eligible join columns, which are usually primary key or foreign key columns for their tables. Primary keys (titles.title_id) join to the corresponding foreign keys (salesdetails.title_id, titleauthors.title_id, and titleeditors.title_id). Without join columns available as links, it is difficult to run queries on multiple tables. For a review of design principles, see Chapter 2, "Designing Databases."

Getting a Good Join

What makes for a good join column? Ideally, a join column is a key column for its table—either a primary key or a foreign key. When a key is composite (made up of more than one column), you can join on all the columns of the key.

Since the primary key logically connects to related foreign key columns in other tables, key columns are usually ideal candidate columns on which to construct a join. Such a join is likely to be useful and logically appropriate because the database designer planned ahead for it.

Primary key/foreign key joins are based on the expectation that foreign keys will be kept consistent with their primary keys, in order to preserve the referential integrity of the database. See "Creating Tables with SQL-92 Constraints" in Chapter 3 for information on how to do that with the REFERENCES and FOREIGN KEY keywords in CREATE and ALTER TABLE statements.

If a join is to have meaningful results, you need to follow some general rules:

- Both tables must be named in the table list in order for the system to perform the join. The FROM clause's table list sets the stage—it puts the system on alert to perform a join.
- The columns must have related meaning. For example, you could join authors' ages (such as 25, 30, 50) to numbers in the `salesdetails` table's `qty_shipped` column, but the results would not be useful. The columns have superficial similarities, but they are not logically connected.
- Columns being joined need not have the same name, although they often will (and if you want to use NATURAL JOIN syntax, they must).
- If there are NULLs in the connecting columns of tables being joined, the NULLs will never join because NULLs represent unknown or inapplicable values (and there is no reason to believe one unknown value matches another). For a review of null values, see "All About NULLs" in Chapter 6.

Performance is often an issue with joins. Here are some performance guidelines:

- For nontrivial amounts of data, join columns should be indexed.
- For best performance, join columns should have exactly the same datatypes, including whether they allow NULLs.

- If the database is not large, or performance is not important, joins are possible as long as the datatypes are compatible—types that the system easily converts from one type into the other (usually any of the numeric type columns—such as INTEGER, DECIMAL, or FLOAT—and any of the character type and date columns—such as CHARACTER, VARCHAR, or DATETIME).

There are two types of join syntax:

- FROM/WHERE
- JOIN keyword (SQL-92)

Both are widely used, although the JOIN keyword syntax is becoming more popular as more and more vendors implement it.

FROM/WHERE Join Syntax

A skeleton version of FROM/WHERE join syntax is this:

SYNTAX

```
SELECT select_list
FROM table_1, table_2 [, table_3]...
WHERE [table_1.]column  join_operator  [table_2.]column
```

The join operator in the first several examples is the equal sign (=). The FROM clause's table list must include at least two tables, and the columns specified in the WHERE clause must be join-compatible. When the join columns have identical names, you must qualify the columns with their table names in the select list and in the WHERE clause.

For example, if you wanted to know the names and positions of the editors of *Secrets of Silicon Valley* (PC8888), you'd need a join on a column that exists in the two relevant tables:

```
SQL
select ed_lname, ed_fname, ed_pos
from editors, titleditors
where editors.ed_id = titleditors.ed_id
   and titleditors.title_id = 'PC8888'
```

ed_lname	ed_fname	ed_pos
==========================	====================	============
DeLongue	Martinella	project
Samuelson	Bernard	project
Kaspchek	Christof	acquisition
[3 rows]		

This join selects the names of editors who are connected to the `title_id` "PC8888" by joining on the `ed_id` column that appears in both the `editors` and the `titleditors` tables. Note that the join columns need not be included in the SELECT list.

SQL-92 Join Syntax

SQL-92 provides some keywords for joins (JOIN, CROSS JOIN, and NATURAL JOIN, which can be combined with INNER, RIGHT OUTER, LEFT OUTER, and FULL OUTER to make the full spectrum of joins). Some or all of these keywords are implemented by an increasing number of systems, including the Adaptive Server Anywhere included with this book. However, the original FROM/WHERE join syntax is still common, and vendors that support the new JOIN keyword syntax also provide it. For this reason, most of the examples in this chapter use the original FROM/WHERE syntax. Examples of the new syntax are provided as translations—the concepts are not different, only the annotation is.

Following are some ANSI syntax alternatives. The FROM clause includes the keyword JOIN. The join columns are listed in a special ON or USING clause. (Our demo database, ASA, supports ON.)

```
SELECT select_list
FROM table_1 JOIN table_2
[ON [table_1.]column  join_operator  [table_2.]column
  | USING (column) ]
```

SYNTAX

The join operator can be the JOIN keyword alone or can be modified by CROSS or NATURAL. When it is, the ON and USING keywords are not allowed.

- A CROSS JOIN uses the WHERE clause to qualify joining columns (if you leave off the WHERE clause, it produces a Cartesian product). For

more information see "Avoiding a Common Source of Errors" in this chapter.
- A NATURAL JOIN works only when the two tables have a single identical column. It assumes the join is on this column, so you don't specify it in the ON, USING, or WHERE clause.

Following are examples of three JOIN keyword variants and their corresponding join column notation (in this case they all produce the same results). The comments (preceded by double dashes) at the beginning of each piece of code mark the elements to look at.

SQL
```
--JOIN keyword and ON clause
select ed_lname, ed_fname, ed_pos
from editors join titleditors
on editors.ed_id = titleditors.ed_id
where titleditors.title_id = 'PC8888'


  CROSS JOIN keyword and WHERE clause
select ed_lname, ed_fname, ed_pos
from editors cross join titleditors
where editors.ed_id = titleditors.ed_id
   and titleditors.title_id = 'PC8888'

--NATURAL JOIN keyword, no join columns specified in WHERE clause
select ed_lname, ed_fname, ed_pos
from editors natural join titleditors
where titleditors.title_id = 'PC8888'
```

ed_lname	ed_fname	ed_pos
===	===	===
DeLongue	Martinella	project
Samuelson	Bernard	project
Kaspchek	Christof	acquisition

[3 rows]

Not all systems support every element of the ANSI join keyword syntax (JOIN, CROSS, and NATURAL). When you specify a join, whether original or ANSI, you must list multiple tables and indicate which columns you are joining (Figure 7.2).

	FROM/WHERE	SQL-92
list tables (must be more than one table)	in FROM clause	in FROM clause
locate JOIN keyword	n/a	in FROM clause
locate join columns	in WHERE clause only	in ON, USING, or WHERE clause, depending on join operator (join columns not needed for NATURAL JOIN)

Figure 7.2 Join Prerequisites

Analyzing a Join

The join operator, which expresses the relationship between the join columns, can be any of the relational operators. Equality is the most common (in which a value in the join column from one table is equal to a value in the join column from another table). For example, if an author calls to ask which editors live in the same city as a publisher's home office, a join query can provide the answer. The following query finds the names of editors who live in the same city as Algodata Infosystems:

```
SQL
select ed_lname, ed_id, editors.city, pub_name, publishers.city
from editors, publishers
where editors.city = publishers.city
   and pub_name = 'Algodata Infosystems'
ed_lname     ed_id          city         pub_name                 city
==========   ============   ==========   ======================   ========
DeLongue     321-55-8906    Berkeley     Algodata Infosystems     Berkeley
Kaspchek     943-88-7920    Berkeley     Algodata Infosystems     Berkeley
[2 rows]
```

A SQL-92 version of the query is

SQL
```
select ed_lname, ed_id, editors.city, pub_name, publishers.city
from editors join publishers
on editors.city = publishers.city
where pub_name = 'Algodata Infosystems'
```

The query, with either syntax, promptly reports that two editors, DeLongue and Kaspchek, live in the same city (Berkeley) as Algodata Infosystems. This was information you didn't know earlier. In fact, all you had to know was the publisher's name, and the join supplied you with all that additional information. You told the system: "Join on the city, whatever that is, and tell me the editors' names, whoever they are."

Improving the Readability of Join Results

When you join tables, the system compares the data in the specified columns and displays the results of the comparison as a table of the qualifying rows. The results show a row for each successful join. Data from any of the tables is duplicated as needed.

Join query results replicate data from qualifying rows as needed in order to regularize the table display. As with any query, the results of a join query display as a table without altering the database tables in any way. The join operation simply permits the system to manipulate data from multiple tables as if it were contained in a single table.

Avoiding Duplication

You don't have to name both join columns in the SELECT list, or even include the join columns in the results at all, in order for the join to succeed. Note that you may need to qualify the name of a join column with its table name in the SELECT list or in the join specification if there is any ambiguity about which column you mean. In the following query, the tables join on `editors.city` and `publishers.city`, and both `city` columns are included in the SELECT list.

SQL
```
select ed_lname, editors.city, publishers.city
from editors, publishers
where editors.city = publishers.city
and pub_name = 'Algodata Infosystems'
```

SQL

```
select ed_lname, editors.city, publishers.city
from editors join publishers
on editors.city = publishers.city
where pub_name = 'Algodata Infosystems'
```

ed_lname	city	city
==========	======	======
DeLongue	Berkeley	Berkeley
Kaspchek	Berkeley	Berkeley
[2 rows]		

However, because the two city columns contain identical information (that's why they join!), there's really no need to include both in the results.

In a more common version of the query, the SELECT list includes only one of the columns, here editors.city.

SQL

```
select ed_lname, editors.city
from editors, publishers
where editors.city = publishers.city
and pub_name = 'Algodata Infosystems'
```

SQL

```
select ed_lname, editors.city
from editors join publishers
on editors.city = publishers.city
where pub_name = 'Algodata Infosystems'
```

ed_lname	city
==========	======
DeLongue	Berkeley
Kaspchek	Berkeley
[2 rows]	

Limiting the Width of the Display

As with any SELECT statement, the columns you name after the SELECT keyword are the columns you want the query results to display, in their desired order.

If you use SELECT *, the columns appear in their CREATE TABLE order. In a query to find the title or titles associated with sales order number 1, you might join the salesdetails table to titles on title_id. The SQL-92 version uses the JOIN keyword in the FROM clause and adds the ON clause for specifying the join columns.

SQL	*SQL*
select *	select *
from titles, salesdetails	from titles **join** salesdetails
where **titles.title_id =**	**on** titles.title_id =
salesdetails.title_id	salesdetails.title_id
and sonum = 1	where sonum = 1

```
title_id
   title
   type          pub_id        price       advance
   ytd_sales contract
   notes
   pubdate                     sonum       qty_ordered          qty_shipped
   title_id    date_shipped
========================================================================
PS2091
   Is Anger the Enemy?
   psychology    0736          21.95       2275.00
   2045          1
   Carefully researched study of the effects of strong emotions on the
   body. Metabolic charts included.
   Jun 15 1998 12:00 am        1           75                   75
   PS2091        Sep 15 1998 12:00 am
[1 row]
```

The preceding query produces a result display that has 1 row and 14 columns. It has two potential problems:

- Indiscriminate use of * queries can make your system do more work than is needed, bringing back more data than you want and forcing the optimizer to avoid an index that might have been available to a query that used only columns "covered" in an index.
- A join that creates a very wide row can present you with results that are hard to read. Choose columns carefully for ad hoc queries.

The order of the tables (or views) in the FROM list affects the results display only when you use SELECT * to specify the select list.

The table list should name all the tables that will participate in any of the query's joins. You can specify a join on more than two tables, as long as you join tables two at a time. There are examples of three-way joins later in this chapter, and, of course, you can go beyond that—most real-life systems do.

Using Aliases in the FROM Clause Table/View List

You can assign each table (or view—see Chapter 9) an alias (an abbreviation for the full table name) in the FROM clause table list, in order to make join queries

* Easier to type
* More readable

Assigning an alias to each table name is particularly helpful when you join on identically named columns, which have to be qualified with the table name each time they're used. Aliases can be letters or numbers in any combination; most people make them short and easy to remember.

Here's how you could use aliases in a query to find authors who live in the same city as some publisher:

```
SQL
select au_lname, au_fname
from authors a, publishers p
where a.city = p.city

au_lname
========================================
Bennet
Carson
[2 rows]
```

```
SQL
select au_lname, au_fname
from authors a join publishers p
on a.city = p.city

au_fname
====================
Abraham
Cheryl
```

If you want to display the city name, you need to qualify it with one of the table name aliases (a or p) in the SELECT list.

Some people make it a rule to qualify all columns. That way, changes in table structures do not introduce ambiguities.

TIP

SQL

```
select a.au_fname as Author, a.zip as AuthorZip, p.pub_name as Publisher
from authors a, publishers p
where a.city = p.city
```

```
Author                AuthorZip Publisher
==================== ========= ====================
Abraham               94705     Algodata Infosystems
Cheryl                94705     Algodata Infosystems
[2 rows]
```

If someone adds a column coincidentally named `zip` to `publishers` (which did not originally have a `zip column`), the query will still run. The qualifier makes it clear that it's `authors.zip` you want to see.

SQL

```
alter table publishers
add zip char(5) null
```

```
select a.au_fname as Author, a.zip as AuthorZip, p.pub_name as Publisher
from authors a, publishers p
where a.city = p.city
```

```
Author                AuthorZip Publisher
==================== ========= ====================
Abraham               94705     Algodata Infosystems
Cheryl                94705     Algodata Infosystems
[2 rows]
```

Without the qualification on the (originally) unambiguous column, you'd get an error.

SQL

```
select au_fname as Author, zip as AuthorZip, pub_name as Publisher
from authors a, publishers p
where a.city = p.city
Error: Column 'zip' found in more than one
table -- need a correlation name.
```

Specifying Join Conditions

The examples so far have illustrated joins based on equality or on matching values in the joining columns. Joins based on equality are indicated with the "=" logical operator in the join column clause (WHERE or ON). Joins can also be constructed on other conditions: The join operator can be any one of the comparison operators or a special operator for specifying an **outer join** (which we'll discuss later).

In addition to the equality operator, the other comparison operators that can be used to specify comparison conditions are shown in Figure 7.3.

Joins Based on Equality

There are two kinds of joins that use the "equal to" operator:

- Equijoins
- Natural joins

The **equijoin** is useful when you're first working with joins. It displays the join column from each table and allows you to see how the join works. **Natural joins** eliminate the duplication and are much more common.

Symbol	Meaning
>	greater than
>=	greater than or equal to
<	less than
<=	less than or equal to
<>	not equal to

Figure 7.3 Comparison Operators

SQL VARIANTS   Transact-SQL also provides the operators !=, !>, and !<, which are equivalent to <>, <=, and >=, respectively.

Equijoins   By definition, an equijoin joins on matching values and displays the join's seam—the connecting column from each table that participates in the join.

This query finds titles that are connected to orders with a particular sales order number:

```
SQL
select title, t.title_id,
    sonum, sd.title_id
from titles t, salesdetails sd
where t.title_id = sd.title_id
    and sonum = 14
```

```
SQL
select title, t.title_id,
    sonum, sd.title_id
from titles t join salesdetails sd
on t.title_id = sd.title_id
where sobum = 14
```

title	title_id	sonum	title_id
===	===	===	===
Emotional Security: A New Algorithm	PS7777	14	PS7777
Prolonged Data Deprivation: Four Case Studies	PS3333	14	PS3333
Life Without Fear	PS2106	14	PS2106
Computer Phobic and Non-Phobic Individuals:			
Behavior Variations	PS1372	14	PS1372

[4 rows]

Natural Joins   Because there's really no need to display information redundantly, you can eliminate the display of one of the connecting columns by restating the query so that it displays the join column only once. Such a display is called a natural join. The natural join version of the previous query follows. (The SQL-92 example on the right uses the word NATURAL because the join is on columns with the same name. The ON or USING clause is not needed in this case.)

```
SQL
select title, t.title_id, sonum
from titles t,
            salesdetails sd
where sonum = 14
and t.title_id = sd.title_id
```

```
SQL
select title, t.title_id, sonum
from titles t natural join
                salesdetails sd
where sonum = 14
```

title	title_id	sonum
===	=============	=====
Emotional Security: A New Algorithm	**PS7777**	14
Prolonged Data Deprivation: Four Case Studies	**PS3333**	14
Life Without Fear	**PS2106**	14
Computer Phobic and Non-Phobic Individuals:		
Behavior Variations	**PS1372**	14

[4 rows]

Now we have a natural join because the column `title_id` does not appear twice in the results. Some systems use the natural join display as the default display for a join because it makes the results more readable. It doesn't matter which `title_id` column you include, but you have to qualify it in the SELECT list with its table name.

Joins Not Based on Equality

Joins not based on equality can be described by their comparison condition, as "less-than join," "greater-than join," and so forth. This example of a less-than join displays orders that were shipped on a date later than the sale (the company attempts to ship all orders on the day received):

SQL
```
select distinct s.sonum, s.stor_id, s.sdate,
 sd.date_shipped
from sales s, salesdetails sd
where s.sdate < sd.date_shipped
 and s.sonum = sd.sonum
```

sonum	stor_id	sdate	date_shipped
=========	=======	====================	====================
1	7066	Sep 13 1998 12:00 am	Sep 15 1998 12:00 am
2	7067	Sep 14 1998 12:00 am	Sep 15 1998 12:00 am
3	7131	Sep 14 1998 12:00 am	Sep 18 1998 12:00 am
4	7131	Sep 14 1998 12:00 am	Sep 18 1998 12:00 am
6	8042	Sep 14 1998 12:00 am	Sep 22 1998 12:00 am
7	6380	Sep 13 1998 12:00 am	Sep 20 1998 12:00 am
9	8042	Mar 11 2001 12:00 am	Mar 28 2001 12:00 am
19	7896	Feb 21 2001 12:00 am	Mar 15 2001 12:00 am
10	7896	Oct 28 2000 12:00 am	Oct 29 2000 12:00 am

```
        11 7896    Dec 12 2000 12:00 am Jan 12 2001 12:00 am
        12 8042    May 22 2000 12:00 am May 24 2000 12:00 am
        14 7131    May 29 2000 12:00 am Jun 13 2000 12:00 am
        15 7067    Jun 15 2000 12:00 am Jun 17 2000 12:00 am
[13 rows]
```

As in this example, unequal joins are often used with an equal join. Unequal joins return nonmatches in some order. This can be more data than makes sense, unless it is paired with an equal join. There are more examples of unequal operators in the section on self-joins later in this chapter.

Joining More Than Two Tables

The design of the `bookbiz` database dictates that you must join three tables (two at a time) in order to obtain complete information about books and their authors—`titleauthors` is an intermediate table that joins with both `authors` and `titles`. For example, to find the titles of all the books of a particular type (`trad_cook`) and the names of their authors, the query is this:

SQL
```
select au_lname, au_fname, title
from authors a, titles t, titleauthors ta
where a.au_id = ta.au_id
  and t.title_id = ta.title_id
  and t.type = 'trad_cook'
```

au_lname	au_fname	title
==============	========	==
Yokomoto	Akiko	Sushi, Anyone?
O'Leary	Michael	Sushi, Anyone?
Gringlesby	Burt	Sushi, Anyone?
Blotchet-Halls	Reginald	Fifty Years in Buckingham Palace Kitchens
Panteley	Sylvia	Onions, Leeks, and Garlic: Cooking Secrets of the Mediterranean

```
[5 rows]
```

When there is more than one join condition in a statement, the join conditions are almost always connected with AND, as in the preceding examples. Connecting two join conditions with OR is rarely justified: The results are not likely to make sense because the conditions are not restrictive enough.

The SQL-92 version of this query is a little different. The related ON clause comes immediately after the FROM listing of each table pair. Join phrases are separated with a comma.

```
SQL
select au_lname, au_fname, title
from authors a join titles t
  on a.au_id = ta.au_id,
titles t join titleauthors ta
  on t.title_id = ta.title_id
where t.type = 'trad_cook'
```

Exploring Exotic Joins

In addition to the joins we've examined so far, there are two specialized kinds of joins:

- Self-joins
- Outer joins

Joining a Table with Itself: The Self-Join

A **self-join** compares values within a single table. You often use a self-join to unravel a complex relationship, such as which employees work for which managers or which parts belong in an assemblage. The critical elements of a self-join are

- Listing the table twice in the FROM clause and assigning a different alias to each
- Joining the table to itself, using the table aliases to qualify the columns
- Adding a condition (often an unequal join on another column) to prevent a row joining itself

The `editors` table uses the editor ID number in two ways: to identify an editor (`ed_id`) and to identify the editor's boss (`ed_boss`). Here's what the relevant data looks like:

SQL

```
select ed_id, ed_fname, ed_lname, ed_pos, ed_boss
from editors
order by ed_id
```

ed_id	ed_fname	ed_lname	ed_pos	ed_boss
321-55-8906	Martinella	DeLongue	project	993-86-0420
527-72-3246	Morningstar	Greene	copy	826-11-9034
712-45-1867	Innes	del Castillo	copy	826-11-9034
777-02-9831	Bernard	Samuelson	project	993-86-0420
777-66-9902	Alfred	Almond	copy	826-11-9034
826-11-9034	Eleanore	Himmel	project	993-86-0420
885-23-9140	Hannah	Rutherford-Hayes	project	993-86-0420
943-88-7920	Christof	Kaspchek	acquisition	(NULL)
993-86-0420	Dennis	McCann	acquisition	(NULL)

[9 rows]

Unraveling Relationships   To find out the names of the bosses, you need to do a self-join, connecting the ed_boss column in editors e1 to the ed_id column in editors e2. This allows you to translate the boss number into a boss name.

SQL

```
select e1.ed_fname, e1.ed_id, e1.ed_pos,  e2.ed_fname as boss_name
from editors e1, editors e2
where e1.ed_boss = e2.ed_id
```

ed_fname	ed_id	ed_pos	boss_name
Alfred	777-66-9902	copy	Eleanore
Morningstar	527-72-3246	copy	Eleanore
Innes	712-45-1867	copy	Eleanore
Martinella	321-55-8906	project	Dennis
Bernard	777-02-9831	project	Dennis
Eleanore	826-11-9034	project	Dennis
Hannah	885-23-9140	project	Dennis

[7 rows]

It turns out that all the copy editors work for Eleanore and all the project editors work for Dennis. Two editors (Dennis and Christof) don't have bosses listed.

Using Not-Equal Comparisons   How would you determine whether more than one author has the same last name? Following is a self-join using an equality operator:

SQL
```
select a1.au_id, a1.au_lname, a2.au_id, a2.au_lname
from authors a1, authors a2
where a1.au_lname = a2.au_lname
```

au_id	au_lname	au_id	au_lname
409-56-7008	Bennet	409-56-7008	Bennet
213-46-8915	Green	213-46-8915	Green
238-95-7766	Carson	238-95-7766	Carson
998-72-3567	Ringer	998-72-3567	Ringer
998-72-3567	Ringer	899-46-2035	Ringer
899-46-2035	Ringer	998-72-3567	Ringer
899-46-2035	Ringer	899-46-2035	Ringer
722-51-5454	DeFrance	722-51-5454	DeFrance
807-91-6654	Panteley	807-91-6654	Panteley
893-72-1158	McBadden	893-72-1158	McBadden
724-08-9931	Stringer	724-08-9931	Stringer
274-80-9391	Straight	274-80-9391	Straight
756-30-7391	Karsen	756-30-7391	Karsen
724-80-9391	MacFeather	724-80-9391	MacFeather
427-17-2319	Dull	427-17-2319	Dull
672-71-3249	Yokomoto	672-71-3249	Yokomoto
267-41-2394	O'Leary	267-41-2394	O'Leary
472-27-2349	Gringlesby	472-27-2349	Gringlesby
527-72-3246	Greene	527-72-3246	Greene
172-32-1176	White	172-32-1176	White
712-45-1867	del Castillo	712-45-1867	del Castillo
846-92-7186	Hunter	846-92-7186	Hunter
486-29-1786	Locksley	486-29-1786	Locksley
648-92-1872	Blotchet-Halls	648-92-1872	Blotchet-Halls
341-22-1782	Smith	341-22-1782	Smith

[25 rows]

Every single author has at least one match: himself or herself. Here's where you may need to add an unequal join on a unique value to make sure a row does not join itself. A not-equal join (<>) can also be stated with the NOT keyword. The expression *NOT column_name = column_name* is equivalent to *column_name <> column_name*, as shown in the comment of the following query:

SQL
```
select a1.au_id, a1.au_lname, a2.au_id, a2.au_lname
from authors a1, authors a2
where a1.au_lname = a2.au_lname
   and a1.au_id <> a2.au_id    /*OR USE and not a1.au_id - a2.au_id*/
```

au_id	au_lname	au_id	au_lname
===========	===============================	===========	===========
998-72-3567	Ringer	899-46-2035	Ringer
899-46-2035	Ringer	998-72-3567	Ringer
[2 rows]			

Now it is clear that there are two authors surnamed Ringer.

Showing the Background: Outer Joins

The joins we've discussed so far include only rows that satisfy the join condition in the results. Occasionally, you may want to display the rows of one table that do *not* satisfy the join condition. An outer join shows you the join rows against the background of rows that did not meet the join conditions. It is convenient for putting results in context and makes visual scans easy. You can use it for finding books that did not sell or authors with no books.

SQL-92 provides language for retrieving either the LEFT (first-named) table for an outer join or the RIGHT (second-named) table. A FULL outer join lets you see non-matching rows from both tables.

Left Outer Join   Recall that the query for authors who live in the same city as a publisher returns two names: Abraham Bennet and Cheryl Carson. To include all the names from the authors table, regardless of whether they qualify for the join, use an outer join. The following SQL-92 form is supported by our sample software, ASA:

SQL

```
select au_fname, au_lname, pub_name
from authors left outer join publishers
on authors.city = publishers.city
```

au_fname	au_lname	pub_name
====================	====================	====================
Abraham	Bennet	Algodata Infosystems
Marjorie	Green	(NULL)
Cheryl	Carson	Algodata Infosystems
Albert	Ringer	(NULL)
Anne	Ringer	(NULL)
Michel	DeFrance	(NULL)
Sylvia	Panteley	(NULL)
Heather	McBadden	(NULL)
Dirk	Stringer	(NULL)
Dick	Straight	(NULL)
Livia	Karsen	(NULL)
Stearns	MacFeather	(NULL)
Ann	Dull	(NULL)
Akiko	Yokomoto	(NULL)
Michael	O'Leary	(NULL)
Burt	Gringlesby	(NULL)
Morningstar	Greene	(NULL)
Johnson	White	(NULL)
Innes	del Castillo	(NULL)
Sheryl	Hunter	(NULL)
Chastity	Locksley	(NULL)
Reginald	Blotchet-Halls	(NULL)
Meander	Smith	(NULL)

[23 rows]

SQL VARIANTS

Vendors generally implemented this feature before the standard defined it, and implementations still vary. Some systems mark the outer join in the FROM clause, and others in the WHERE clause. Check your reference manuals for information. Transact-SQL uses the WHERE clause and *= to include all rows from the first-named table or =* to include all rows from the second-named table.

Transact-SQL
```
select au_fname, au_lname, pub_name
from authors, publishers
where authors.city *= publishers.city
```

SQL Anywhere and Microsoft SQL Server support this form in addition to SQL-92 RIGHT/LEFT OUTER JOIN.

Oracle uses a plus mark after the table that must be expanded (filled with nulls for this report)—annotating the opposite table from Transact-SQL.

Oracle
```
SQL> select au_fname, au_lname, pub_name
  2  from authors a, publishers p
  3  where a.city = p.city (+);
```

Informix adds the word OUTER to the FROM clause.

Informix
```
select au_fname, au_lname, pub_name
from publishers p, outer authors a
where a.city = p.city
```

The LEFT OUTER JOIN operator (however it is written) tells the system to include all the rows from the first table in the join specification (here, authors) in the results, whether there is a match on the city column in the publishers table. The outer join results show "no match" for most of the authors listed, as the results indicate with null values in the pub_name column.

You can specify that an outer join show nonmatching rows either from the first table in the join specification (a "left" outer join) or from the second table (a "right" outer join).

Right Outer Join Substituting the right outer join operator shows the publishers that do not coexist in the same city with any authors, as well as the publisher that did satisfy the join condition:

SQL

```
select au_fname, au_lname, pub_name
from authors right outer join publishers
on authors.city = publishers.city
```

au_fname	au_lname	pub_name
===========	================	=============================
(NULL)	(NULL)	New Age Books
(NULL)	(NULL)	Binnet & Hardley
Abraham	Bennet	Algodata Infosystems
Cheryl	Carson	Algodata Infosystems

[4 rows]

Full Outer Join   A full outer join returns all qualifying rows—two rows in which author and publisher are in the same city, two rows for publishers who have no matching city in the authors table, and twenty-one rows for authors who have no matching city in the publishers table, for a total of twenty-five rows. Compare the results of the following query to the results of the right and left outer joins:

SQL Server

```
select au_fname, au_lname, pub_name
from authors full outer join publishers
on authors.city = publishers.city
```

au_fname	au_lname	pub_name
Abraham	Bennet	Algodata Infosystems
Marjorie	Green	NULL
Cheryl	Carson	Algodata Infosystems
Albert	Ringer	NULL
Anne	Ringer	NULL
Michel	DeFrance	NULL
Sylvia	Panteley	NULL
Heather	McBadden	NULL
Dirk	Stringer	NULL
Dick	Straight	NULL
Livia	Karsen	NULL
Stearns	MacFeather	NULL
Ann	Dull	NULL
Akiko	Yokomoto	NULL

```
Michael      O'Leary          NULL
Burt         Gringlesby       NULL
Morningstar  Greene           NULL
Johnson      White            NULL
Innes        del Castillo     NULL
Sheryl       Hunter           NULL
Chastity     Locksley         NULL
Reginald     Blotchet-Halls   NULL
Meander      Smith            NULL
NULL         NULL             New Age Books
NULL         NULL             Binnet & Hardley
(25 row(s) affected)
```

Outer Joins and Other Conditions   As in any join, the results of an outer join can be restricted by comparison to a constant. This means that you can zoom in on precisely the value or values you want to see and use the outer join to show the rows that didn't make the cut. Let's look at the plain join first, and then compare it to the outer join. For example, if you wanted to find out which title had sold more than fifty copies from any store, you'd use this query:

SQL
```
select sonum, title
from salesdetails sd, titles t
where qty_ordered > 50
and sd.title_id = t.title_id
```
```
      sonum title
=========== ==========================================
          1 Is Anger the Enemy?
[1 row]
```

To show, in addition, the titles that didn't sell more than fifty copies in any store, you'd use an outer join query:

SQL
```
select sonum, title
from salesdetails sd right outer join titles t
on sd.title_id = t.title_id
and qty_ordered > 50
```

```
    sonum title
========== ======================================================
    (NULL) Secrets of Silicon Valley
    (NULL) The Busy Executive's Database Guide
    (NULL) Emotional Security: A New Algorithm
    (NULL) Prolonged Data Deprivation: Four Case Studies
    (NULL) Cooking with Computers: Surreptitious Balance Sheets
    (NULL) Silicon Valley Gastronomic Treats
    (NULL) Sushi, Anyone?
    (NULL) Fifty Years in Buckingham Palace Kitchens
    (NULL) But Is It User Friendly?
    (NULL) You Can Combat Computer Stress!
         1 Is Anger the Enemy?
    (NULL) Life Without Fear
    (NULL) The Gourmet Microwave
    (NULL) Onions, Leeks, and Garlic:
           Cooking Secrets of the Mediterranean
    (NULL) The Psychology of Computer Cooking
    (NULL) Straight Talk About Computers
    (NULL) Computer Phobic and Non-Phobic Individuals:
           Behavior Variations
    (NULL) Net Etiquette
[18 rows]
```

Avoiding a Common Source of Errors

It's not all that uncommon to make a mistake in a join statement that results in an incomprehensible report. If your join results seem to contain too many rows and include a great many duplicate rows, you probably need to restate your join query. The excess output—although it is not what you intended—does reveal something about the way a relational system processes joins. Garbage results from a join generally mean that your query is displaying the cross (Cartesian) product.

Understanding the Cartesian Product

Conceptually speaking, the first step in processing a join is to form the **Cartesian product** of the tables—all the possible combinations of the rows from each of the tables. Once the system obtains the Cartesian product, it uses the columns in the SELECT list for the projection and the conditions in the WHERE clause for the selection to eliminate the rows that do not satisfy the join.

The Cartesian product is the matrix of all the possible combinations that could satisfy the join condition. If there is only one row in each table, there is only one possible combination. To show the product of two tables having one row each, we use data values of a, b in one table and c, d in the other, with the column names *one*, *two* in the first table and *three*, *four* in the second table:

```
one two
--- ---
a   b
```

```
three four
----- ----
c     d
```

The Cartesian product is

```
one two three four
--- --- ----- ----
a   b   c     d
```

If you have two rows in each table, the Cartesian product is four rows (2×2):

```
First table (test)
one two
--- ---
a   b
c   d
```

```
Second table (test2)
three four
----- ----
c     d
e     f
```

```
Cartesian product
one two three four
--- --- ----- ----
a   b   c     d
a   b   e     f
c   d   c     d
c   d   e     f
(4 rows affected)
```

The number of rows in the Cartesian product increases geometrically in direct relation to the number of rows in the two tables. It equals the number of rows in the first table times the number of rows in the second table. As soon as you have any significant amount of data, a Cartesian product can produce an overwhelming volume of rows and columns. Whenever you get results that seem too large, scrutinize your join.

TIP

All you have to do in order to create a Cartesian product right at your own terminal is to set up a join on two tables and *omit the join condition.* The query that produced the preceding Cartesian product was

```
select *
from test, test2
```

Using the Cartesian Product

Valid joins are essential to producing comprehensible multitable query results, unless one of the tables contains a single row—perhaps a system variable or a stored value. In that case, you can use a Cartesian product between two tables without fear. For example, test3 contains the current tax rate.

```
SQL
create table test3
(rate decimal not null,
date_start date not null default current date)
[table created]
insert test3 (rate)
values (.08)
[1 row]
```

You can use `test3` with `titles` without a join to calculate the base-plus-tax price of books.

SQL
```
select title_id as Book, price as BasePrice, price + ( price * rate)
as TaxPrice
from titles, test3
where type = 'business'
order by title_id
```

Book	BasePrice	TaxPrice
BU1032	29.99	32.39
BU1111	21.95	23.71
BU2075	12.99	14.03
BU7832	29.99	32.39

[4 rows]

Constraining the Cartesian Product

Single-row tables, however, are not the norm. Without a valid join, precisely stated and refined, a query on multiple tables with multiple rows can produce an uncontrolled display of the whole set of possible connections between the tables.

In the `bookbiz` database, the Cartesian product of the `publishers` table (3 rows) and the `authors` table (23 rows) shows a results display of 69 rows (3 rows × 23 rows). This result is not only excessive but downright misleading because it seems to imply that every author in the database has a relationship with every publisher in the database—which is not true at all. Getting the Cartesian product represents a failure of communication between you and your system.

Going Beyond Joins: UNION, INTERSECT, MINUS

The relational model calls for three more operations: UNION, INTERSECT, and MINUS (see Figure 7.4). These correspond to the set operations union, **intersection**, and difference.

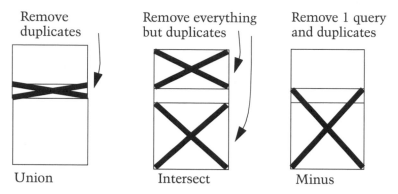

Figure 7.4 UNION, INTERSECT, MINUS

- UNION returns results from sets of queries. By default, it removes duplicate rows so you see all unique rows and one copy (not two) of duplicates.
- INTERSECT returns common results from sets of queries—that is, only the duplicates.
- MINUS returns results from sets of queries. It shows the rows from one query or another, without the values that appear in the other query.

UNION is widely supported; the other two less so.

UNION

Although UNION isn't a join, it is a way of combining data from multiple tables into one display. UNION is useful when you want to see similar data from two or more tables in one display. The simplified syntax is this:

```
select_statement
UNION
select_statement
```

SYNTAX

Following is a query that will give you a list of all the authors and editors who live in Oakland or Berkeley:

SQL
```
select au_fname, au_lname, city
from authors
where city in ('Oakland', 'Berkeley')
union
select ed_fname, ed_lname, city
from editors
where city in ('Oakland', 'Berkeley')
```

Notice that the two SELECT lists contain the same number of items and the datatypes are compatible. Check your documentation for specifics on what datatype combinations you can use.

When you examine the query results, you'll see that there are seven rows from `authors` and three from `editors` (those for Bernard, Christof, and Martinella). The UNION display uses the column names from the first SELECT list only:

Results

au_fname	au_lname	city
Abraham	Bennet	Berkeley
Marjorie	Green	Oakland
Cheryl	Carson	Berkeley
Dirk	Stringer	Oakland
Dick	Straight	Oakland
Livia	Karsen	Oakland
Stearns	MacFeather	Oakland
Martinella	DeLongue	Berkeley
Bernard	Samuelson	Oakland
Christof	Kaspchek	Berkeley

[10 rows]

UNION Rules   Although each SELECT statement can have its own WHERE clause, the query as a whole takes only one ORDER BY clause. It comes in its normal position but must be in the last SELECT statement. It applies to all the output.

Following is a query that makes the display more readable by "generalizing" the column names in the first SELECT statement. There's no need to change those names in the second list because the display is set up based on the names in the first select list only. The query also contains an ORDER BY clause to sort the results by city.

SQL

```
select au_fname as First_name, au_lname as Last_name,
    city as City
from authors
where city in ('Oakland', 'Berkeley')
union
select ed_fname, ed_lname, city
from editors
where city in ('Oakland', 'Berkeley')
order by 3
```

First_name	Last_name	City
====================	=============================	========
Abraham	Bennet	Berkeley
Cheryl	Carson	Berkeley
Christof	Kaspchek	Berkeley
Martinella	DeLongue	Berkeley
Bernard	Samuelson	Oakland
Dick	Straight	Oakland
Dirk	Stringer	Oakland
Livia	Karsen	Oakland
Marjorie	Green	Oakland
Stearns	MacFeather	Oakland

[10 rows]

By default, UNION removes duplicate rows from the results display. This can be confusing when there is only one column in the query. For example, the `authors` table lists 23 cities, and the `publishers` table lists 3. A UNION shows only 18 rows.

SQL

```
select count(city)
from authors
count(authors.city)
====================
        23
```

SQL
```
select count(city)
from publishers
count(publishers.city)
======================
                     3
```

SQL
```
select city
from authors
union
select city
from publishers
city
====================
Berkeley
Oakland
Salt Lake City
Gary
Rockville
Vacaville
Palo Alto
Walnut Creek
San Jose
Covelo
Nashville
Menlo Park
Ann Arbor
San Francisco
Corvallis
Lawrence
Boston
Washington
[18 rows]
```

Why only 18 rows? UNION removes all the duplicates from the display, no matter which table they were derived from. Because authors has 16 distinct entries for city and publishers has 3, with one duplicating an authors city, the union of the two comes to 18.

To display all rows, including duplicates, add the keyword ALL after UNION. In many cases, you'll get better performance because there is one fewer sort. Check your implementation's documentation for other rules applying to UNION.

If I Had a UNION   One final wrinkle: You can use UNION as a kind of IF statement to display different values for one field, depending on what's in another. Without UNION, you'd have to use several queries or some procedural elements to get the same effect.

For example, it's time to reduce inventory. You need to produce a list of books showing discount percent and new prices. Books under $15.00 are reduced by 20 percent; those between $15.00 and $25.00 are reduced by 10 percent; and those above $25.00 are reduced by 30 percent. Without UNION, you'd have to write three separate queries and put the results into a new table.

Here's a UNION query that will do it in one pass:

```
SQL
select '20% off' as Discount, title as Book,
       price as OldPrice, price * .80 as NewPrice
from titles
where price < 15.00
union
select '10% off', title, price, price * .90
from titles
where price between 15.00 and 25.00
union
select '30% off', title, price, price * .70
from titles
where price > 25.00
```

Discount	Book	OldPrice	NewPrice
20% off	You Can Combat Computer Stress!	12.99	10.39
20% off	The Gourmet Microwave	12.99	10.39
10% off	Emotional Security: A New Algorithm	17.99	16.19
10% off	Cooking with Computers: Surreptitious Balance Sheets	21.95	19.76
10% off	Fifty Years in Buckingham Palace Kitchens	21.95	19.76
10% off	Is Anger the Enemy?	21.95	19.76
10% off	Life Without Fear	17.00	15.30
30% off	Secrets of Silicon Valley	40.00	28.00

30% off	The Busy Executive's Database Guide	29.99	20.99
30% off	Prolonged Data Deprivation:		
	Four Case Studies	29.99	20.99
30% off	Silicon Valley Gastronomic Treats	29.99	20.99
30% off	Sushi, Anyone?	29.99	20.99
30% off	But Is It User Friendly?	42.95	30.07
30% off	Onions, Leeks, and Garlic:		
	Cooking Secrets of the Mediterranean	40.95	28.67
30% off	Straight Talk About Computers	29.99	20.99
30% off	Computer Phobic and Non-Phobic		
	Individuals: Behavior Variations	41.59	29.11

[16 rows]

Add an ORDER BY clause if you want to see the output sorted by price. You can do similar work with CASE and DECODE, discussed in Chapter 11.

INTERSECT and MINUS

Although long discussed as part of the relational model, INTERSECT and MINUS are not widely implemented as keywords. You may be able to get the same effect with other code.

Oracle is one system that supports INTERSECT and MINUS. The first query shows the intersection on city between authors and publishers. Berkeley is the only shared location.

```
Oracle
SQL> select city
  2  from authors
  3  intersect
  4  select city
  5  from publishers;

CITY
--------------------
Berkeley
```

The following MINUS queries have different results. The first returns all the cities from authors, except those that appear in publishers.

```
Oracle
SQL> select city
  2  from authors
  3  minus
  4  select city
  5  from publishers;
CITY
--------------------
Ann Arbor
Corvallis
Covelo
Gary
Lawrence
Menlo Park
Nashville
Oakland
Palo Alto
Rockville
Salt Lake City
San Francisco
San Jose
Vacaville
Walnut Creek
15 rows selected.
```

The second reverses the order of the two queries. It displays all publisher cities, except those in the authors table.

```
Oracle
SQL> select city
  2  from publishers
  3  minus
  4  select city from authors;
CITY
--------------------
Boston
Washington
[2 rows]
```

Summary

Once you master joins, the relational model is yours. Nothing beats practice: Take a little time to pose and run join queries on all the tables in the database. In this chapter we discussed

- The definition of a join
- The use of joins, so basic to the relational model, for uniting data from separate tables and providing flexibility for the growth of the database
- The requirements for good joins, including name, null status, and datatype issues and syntax (original FROM WHERE style and SQL-92 JOIN keyword syntax)
- Hints for making your join results easier to read
- Creating simple joins with comparison operators
- Exploring more complex joins—self-joins and outer joins
- Reviewing the dreaded Cartesian product
- Looking at other ways of associating data from multiple tables: UNION, INTERSECT, MINUS

In the next chapter we turn our attention to subqueries, the other method that relational systems provide for querying multiple tables. Although joins and subqueries are often interchangeable, there are some cases in which only a subquery yields the desired results.

Chapter 8

Structuring Queries with Subqueries

In This Chapter

- What Is a Subquery?
- How Do Subqueries Work?
- Joins or Subqueries?
- Subquery Rules
- Subqueries Returning Zero or More Values
- Subqueries Returning a Single Value
- Subqueries Testing Existence
- Subqueries in Multiple Levels of Nesting
- Subqueries In UPDATE, DELETE, and INSERT Statements
- Subqueries in FROM and SELECT clauses

What Is a Subquery?

A subquery is an additional method for handling multitable manipulations. It is a SELECT statement that nests

- Inside the WHERE or HAVING (and in some systems, SELECT or FROM) clause of another SELECT statement;
- Inside an INSERT, UPDATE, or DELETE statement; or
- Inside another subquery.

The ability to nest SQL statements is the reason that SQL was originally called the Structured Query Language. The term subquery is sometimes used to refer to an entire set of statements that includes one or more subqueries, as well as to an individual nestling. Each enclosing statement, the next level up in a subquery, is the outer level for its inner subquery.

243

Subqueries are a complex topic because there are two processing types—**simple subqueries** (or **noncorrelated subqueries**) and **correlated subqueries**—and three subquery-to-outer-clause connection possibilities. After looking at general subquery syntax, we'll examine how noncorrelated and correlated subqueries work, and compare them to joins. Then we'll dive into the connection issue, looking at noncorrelated and correlated examples of each.

Simplified Subquery Syntax

A simplified form of the subquery syntax (Figure 8.1) shows how a subquery nests in a SELECT statement. (Most of the examples in this chapter use this kind of WHERE clause subquery structure.)

SYNTAX

Other query search conditions (including joins) can appear in the outer query WHERE clause, either before or after the inner query.

How Do Subqueries Work?

Subqueries return results from an inner query to an outer clause and come in two basic flavors: simple and correlated. The first is evaluated (conceptually) from the inside out. That is, the outer query takes an action based on the results of the inner query. You can think of the second type of subquery—the correlated subquery—as working the opposite way: The outer SQL statement provides the values for the inner subquery to use in its evaluation. Then the subquery results are passed back to the outer query. You use a correlated subquery when you need to look at the data row by row.

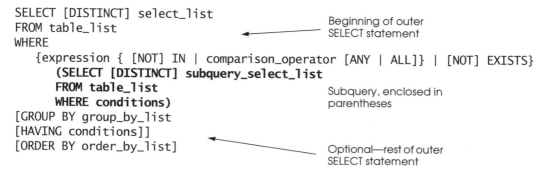

```
SELECT [DISTINCT] select_list
FROM table_list                        Beginning of outer
WHERE                                   SELECT statement
    {expression { [NOT] IN | comparison_operator [ANY | ALL]} | [NOT] EXISTS}
        (SELECT [DISTINCT] subquery_select_list
        FROM table_list
        WHERE conditions)              Subquery, enclosed in
                                       parentheses
[GROUP BY group_by_list]
[HAVING conditions]]
[ORDER BY order_by_list]               Optional—rest of outer
                                       SELECT statement
```

Figure 8.1 A Subquery in an Outer SELECT

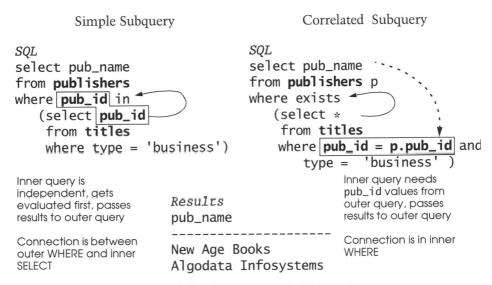

Figure 8.2 Simple and Correlated Subqueries

Figure 8.2 compares a simple and a correlated subquery that produce identical results. Both find the names of the publishers who produce business books. The EXISTS operator is used almost exclusively with correlated subqueries. You'll find more information on it in "Subqueries Testing Existence" later in this chapter.

As with many subqueries, you could also formulate this as a join query (see "Joins or Subqueries" later in this chapter for information on when to use what). To show publisher names only once, add DISTINCT to the SELECT list.

SQL
```
select distinct pub_name
from publishers p, titles t
where p.pub_id = t.pub_id
and type = 'business'
```

Simple Subquery Processing

Conceptually, the outer query and the simple subquery (or inner query) are evaluated in two steps:

1. The inner query returns the identification numbers of those publishers
    that have published business books (1389 and 0736):

    SQL
    ```
    select pub_id
    from titles
    where type = 'business'

    pub_id
    ======
    1389
    1389
    0736
    1389
    [4 rows]
    ```

2. These values are substituted into the outer query, which finds the
    names that go with the identification numbers in the publishers table:

    SQL
    ```
    select pub_name
    from publishers
    where pub_id in ('1389', '0736')

    pub_name
    =========================================
    New Age Books
    Algodata Infosystems
    (2 rows affected)
    ```

Qualifying Column Names In subqueries, column names are implicitly qualified by the FROM clause table at the same level. This means

*   The pub_id column in the outer query WHERE clause is
    publishers.pub_id.
*   The pub_id column in the subquery select list is titles.pub_id.

Here's what the query looks like with these qualifications spelled out:

SQL
```
select pub_name
from publishers
where publishers.pub_id in
    (select titles.pub_id
     from titles
     where type = 'business')
```

It is never wrong to state the table name explicitly, and you can always override implicit assumptions about table names with explicit qualifications.

Correlated Subquery Processing

Correlated subqueries are not as neat, but they are very valuable (they can handle problems you can't easily approach with joins or simple subqueries). For now, just understand the syntax, and get an idea of how correlated subqueries work. As you experiment, you'll become comfortable with them.

In the correlated subquery, the inner query cannot be evaluated independently: It references the outer query and is executed once for each qualified row in the outer query. In the example in Figure 8.2, the outer table (publishers) has three rows, so the inner query will run three times.

Conceptually, the processing follows these steps:

1. The outer query finds the first name in the publishers table (for example, New Age Books).

    SQL
    ```
    select pub_name
    from publishers p

    pub_name
    =======================================
    New Age Books
    Binnet & Hardley
    Algodata Infosystems
    [3 rows]
    ```

2. The inner query joins the associated `publishers.pub_id` (0736) to `titles.pub_id` to find qualifying rows in the `titles` table (it finds six). Only one of the six is a business book. (The relevant columns follow.)

SQL
```
select *
from titles
where pub_id = '0736'
   and type = 'business'
```

```
title_id ... type     ... pub_id
============ ========== ==========
BU2075       business   0736
[1 row]
```

3. The inner query passes this information back to the outer: New Age Books qualifies.

4. The outer query then goes to work again, this time passing the `pub_id` of the second row in `publishers` (Binnet & Hardley, 0877) to the inner query.

5. Using this value, the inner query finds no rows with the correct type and signals "no rows found" to the outer query. Binnet & Hardley does not qualify.

6. The subquery runs the third time with a `publishers.pub_id` of 1389 (Algodata Infosystems) and finds six more rows. Three of them have **type** "business." Algodata Infosystems will be in the final result set.

Qualifying Column Names   Correlated queries require explicit naming for columns from the outer query (you can use aliases, as `p.pub_id` for `publishers.pub_id` in Figure 8.2). Columns belonging to the inner query table are implicitly qualified by it.

However, you can always specify both tables:

SQL
```
select pub_name
from publishers
```

```
where exists
   (select *
    from titles
    where titles.pub_id = publishers.pub_id and
       type = 'business' )
```

Simple-Correlated Performance Issues

In the example query, the simple, noncorrelated subquery traversed the `titles` table once. The correlated subquery accessed the `titles` table once for every qualified row in the `publisher` table, or a total of three times. In most cases, it is more efficient to use simple subqueries. However, if you need to look at the data row by row, a correlated subquery is the answer.

Joins or Subqueries?

As you develop your SQL style, you will use both joins and subqueries for your multitable queries. They can often be used interchangeably to solve a given problem; in these cases, whether you use a join or a subquery is simply a matter of individual preference. Some SQL users automatically reach for a subquery, while others prefer joins. However, each has particular advantages and disadvantages.

Subqueries!

For example, consider the problem of listing all books with prices equal to the minimum book price. Using joins, you'd do the job in two steps:

1. Find the minimum price.

   SQL
   ```
   select min (price)
   from titles
   ```

   ```
   min(titles.price)
   =================
               12.99
   ```

2. Get the names of all books selling for this price.

SQL
```
select title, price
from titles
where price = 12.99
title                                      price
====================================  ======
You Can Combat Computer Stress!       12.99
The Gourmet Microwave                 12.99
[2 rows]
```

With a subquery, you need only one statement:

SQL
```
select title, price
from titles
where price =
    ( select min (price)
    from titles )
```

The ability to calculate an aggregate value on the fly and feed it back to the outer query for comparison is a subquery advantage; a join can't compete.

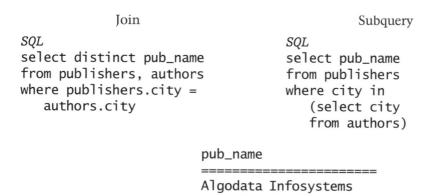

Join	Subquery

SQL
`select distinct pub_name`
`from publishers, authors`
`where publishers.city =`
`   authors.city`
	SQL
	`select pub_name`
	`from publishers`
	`where city in`
	`       (select city`
	`        from authors)`

```
pub_name
========================
Algodata Infosystems
```

Figure 8.3 Comparing a Join and a Subquery

Joins!

But joins also have some special strengths. For example, the two queries in Figure 8.3 (both search for the names of publishers located in the same city as some author) return identical results.

However, the join gives more options because you can edit it to display results from both tables, which is not possible with the subquery.

SQL
```
select pub_name, au_fname, au_lname
from publishers, authors
where publishers.city =
    authors.city
```

pub_name	au_fname	au_lname
===	===	===
Algodata Infosystems	Abraham	Bennet
Algodata Infosystems	Cheryl	Carson
[2 rows]		

The subquery can display information from the outer table (`publishers`) only, so it reports the name of the publisher once and stops there. When you want results to include information from both tables, use a join.

Subqueries vs. Self-Joins?

Many statements in which the subquery and the outer query refer to the same table can be alternatively stated as self-joins. For example, you can find authors who live in the same city as Livia Karsen by using a subquery:

SQL
```
select au_lname, au_fname, city
from authors
where city in
    (select city
     from authors
     where au_fname = 'Livia'
     and au_lname = 'Karsen')
```

au_lname	au_fname	city
==========	==========	======
Green	Marjorie	Oakland
Stringer	Dirk	Oakland
Straight	Dick	Oakland
Karsen	Livia	Oakland
MacFeather	Stearns	Oakland
[5 rows]		

Or you can use a self-join:

SQL

```
select au1.au_lname, au1.au_fname, au1.city
from authors au1, authors au2
where au1.city = au2.city
    and au2.au_lname = 'Karsen'
    and au2.au_fname = 'Livia'
```

Which Is Better?

Deciding whether to use a subquery or a join when you are working with multiple tables is usually a matter of style. Most people find one—or the other—more intuitive. (Programmers, for example, often prefer subqueries because subqueries are like subroutines.) Nonetheless, there are times when you must choose:

- Subqueries shine when you need to compare aggregates to other values.
- Joins star when you're displaying results from multiple tables.

Subquery Rules

Now that you've explored simple and correlated subqueries and have compared them to joins, look more closely at the rules governing subqueries. They primarily concern the SELECT list of the nested subquery, with some additional restrictions on functions that you can specify in a subquery. Your SQL dialect may have more or fewer restrictions, but here are some of the common ones:

- The SELECT list of an inner subquery introduced with a comparison operator or IN can include only one expression or column name. The column you name in the WHERE clause of the outer statement must be join-compatible with the column you name in the subquery SELECT list.
- Subqueries introduced by an unmodified comparison operator (a comparison operator not followed by the keyword ANY or ALL) cannot include GROUP BY and HAVING clauses unless you determine in advance that the grouping returns a single value.
- The SELECT list of a subquery introduced with EXISTS almost always consists of the asterisk (*). There is no need to specify column names because you are testing only for the existence (or nonexistence) of any rows that meet the criteria. (You can qualify the rows in the nested subquery WHERE clause.) The SELECT list rules for a subquery introduced with EXISTS are otherwise identical to those for a standard select list.
- Subqueries cannot manipulate their results internally. That is, a subquery cannot include the ORDER BY clause (or the Transact-SQL INTO keyword). The optional DISTINCT keyword may effectively order the results of a subquery because some systems eliminate duplicates by first ordering the results.

A survey of the three main types of subquery connections will clarify these restrictions and the reasons for them. These connections involve

1. Subqueries that return zero or any number of items (introduced with IN or with a comparison operator modified by ANY or ALL)

2. Subqueries that return a single value (introduced with an unmodified comparison operator)

3. Subqueries that are an existence test (introduced with EXISTS)

For each connection type, subqueries can be simple or correlated. However, EXISTS is the connector of choice for most correlated subqueries and is seldom used for simple subqueries.

Subqueries Returning Zero or More Values

This group includes subqueries introduced with IN, NOT IN, or a comparison operator and ANY or ALL. There is no limit on the number of rows these subqueries can return. (Subqueries introduced with an unmodified comparison operator can return no more than one row.)

Subqueries Introduced with IN

Subqueries introduced with the keyword IN take the following general form:

SYNTAX

```
Start of SELECT, INSERT, UPDATE, DELETE statement; or
    subquery
WHERE expression [NOT] IN
    (subquery)
[End of SELECT, INSERT, UPDATE, DELETE statement; or
    subquery]
```

The result of the inner subquery is a list of zero or more values. Once the subquery returns results, the outer query makes use of them.

Here's an example of a statement that you could formulate either with a subquery or with a join. The English version of the query is "Find the names of all second authors who live in California and receive less than 30 percent of the royalties on the books they coauthor." Using a subquery, the statement is

```
SQL
select au_lname, au_fname
from authors
where state = 'CA'
and au_id in
    (select au_id
     from titleauthors
     where royaltyshare < .30
     and au_ord = 2)
```

au_lname	au_fname
MacFeather	Stearns

[1 row]

The inner query is evaluated, producing a list of the IDs of the two second authors who meet the qualification of earning less than 30 percent of the royalties. The system then evaluates the outer query.

Notice that it's legal to include more than one condition in the WHERE clause of both the inner and the outer query. A subquery can even include a join—joins and subqueries are by no means mutually exclusive.

Using a join, the query is expressed like this:

SQL
```
select au_lname, au_fname
from authors, titleauthors
where state = 'CA'
        and authors.au_id = titleauthors.au_id
        and royaltyshare < .30
        and au_ord = 2
```

Which authors are both sole authors and coauthors is a question that may be easier to read and understand as a subquery, although you can get the same information with a complex join.

SQL
```
select authors.au_id, au_lname, au_fname
from authors, titleauthors
where royaltyshare < 1.0
and authors.au_id = titleauthors.au_id
and authors.au_id in
    (select distinct authors.au_id
     from authors, titleauthors
     where titleauthors.royaltyshare = 1.0
     and authors.au_id = titleauthors.au_id)
```

au_id	au_lname	au_fname
213-46-8915	Green	Marjorie
998-72-3567	Ringer	Albert

[2 rows]

First the inner query selects the identification numbers of authors whose royalty share is equal to 100 percent, and then the outer query compares these IDs to its selection of authors whose royalty share is less than 100 percent.

Here's a join that finds the same information. The select list is a little different in order to list both royalty values (not possible with the subquery version where you'd be able to display only one):

SQL
```
select a1.au_id, au_lname, ta1.royaltyshare, ta2.royaltyshare
from authors a1, titleauthors ta1, titleauthors ta2
```

```
where ta1.royaltyshare < 1.0
    and a1.au_id = ta1.au_id
    and a1.au_id = ta2.au_id
    and ta2.royaltyshare = 1.0
au_id         au_lname                          royaltyshare royaltyshare
===========  =============================  ============  ============
213-46-8915  Green                                   .40          1.00
998-72-3567  Ringer                                  .50          1.00
[2 rows]
```

Subqueries Introduced with NOT IN

Subqueries introduced with NOT IN also return a list of zero or more values for the outer query's use. This query finds the names of the publishers who have *not* published business books (the inverse of an earlier example). This kind of query—returning rows that do *not* have a match in another table—is what Oracle calls an **anti-join**.

```
SQL
select distinct pub_name
from publishers
where pub_id not in
    (select pub_id
     from titles
     where type = 'business')
pub_name
==========================================
Binnet & Hardley
[1 row]
```

The query is exactly the same as the earlier one except that NOT IN is substituted for IN. However, you cannot convert this NOT IN statement to a "not equal" join. The analogous "not equal" join has a different meaning: It finds the names of publishers who have published *some* book that is not a business book.

SQL
```
select distinct pub_name
from publishers, titles
where publishers.pub_id = titles.pub_id
and type <> 'business'
pub_name
============================================
New Age Books
Binnet & Hardley
Algodata Infosystems
[3 rows]
```

To refresh your memory about joins based on inequality, refer to Chapter 7.

Correlated Subqueries Introduced with IN

You can find the names of all authors who earn 100 percent royalty on a book with the following statement:

SQL
```
select au_lname, au_fname
from authors
where 1.00 in
    (select royaltyshare
     from titleauthors
     where au_id = authors.au_id)
order by au_lname
au_lname                              au_fname
================================ ====================
Blotchet-Halls                        Reginald
Carson                                Cheryl
del Castillo                          Innes
Green                                 Marjorie
Locksley                              Chastity
Panteley                              Sylvia
Ringer                                Albert
Straight                              Dick
White                                 Johnson
[9 rows]
```

You could get the same results and probably get better performance with a simple subquery.

```
SQL
select au_lname, au_fname
from authors
where au_id in
  (select au_id
   from titleauthors
   where royaltyshare = 1.00)
order by au_lname
```

Why better performance? In the correlated subquery you traverse the `titleauthors` table nine times—once for each qualifying row in the outer table. In the simple version, you read it only once. When you have a choice between a simple and a correlated subquery, choose the simple one. The simple subquery has the connection in the outer WHERE and the inner SELECT clauses. The correlated subquery has the connection in the inner WHERE clause.

Correlated IN Subqueries on a Single Table You can use a correlated subquery introduced with IN on a single table—for example, to find which types of books are common to more than one publisher:

```
SQL
select distinct t1.type
from titles t1
where t1.type in
  (select t2.type
   from titles t2
   where t1.pub_id <> t2.pub_id)

type
============
business
[1 row]
```

Aliases are required here to distinguish the two different roles in which the titles table appears. This nested query is equivalent to the following self-join statement:

SQL

```
select distinct t1.type
from titles t1, titles t2
where t1.type = t2.type
and t1.pub_id <> t2.pub_id
```

Correlated IN Subqueries in a HAVING Clause   You can also use a correlated subquery in a HAVING clause. This kind of formulation will, for example, find types of books in which the maximum advance is at least twice the average advance for that type.

SQL

```
select t1.type
from titles t1
group by t1.type
having max(t1.advance) in
  (select 2 * avg(t2.advance)
   from titles t2
   where t1.type = t2.type)

type
============
mod_cook
[1 row]
```

In this case, the subquery is evaluated once for each group defined in the outer query—once for each type of book.

Subqueries Introduced with Comparison Operators and ANY or ALL

Another kind of subquery, which returns any number of rows (including none) for the outer query, uses a comparison operator modified with keywords ALL or ANY. Subqueries introduced with a modified comparison operator take the following general form:

```
Start of SELECT, INSERT, UPDATE, DELETE statement; or
    subquery
WHERE expression comparison_operator [ANY | ALL]
    (subquery)
[End of SELECT, INSERT, UPDATE, DELETE statement; or subquery]
```

Understanding ALL and ANY Using the ">" comparison operator as an example, "> ALL" means greater than every value—in other words, greater than the largest value. In this way, "> ALL (1, 2, 3)" means greater than 3. "> ANY" means greater than at least one value—in other words, greater than the minimum. So "> ANY (1, 2, 3)" means greater than 1. Figure 8.4 compares ANY and ALL.

   ALL and ANY can be tricky because computers won't tolerate the ambiguity that these words sometimes have in English.

Subqueries with ALL For example, you might ask the question: Which books commanded an advance greater than any book published by New Age Books? This question can be paraphrased to make the SQL "translation" of it clearer: Which books commanded an advance greater than the largest advance paid by New Age Books? The ALL keyword (*not* the ANY keyword) is what's required here:

ALL	Results	ANY	Results
> ALL (1, 2, 3)	>3	> ANY (1, 2, 3)	>1
< ALL (1, 2, 3)	<1	< ANY (1, 2, 3)	<3
= ALL (1, 2, 3)	=1 and =2 and =3 (all at the same time)	= ANY (1, 2, 3)	=1 or =2 or =3

Figure 8.4 Comparing ALL and ANY

SQL
```
select title
from titles
where advance > all
   (select advance
    from publishers, titles
    where titles.pub_id = publishers.pub_id
    and pub_name = 'New Age Books')
title
===========================================================
The Gourmet Microwave
[1 row]
```

For each title, the inner query finds a list of advance amounts paid by New Age. The outer query looks at the largest value in the list and determines whether the title currently being considered has commanded an even bigger advance.

If an inner subquery introduced with a comparison operator and ALL (> ALL = ALL) returns NULL as one of its values, the entire query fails. For example, the advances for Algodata Infosystems books look like this:

SQL
```
select advance
from publishers, titles
where titles.pub_id = publishers.pub_id
   and pub_name = 'Algodata Infosystems'
      advance
   ============
      8000.00
      5000.00
      5000.00
      7000.00
      5000.00
       (NULL)
[6 rows]
```

If you query for advances greater than all of those provided by Algodata Infosystems, you get no results, because it's impossible to tell what's greater than NULL.

SQL
```
select title
from titles
where advance > all
   (select advance
    from publishers, titles
    where titles.pub_id = publishers.pub_id
    and pub_name = 'Algodata Infosystems')
title
=========================================================

[0 rows]
```

Check your system to see what happens when an inner query returns no results, as in the following example, with a false condition (there is no publisher called "Demo Books").

SQL
```
select title
from titles
where advance > all
   (select advance
    from publishers, titles
    where titles.pub_id = publishers.pub_id
    and pub_name = 'Demo Books')
```

Subqueries with ANY A query with ANY finds values greater than "some" value of a subquery. The following query finds the titles that got an advance larger than the minimum advance amount ($5,000) paid by Algodata Infosystems.

SQL
```
select title, advance
from titles
where advance > any
   (select advance
    from titles, publishers
    where titles.pub_id = publishers.pub_id
    and pub_name = 'Algodata Infosystems')
```

title	advance
Secrets of Silicon Valley	8000.00
Sushi, Anyone?	8000.00
But Is It User Friendly?	7000.00
You Can Combat Computer Stress!	10125.00
Life Without Fear	6000.00
The Gourmet Microwave	15000.00
Onions, Leeks, and Garlic:	
Cooking Secrets of the Mediterranean	7000.00
Computer Phobic and Non-Phobic Individuals:	
Behavior Variations	7000.00

[8 rows]

For each title, the inner query finds a list of advance amounts paid by Algodata. The outer query looks at all the values in the list and determines whether the title currently being considered has commanded an advance larger than any of those amounts.

If the subquery does not return any values, the entire query fails.

Comparing IN, ANY, and ALL   The "= ANY" operator is exactly equivalent to IN. For example, to find authors that live in the same city as some publisher, you can use either IN or = ANY:

> *SQL*
> ```
> select au_lname, au_fname, city
> from authors
> where city in
>    (select city
>     from publishers)
> order by city
> ```

or

> *SQL*
> ```
> select au_lname, au_fname, city
> from authors
> where city = any
>    (select city
>     from publishers)
> order by city
> ```

au_lname	au_fname	city
==========	==========	======
Carson	Cheryl	Berkeley
Bennet	Abraham	Berkeley
[2 rows]		

However, the "< > ANY" operator (or "!= ANY" operator, depending on the syntax your system uses) is different from NOT IN. "< > ANY" means "not = a *or* not = b *or* not = c." NOT IN means "not = a *and* not = b *and* not = c." Suppose you want to find the authors who live in a city where no publisher is located. You might try this query:

SQL
```
select au_lname, au_fname
from authors
where city <> any
    (select city
      from publishers)
```

au_lname	au_fname	city
==========	==========	======
Bennet	Abraham	Berkeley
Green	Marjorie	Oakland
Carson	Cheryl	Berkeley
Ringer	Albert	Salt Lake City
Ringer	Anne	Salt Lake City
DeFrance	Michel	Gary
Panteley	Sylvia	Rockville
McBadden	Heather	Vacaville
Stringer	Dirk	Oakland
Straight	Dick	Oakland
Karsen	Livia	Oakland
MacFeather	Stearns	Oakland
Dull	Ann	Palo Alto
Yokomoto	Akiko	Walnut Creek
O'Leary	Michael	San Jose
Gringlesby	Burt	Covelo
Greene	Morningstar	Nashville
White	Johnson	Menlo Park
del Castillo	Innes	Ann Arbor

Hunter   Sheryl   Palo Alto
Locksley   Chastity   San Francisco
Blotchet-Halls   Reginald   Corvallis
Smith   Meander   Lawrence
[23 rows]

The results include all 23 authors. This is because every author lives in *some* city where no publisher is located; each author lives in one and only one city. The inner query finds all the cities in which publishers are located, and then, for *each* city, the outer query finds the authors who don't live there. Here's what happens when you substitute NOT IN in this query:

SQL
```
select au_lname, au_fname, city
from authors
where city not in
    (select city
     from publishers)
order by city
```

au_lname	au_fname	city
==========	==========	======
del Castillo	Innes	Ann Arbor
Blotchet-Halls	Reginald	Corvallis
Gringlesby	Burt	Covelo
DeFrance	Michel	Gary
Smith	Meander	Lawrence
White	Johnson	Menlo Park
Greene	Morningstar	Nashville
Green	Marjorie	Oakland
Stringer	Dirk	Oakland
Straight	Dick	Oakland
Karsen	Livia	Oakland
MacFeather	Stearns	Oakland
Dull	Ann	Palo Alto
Hunter	Sheryl	Palo Alto
Panteley	Sylvia	Rockville
Ringer	Albert	Salt Lake City
Ringer	Anne	Salt Lake City
Locksley	Chastity	San Francisco

```
O'Leary           Michael         San Jose
McBadden          Heather         Vacaville
Yokomoto          Akiko           Walnut Creek
[21 rows]
```

These are the results you want. They include all the authors except Cheryl Carson and Abraham Bennet who live in Berkeley where Algodata Infosystems is located.

Subqueries Returning a Single Value

A subquery introduced with an **unmodified comparison operator** (a comparison operator not followed by ANY or ALL) *must* resolve to a single value. (If it doesn't, you'll get an error message, and the query won't be processed.) These subqueries take this general form:

SYNTAX

```
Start of SELECT, INSERT, UPDATE, DELETE statement; or
    subquery
WHERE expression comparison_operator
    (subquery)
[End of SELECT, INSERT, UPDATE, DELETE statement; or
    subquery]
```

Ideally, in order to use this kind of subquery, you must be familiar enough with your data and with the nature of the problem to know that the subquery will return exactly one value. When you expect more than one value, use IN or a modified comparison operator. Why not use IN or a modified comparison operator all the time? Unmodified comparison operators offer better performance in most cases.

For example, if you suppose each publisher to be located in only one city and you wish to find the names of authors who live in the city where Algodata Infosystems is located, you can write a SQL statement with a subquery introduced with the simple comparison operator "=":

```
SQL
select au_lname, au_fname
from authors
```

```
where city =
   (select city
    from publishers
    where pub_name = 'Algodata Infosystems')
```

au_lname	au_fname
================================	====================
Bennet	Abraham
Carson	Cheryl
[2 rows]	

Aggregate Functions Guarantee a Single Value

Comparison operator subqueries often include aggregate functions because these functions are guaranteed to return a single value. For example, to find the names of all books with prices that are higher than the current minimum price, you can use the following query:

SQL
```
select title
from titles
where price >
   (select min(price)
    from titles)
```

```
title
================================================================
Secrets of Silicon Valley
The Busy Executive's Database Guide
Emotional Security: A New Algorithm
Prolonged Data Deprivation: Four Case Studies
Cooking with Computers: Surreptitious Balance Sheets
Silicon Valley Gastronomic Treats
Sushi, Anyone?
Fifty Years in Buckingham Palace Kitchens
But Is It User Friendly?
Is Anger the Enemy?
Life Without Fear
Onions, Leeks, and Garlic: Cooking Secrets of the Mediterranean
```

```
Straight Talk About Computers
Computer Phobic and Non-Phobic Individuals: Behavior Variations
[14 rows]
```

First the inner query finds the minimum price in the `titles` table; then the outer query uses this value to select qualifying titles.

GROUP BY and HAVING Must Return a Single Value

Comparison operator subqueries cannot include GROUP BY and HAVING clauses unless you know that they return a single value. For example, this query finds the books priced the same as the lowest-priced book in any category in which the minimum price is one-200th of the minimum advance. The subquery finds one qualifying row so there is no problem.

```
SQL
select title, type, price
from titles
where price =
    (select min(price)
    from titles
    group by type
    having min (price) < min(advance) /200  )
```

title	type	price
===	================	=======
You Can Combat Computer Stress!	business	12.99
The Gourmet Microwave	mod_cook	12.99
[2 rows]		

If you modify the HAVING clause to look for categories in which the minimum price is one-100th of the minimum advance, you get an error message. The subquery actually finds four rows, and `price` can't be equal to all of them.

Correlated Subqueries with Comparison Operators

To find sales where the quantity ordered is less than the average order for sales of that title, use the following query:

SQL
```
select s1.sonum, s1.title_id, s1.qty_ordered
from salesdetails s1
where qty_ordered <
  (select avg(qty_ordered)
   from salesdetails s2
   where s1.title_id - s2.title_id)
order by title_id
```

sonum	title_id	qty_ordered
8	BU1032	5
5	MC3021	15
2	PS2091	10
3	PS2091	20
7	PS2091	3

[5 rows]

The outer query selects the rows of the `salesdetails` table (that is, of `s1`) one by one. The subquery calculates the average quantity for each order being considered for selection in the outer query. For each possible value of `s1`, the system evaluates the subquery and includes the row in the results if the quantity is less than the calculated average for that table.

In this query and in the next one, a correlated subquery mimics a GROUP BY statement. It is not necessary to group by type explicitly because the self-join in the WHERE clause of the subquery effectively evaluates average prices by type. To find titles whose price is greater than the average for books of its type, the query is this:

SQL
```
select t1.type, t1.title
from titles t1
where t1.price >
  (select avg(t2.price)
   from titles t2
   where t1.type = t2.type)
```

```
type              title
============      ==================================================================
business          The Busy Executive's Database Guide
psychology        Prolonged Data Deprivation: Four Case Studies
mod_cook          Silicon Valley Gastronomic Treats
popular_comp      But Is It User Friendly?
trad_cook         Onions, Leeks, and Garlic: Cooking Secrets of
                  the Mediterranean
business          Straight Talk About Computers
psychology        Computer Phobic and Non-Phobic Individuals:
                  Behavior Variations

[7 rows]
```

For each possible value of t1, the system evaluates the subquery and includes the row in the results if the price value in that row is greater than the calculated average.

Subqueries Testing Existence

When a subquery is introduced with the keyword EXISTS, the subquery functions as an "existence test." The EXISTS keyword in a WHERE clause tests for the existence or nonexistence of data that meets the criteria of the subquery.

A subquery introduced with EXISTS takes this general form:

SYNTAX

```
Start of SELECT, INSERT, UPDATE, DELETE statement; or
    subquery
WHERE [NOT] EXISTS
    (subquery)
[End of SELECT, INSERT, UPDATE, DELETE statement; or
    subquery]
```

To find the names of all the publishers that publish business books, the query is this:

```
SQL
select distinct pub_name
from publishers
```

```
where exists
   (select *
    from titles
    where pub_id = publishers.pub_id
    and type = 'business')
pub_name
=========================================
New Age Books
Algodata Infosystems
[2 rows]
```

EXISTS tests for the presence or absence of the "empty set" of rows.

- If the subquery returns at least one row, the subquery evaluates to "true." This means that an EXISTS phrase will succeed and a NOT EXISTS phrase will fail.
- If the subquery returns the empty set (no rows), the subquery evaluates to "false." This means that a NOT EXISTS phrase will succeed and an EXISTS phrase will fail.

In the preceding query, the first publisher's name is Algodata Infosystems, with an identification number of 1389. Does Algodata Infosystems pass the existence test? That is, are there any rows in the `titles` table in which `pub_id` is 1389 and `type` is business? If so, Algodata Infosystems should be one of the values selected. The same process is repeated for each of the other publishers' names.

Notice that the syntax of subqueries introduced with EXISTS differs a bit from the syntax of other subqueries, in these ways:

- The keyword EXISTS is not preceded by a column name, a constant, or another expression.
- The select list of a subquery introduced by EXISTS almost always consists of an asterisk (*). There is no real point in listing column names because you are simply testing for the existence of rows that meet the subquery's conditions and these are spelled out in the subquery WHERE clause, not in the subquery SELECT clause.

The EXISTS keyword is very important because there is often no alternative, nonsubquery formulation. In practice, an EXISTS subquery is almost always a correlated subquery. Instead of having the outer query operate on values that the inner query supplies, the outer query presents values, one by one, that the inner query tests.

You can use EXISTS to express all "list" subqueries that would use IN, ANY, or ALL. Some examples of statements using EXISTS and their equivalent alternatives follow.

Figure 8.5 shows two queries that find titles of books published by any publisher located in a city that begins with the letter *B*. Both queries produce the same results. The results show that twelve of the books in the `titles` table are published by a publisher located in either Boston or Berkeley.

```
Results:
title
=============================================================================
Emotional Security: A New Algorithm
Prolonged Data Deprivation: Four Case Studies
You Can Combat Computer Stress!
Is Anger the Enemy?
Life Without Fear
Computer Phobic and Non-Phobic Individuals: Behavior Variations
Secrets of Silicon Valley
The Busy Executive's Database Guide
Cooking with Computers: Surreptitious Balance Sheets
But Is It User Friendly?
Straight Talk About Computers
Net Etiquette
[12 rows]
```

SQL
```
select title
from titles
where pub_id in
    (select pub_id
     from publishers
     where city like 'B%')
```

SQL
```
select title
from titles
where exists
    (select *
     from publishers
     where pub_id = titles.pub_id
     and city like 'B%')
```

Figure 8.5 Comparing Subqueries with IN and EXISTS

NOT EXISTS Seeks the Empty Set

NOT EXISTS is the inverse of EXISTS. NOT EXISTS queries succeed when the subquery returns no rows.

For example, to find the names of publishers that do not publish business books, the query is this:

SQL
```
select pub_name
from publishers
where not exists
   (select *
    from titles
    where pub_id = publishers.pub_id
    and type = 'business')
pub_name
========================================
Binnet & Hardley
[1 row]
```

The following query finds the titles for which there have been no sales:

SQL
```
select title
from titles
where not exists
   (select title_id
    from salesdetails
    where title_id = titles.title_id)
title
============================================================
The Psychology of Computer Cooking
Net Etiquette
[2 rows]
```

Using EXISTS to Find Intersection and Difference

Subqueries introduced with EXISTS and NOT EXISTS can be used for two set theory operations: **intersection** and **difference**. The intersection of two sets contains all elements that belong to both of the two original sets. The difference contains the elements that belong only to the first of the two sets. (See "Going Beyond Joins: UNION, INTERSECT, MINUS" in Chapter 7 for more information.)

The intersection of `authors` and `publishers` over the `city` column is the set of cities in which both an author and a publisher are located:

```
SQL
select distinct city
from authors
where exists
  (select *
   from publishers
   where authors.city = publishers.city)

city
====================
Berkeley
[1 row]
```

The difference between `authors` and `publishers` over the `city` column is the set of cities where an author lives but no publisher is located (that is, all the cities except Berkeley):

```
SQL
select distinct city
from authors
where not exists
  (select *
   from publishers
   where authors.city = publishers.city)

city
====================
Oakland
Salt Lake City
Gary
Rockville
Vacaville
```

```
Palo Alto
Walnut Creek
San Jose
Covelo
Nashville
Menlo Park
Ann Arbor
San Francisco
Corvallis
Lawrence
[15 rows]
```

EXISTS Alternatives

Sometimes you'll see code like the following, in which the results of a subquery are greater than zero:

```
SQL
select distinct city
from authors
where
  (select count(*)
   from publishers
   where authors.city = publishers.city) > 0
```

This is equivalent to the EXISTS intersection query in the previous section (there are more than zero rows). However, performance is slower with COUNT(*). EXISTS stops processing as soon as one "true" result row is returned. COUNT(*) requires counting all the qualifying rows and comparing that number to the value.

The COUNT(*) version of NOT EXISTS has the same performance issues. Following is an example that does the same as the NOT EXISTS difference query you saw earlier.

```
SQL
select distinct city
from authors
where
  (select count(*)
   from publishers
   where authors.city = publishers.city) = 0
```

Subqueries in Multiple Levels of Nesting

A subquery can itself include one or more subqueries. You can nest any number of subqueries.

An example of a problem that can be solved using a statement with multiple levels of nested queries is "Find the names of authors who have participated in writing at least one popular computing book."

SQL
```
select au_lname, au_fname
from authors
where au_id in
  (select au_id
   from titleauthors
   where title_id in
      (select title_id
       from titles
       where type = 'popular_comp') )
```

au_lname	au_fname
======================================	==================
Carson	Cheryl
Dull	Ann
Hunter	Sheryl
Locksley	Chastity
(4 rows affected)	

The innermost query returns the title ID numbers PC1035, PC8888, and PC9999. The query at the next level is evaluated with these title IDs and returns the author ID numbers. Finally, the outer query uses the author IDs to find the names of the authors.

You can also express this query as a join:

SQL
```
select au_lname, au_fname
from authors, titles, titleauthors
where authors.au_id = titleauthors.au_id
  and titles.title_id = titleauthors.title_id
  and type = 'popular_comp'
```

Subqueries in UPDATE, DELETE, and INSERT Statements

Subqueries can nest in UPDATE, DELETE, and INSERT statements as well as in SELECT statements.

The following query doubles the price of all books published by New Age Books. The statement updates the `titles` table; its subquery references the `publishers` table. If you are following along, use transaction control statements to roll back changes to the data. On the demo system, start with a COMMIT. Run the UPDATE, DELETE, or INSERT, and check your data with a SELECT. Then execute a ROLLBACK command to cancel the changes.

SQL
```
update titles
set price = price * 2
where pub_id in
  (select pub_id
   from publishers
   where pub_name = 'New Age Books')
```

SQL VARIANTS   An equivalent UPDATE statement using a join (for systems that allow a FROM clause in UPDATE) is this:

Transact-SQL
```
update titles
set price = price * 2
from titles, publishers
where titles.pub_id = publishers.pub_id
  and pub_name = 'New Age Books'
```

You can remove all records of sales orders for business books with this nested SELECT statement:

SQL
```
delete salesdetails
where title_id in
  (select title_id
   from titles
   where type = 'business')
```

An equivalent DELETE statement using a join (for systems that allow a FROM clause listing multiple tables in DELETE) is this:

```
Transact-SQL
delete salesdetails
from salesdetails, titles
where salesdetails.title_id = titles.title_id
  and type = 'business'
```

Subqueries in FROM and SELECT Clauses

The ANSI standard allows a subquery in the FROM clause, and some systems permit them in SELECT. The work these two subqueries do is different. We present them together because they are outside the WHERE and HAVING clauses, where you will find most subqueries.

Subqueries in the FROM Clause

Let's say you want to look at the number of sales orders each store has produced. You write a query like this:

```
SQL
select stor_id, count(sonum)
from sales
group by stor_id

stor_id count(sales.sonum)
======= ==================
7066                     2
7067                     2
7131                     3
8042                     4
6380                     2
7896                     3
[6 rows]
```

To see just the highest value, you might consider adding a HAVING clause with a nested aggregate:

SQL
```
select stor_id, count(sonum)
from sales
group by stor_id
having  count (sonum)  = max (count (sonum ) )
```

However, in most systems, you'll get an error message or no rows: Nested aggregates are prohibited.

SQL VARIANTS   Some versions of Transact-SQL allow nested aggregates in the HAVING clause and return the results you'd expect:

Adaptive Server Enterprise
```
stor_id
------- -----------
8042                 4
(1 row affected)
```

So what do you do if you want to find the store with the largest number of orders? Try a FROM subquery. It creates a "virtual view" (see Chapter 9 for a discussion of views).

- Use a subquery in the outer FROM to define a subset of data with a single column.
- Assign column display labels (HiNum) and table aliases (s) to the FROM subquery.
- Use the subquery column as an argument to an aggregate in the outer query.

SQL
```
select max ( s.HiNum )
from  (select count(sonum) as HiNum
         from sales
         group by stor_id) s
max(s.HiNum)
============
           4
[1 row]
```

To include store numbers in the results, create a new query with grouping by stores. Then move the original query (with its FROM subquery) to the outer HAVING clause.

SQL
```
select stor_id, count(*)
from sales
group by stor_id
having count(*) =
        ( select max (s.HiNum)
          from  ( select count(*) as HiNum
                    from sales
                    group by stor_id ) s
        )
stor_id     count(*)
=======  ============
8042               4
[1 row]
```

Subqueries in the SELECT Clause

Some systems allow subqueries in the SELECT statement where the sub-queries act as SELECT list expressions. In the following query, you use SELECT clause correlated subqueries to find principal and second authors. Each subquery joins the outer table in the subquery WHERE clause, which specifies the authors included in the subquery results.

Transact-SQL, Adaptive Server Anywhere:
```
select distinct title_id,
    (select au_id
        from titleauthors
        where au_ord = 1 and title_id = t.title_id) as first_author,
    (select au_id
        from titleauthors
        where au_ord = 2 and title_id = t.title_id) as second_authors,
    (select au_id
        from titleauthors
        where au_ord = 3 and title_id = t.title_id) as third_author
from titleauthors t
```

title_id	first_author	second_authors	third_author
BU1032	409-56-7008	213-46-8915	(NULL)
PS7777	486-29-1786	(NULL)	(NULL)
PC9999	486-29-1786	(NULL)	(NULL)
MC2222	712-45-1867	(NULL)	(NULL)
PS3333	172-32-1176	(NULL)	(NULL)
PC1035	238-95-7766	(NULL)	(NULL)
BU2075	213-46-8915	(NULL)	(NULL)
PS2091	998-72-3567	899-46-2035	(NULL)
PS2106	998-72-3567	(NULL)	(NULL)
MC3021	722-51-5454	899-46-2035	(NULL)
TC3218	807-91-6654	(NULL)	(NULL)
BU7832	274-80-9391	(NULL)	(NULL)
PC8888	427-17-2319	846-92-7186	(NULL)
PS1372	756-30-7391	724-80-9391	(NULL)
BU1111	724-80-9391	267-41-2394	(NULL)
TC7777	672-71-3249	267-41-2394	472-27-2349
TC4203	648-92-1872	(NULL)	(NULL)

[17 rows]

You'll find an example of doing the same kind of work, much more efficiently, with the CASE function in Chapter 11.

Summary

This chapter has explored subqueries, including the following:

- What subqueries are and where they appear
- How simple and correlated subqueries work
- Hints on when to use subqueries and when to stick with joins
- Subquery rules, restrictions, and limitations

After these preliminaries, we looked at operators:

- IN or NOT IN can return any number of rows
- Comparison operators (=, >, etc.) must return no more than one row
- EXISTS and NOT EXISTS test existence and are mostly used with correlated subqueries

Finally, we considered some advanced issues:

- Subqueries within subqueries—nested subqueries
- Subqueries in UPDATE, DELETE, and INSERT statements
- Subqueries in SELECT and FROM

Now that you can write plain and fancy queries using joins and subqueries, you have most of the power of the SQL language at your command. The remaining issues are how to customize your view of your data, how to preserve database integrity and security, and how to use functions for specific data manipulations.

Views, covered in the next chapter, are a means of naming a specific selection of data from one or more tables so that it can be treated as a virtual table. Views can also be used as a security mechanism (discussed in Chapter 10).

Chapter 9

Creating and Using Views

In This Chapter

- With a View Toward Flexibility
- View Commands
- Advantages of Views
- How Views Work
- Data Modification Through Views
- Creating Copies of Data

With a View Toward Flexibility

Like the join operation, the view is a hallmark of the relational model. A view creates a virtual table from a SELECT statement and opens up a world of flexibility for data analysis and manipulation. You can think of a view as a movable frame or window through which you can see data. This metaphor explains why people speak of looking at data or of changing data "through" a view.

Previous chapters have demonstrated how to use a SELECT statement to choose rows, combine tables, add display labels, form groups, and make calculations until you've derived specific information in a specific form. Creating a view based on a SELECT statement gives you an easy way to examine and handle just the data you (or others) need—no more, no less. In effect, a view "freezes" a SELECT statement.

Views are not separate copies of the data in the table(s) or view(s) from which they're derived. In fact, views are called virtual tables because they do not exist as independent entities in the database as "real" tables do. (The ANSI term for a view is a **viewed table**; a native database table is a base table.) You can query views much as you query tables. Modifying data through views is restricted, however (see "Data Modification Through Views" later in this chapter).

The system catalogs store the *definition* of the view—the view's name and SELECT statement. When a user calls a view, the database system associates the appropriate data with it. A view presents the end result of this process, hiding all its technical underpinnings. A view's beauty lies in its transparency: Naive users aren't frightened by joins, crafty users aren't tempted to look at (or try to alter) data that is none of their business, and impatient users aren't slowed down by the need to type long SQL statements.

View Commands

Like tables, views have CREATE and DROP commands. (DROP VIEW applies only to the view, not to the underlying base table.) You access the data with SELECT statements.

Creating Views

Here's the simplified syntax of a view definition statement:

```
CREATE VIEW view_name [(column_name [, column_name]...)]
AS
SELECT_statement
```

SYNTAX

- Follow your system's rules for identifiers when you name the view.
- Specify view column names if the column is calculated or if multiple columns have the same name. Otherwise, columns inherit names from the SELECT clause.
- Define the columns and rows of the view in the SELECT statement.

The following example creates a view that displays the names of authors who live in Oakland, California, and their books. The view is named `oaklanders`. Its SELECT statement pulls data from three tables.

```
SQL
create view oaklanders (FirstName, LastName, Book)
as
select au_fname, au_lname, title
from authors, titles, titleauthors
where authors.au_id = titleauthors.au_id
  and titles.title_id = titleauthors.title_id
  and city = 'Oakland'
```

As you've seen, the SELECT statement doesn't need to be a simple selection of the rows and columns of one particular table. You can create a view using any of these objects or combinations of objects:

- A single table
- More than one table
- Another view
- Multiple views
- Combinations of views and tables

The SELECT statement can have almost any complexity, using projection and selection to define the columns and rows you want to include and including GROUP BY and HAVING clauses. In multiple-object views, you can use joins, subqueries, or combinations of the two to construct connections in the tables and views underlying the view.

In spite of the many kinds of views that can be created, there are always limits, varying from SQL to SQL. Basically, restrictions have two sources:

- Elements not allowed in CREATE VIEW statements (ORDER BY and sometimes UNION). Check your system manuals for specifics.
- Elements permitted in CREATE VIEW statements (computed columns, aggregates) that can limit the data modification permitted through the view because of the problem of interpreting data modification statements.

The view-updating problem is explained and illustrated later in this chapter. If you want users to be able to perform most functions through a view, you may decide to modify a perfectly legal CREATE VIEW statement to avoid these limitations.

Displaying Data Through Views

Creating a view doesn't produce a display. When SQL receives a CREATE VIEW command, it does not actually execute the SELECT statement that follows the keyword AS. Instead, it stores the SELECT statement in the system catalogs.

In order to see data through the view, query the view, just as you would a table.

SQL
```
select *
from oaklanders
```

FirstName	LastName	Book
===========	==========	==
Marjorie	Green	The Busy Executive's Database Guide
Stearns	MacFeather	Cooking with Computers: Surreptitious Balance Sheets
Marjorie	Green	You Can Combat Computer Stress!
Dick	Straight	Straight Talk About Computers
Livia	Karsen	Computer Phobic and Non-Phobic Individuals: Behavior Variations
Stearns	MacFeather	Computer Phobic and Non-Phobic Individuals: Behavior Variations
[6 rows]		

A view in a SELECT statement works just like a table. You can

- Change the order of the columns in the display;
- Add display labels;
- Limit the rows with WHERE conditions;
- Group rows;
- Limit group results with HAVING;
- Sort the results.

For example, you could write a query of oaklanders like this, changing the position of columns, adding display labels, and sorting the results:

SQL
```
select Book as Title,    LastName as Surname
from oaklanders
order by Title
```

Title	Surname
==	==========
Computer Phobic and Non-Phobic Individuals: Behavior Variations	Karsen
Computer Phobic and Non-Phobic Individuals: Behavior Variations	MacFeather
Cooking with Computers: Surreptitious Balance Sheets	MacFeather

```
Straight Talk About Computers                          Straight
The Busy Executive's Database Guide                    Green
You Can Combat Computer Stress!                        Green
[6 rows]
```

Here's a query of the `oaklanders` view with aggregates, GROUP BY, and HAVING:

SQL.
```
select LastName, count(Book)
from oaklanders
group by LastName
having count(Book) > 1
LastName                                    count(titles.title)
========================================    ====================
Green                                                          2
MacFeather                                                     2
[2 rows]
```

Dropping Views

The command for removing views is:

```
DROP VIEW view_name
```

If a view depends on a table (or on another view) that has been dropped, you won't be able to use the view. However, if you create a new table (or view) with the same name to replace the dropped one, you may be able to use the view again, as long as the columns referenced in the view definition still exist. Check your system's reference manuals for details.

Advantages of Views

To clarify the advantages of using views, consider several possible users of the `bookbiz` database. Let's say that the promotion manager needs to know which authors are connected to which books and who has first, second, and third billing on the cover. Prices, sales, advances, royalties, and personal addresses are not of interest, but the promotion manager does need some information from each of the three tables: `titles`, `authors`, and `titleauthors`. Without a view, a query something like the following might be used:

SQL
```
select titles.title_id, au_ord, au_lname, au_fname
from authors, titles, titleauthors
where authors.au_id = titleauthors.au_id and
      titles.title_id = titleauthors.title_id
```

This query involves a lot of typing, and there are any number of places where an error might slip in. Quite a bit of knowledge of the database is required, too. Creating a view called books that is based on this SELECT statement would facilitate the use of this particular set of data. Here's the statement that creates the view (unlike the oaklanders view, this one inherits column names from the SELECT clause):

SQL
```
create view books
as
select titles.title_id, au_ord, au_lname, au_fname
from authors, titles, titleauthors
where authors.au_id = titleauthors.au_id and
      titles.title_id = titleauthors.title_id
```

Now the promotion manager can use the view to get the same results without thinking about joins or select lists or search conditions:

SQL
```
select *
from books
```

title_id	au_ord	au_lname	au_fname
==========	========	==============================	==========
PC8888	1	Dull	Ann
PC8888	2	Hunter	Sheryl
BU1032	1	Bennet	Abraham
BU1032	2	Green	Marjorie
PS7777	1	Locksley	Chastity
PS3333	1	White	Johnson
BU1111	1	MacFeather	Stearns
BU1111	2	O'Leary	Michael

```
MC2222          1 del Castillo                Innes
TC7777          1 Yokomoto                    Akiko
TC7777          2 O'Leary                     Michael
TC7777          3 Gringlesby                  Burt
TC4203          1 Blotchet-Halls              Reginald
PC1035          1 Carson                      Cheryl
BU2075          1 Green                       Marjorie
PS2091          1 Ringer                      Albert
PS2091          2 Ringer                      Anne
PS2106          1 Ringer                      Albert
MC3021          1 DeFrance                    Michel
MC3021          2 Ringer                      Anne
TC3218          1 Panteley                    Sylvia
BU7832          1 Straight                    Dick
PS1372          1 Karsen                      Livia
PS1372          2 MacFeather                  Stearns
PC9999          1 Locksley                    Chastity
[25 rows]
```

An accountant might want to create a different view. Author order on the title page doesn't matter, just the bottom line: To whom should checks be written and for how much. The query involves computing how many books were sold at what price, with what percentage rate for each author:

SQL
```
select au_lname, au_fname,
  sum(price*ytd_sales*royalty*royaltyshare) as Total_Income
from authors, titles, titleauthors, roysched
where authors.au_id = titleauthors.au_id
  and titles.title_id = titleauthors.title_id
  and titles.title_id = roysched.title_id
  and ytd_sales between lorange and hirange
group by au_lname, au_fname
```

If the accountant uses this SELECT statement to create a view named royaltychecks, the equivalent query is this:

SQL
```
select *
from royaltychecks
```

The results (who gets a check and for how much) are as follows:

```
Results
au_lname                au_fname                Total_Income
==================      ======================  ================
Bennet                  Abraham                         7368.54
Blotchet-Halls          Reginald                       46390.01
Carson                  Cheryl                         60336.16
DeFrance                Michel                         43346.33
del Castillo            Innes                           7312.76
Dull                    Ann                             8190.00
Green                   Marjorie                       48688.14
Gringlesby              Burt                            3684.27
Hunter                  Sheryl                          8190.00
Karsen                  Livia                           1169.72
Locksley                Chastity                        6001.46
MacFeather              Stearns                         5494.60
O'Leary                 Michael                         7087.40
Panteley                Sylvia                          1535.63
Ringer                  Albert                          2881.97
Ringer                  Anne                           17142.04
Straight                Dick                           12280.91
White                   Johnson                        12211.93
Yokomoto                Akiko                           4912.36
(19 rows affected)
```

Finally, consider an executive at the parent publishing company who needs to find out how the different categories of books are doing at each subsidiary. The executive can use a query something like this:

```
SQL
select pub_id, type, sum(price*ytd_sales),
    avg(price), avg(ytd_sales)
from titles
group by pub_id, type
```

However, the executive may not want to bother with anything so complex. A much simpler query is

```
SQL
select *
from currentinfo
```

PUB#	TYPE	INCOME	AVG_PRICE	AVG_SALES
1389	popular_comp	540901.00	41.48	6437.50
1389	business	330696.30	27.31	4022.00
0736	psychology	244504.92	25.70	1987.80
0877	mod_cook	349915.22	21.49	12139.00
0877	trad_cook	469522.50	30.96	6522.00
0736	business	243198.78	12.99	18722.00
0877	(NULL)	(NULL)	(NULL)	(NULL)

[7 rows]

Using this view, the busy executive can quickly see which publishing lines are making money, and he or she can compare the relationship among income, average price, and average sales.

SQL VARIANTS

You might see some formatting differences in results, depending on what datatypes your systems uses and how your system displays numbers. Microsoft SQL Server, for example, shows AVG_SALES values as whole numbers:

SQL Server

PUB#	TYPE	INCOME	AVG_PRICE	AVG_SALES
0877	NULL	NULL	NULL	NULL
0736	business	243198.7800	12.9900	18722
1389	business	330696.3000	27.3100	4022
0877	mod_cook	349915.2200	21.4900	12139
1389	popular_comp	540901.0000	41.4750	6437
0736	psychology	244504.9200	25.7040	1987
0877	trad_cook	469522.5000	30.9633	6522

(7 row(s) affected)

As the previous examples demonstrate, you can use views to focus, simplify, and customize each user's perception of the database. In addition, views provide a security mechanism. Finally, they can protect users from the effects of changes in the database structure, providing independence.

Focus, Simplification, and Customization

Views allow the promotion manager, the accountant, and the executive in the previous examples to focus in on the particular data and tasks. No extraneous or distracting information gets in the way.

Working with the data is simpler, too. When favorite joins, projections, and/or selections are already defined as views, it's relatively simple to add other clauses. Constructing the entire underlying query, on the other hand, could be a daunting prospect.

Views are a good way of customizing a database or tailoring it to suit a variety of users with dissimilar interests and skill levels. Our three users see the data in different ways, even when they're looking at the same three tables at the same time.

Security

Views provide security by hiding sensitive or irrelevant parts of the database. If permissions are set up properly, the accountant can find out how big an author's check should be, but can't look at the underlying figures or compare his or her own paycheck to a coworker's. You can restrict the accountant's access in the database to just those views that are relevant to accounting. Using views as a security mechanism is discussed in more detail in Chapter 10.

Independence

Finally, there's the issue of independence. From time to time, you may have to modify the structure of the database, but there's no reason that users should suffer from these changes. For example, say you split the `titles` table into two new tables and drop `titles`. The new tables are shown in Figure 9.1.

Notice that the old `titles` table can be regenerated by joining the `title_id` columns of the two new tables. To shield the changed structure of the database from users, you can create a view that is the join of the two new tables (Figure 9.2). You can even name it `titles` (although here it's called

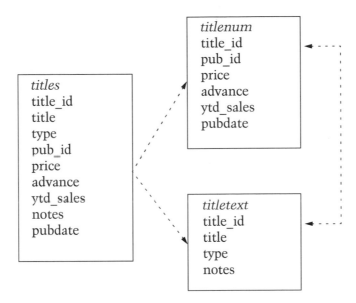

Figure 9.1 Splitting a Table into Two Tables

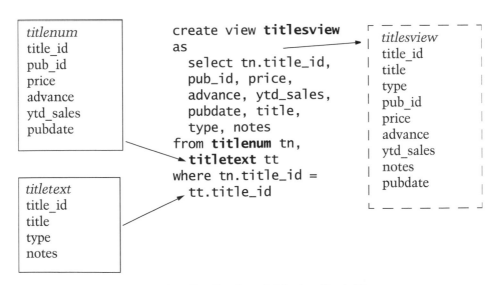

Figure 9.2 Uniting Two Base Tables in a Single View

`titlesview`). In most systems, doing so means you won't have to change any views that were based wholly or in part on the old `titles`.

Restrictions on updating data through views (explained later in this chapter) limit the independence of this kind of view. Certain data modification statements on the new `titles` may not be allowed.

How Views Work

What actually happens in the database when you create a view, and what happens when you use it?

Creating a view means defining it in terms of its base tables. The definition of the view is stored in the system catalogs without any data. When you query or perform data modification commands through the view, you are accessing the data that is stored in association with the underlying tables. In other words, creating a view does not generate a copy of the data, neither at the time the view is defined nor at the time the view is accessed.

When you query a view, it looks exactly like any other database table. You can display it in much the same way as you can any other table, with few restrictions.

Changing data through a view has some limitations (explained later in this chapter). For now, consider the simplest case: a view based on a single table. When you modify the data you see through a view, you are actually changing the data in the underlying base table. Conversely, when you change the data in the base tables, these changes are automatically reflected in the views derived from them.

Suppose you are interested only in books priced higher than $15 and for which an advance of more than $5,000 was paid. This straightforward SELECT statement would find the rows that qualify:

SQL
```
select *
from titles
where price > $15
  and advance > $5000
```

Now suppose you have a slew of retrieval and update operations to do on this collection of data. You could, of course, combine the conditions shown in the previous query with any command that you issue. However, for convenience, you can create a view in which just the records of interest are visible:

SQL

```
create view hiprice
as
select *
from titles
where price > $15
  and advance > $5000
```

When SQL receives this command, it does not actually execute the SELECT statement that follows the keyword AS. Instead, it stores the SELECT statement (which is, in fact, the definition of the view hiprice) in the system catalogs.

Now, when you display or operate on hiprice, SQL combines your statement with the stored definition of hiprice. For example, you can change all the prices in hiprice just as you can change any other table:

SQL

```
update hiprice
set price = price*2
```

SQL actually finds the view definition in the system catalogs and converts this update command into the following statement:

SQL

```
update titles
set price = price*2
where price > $15
  and advance > $5000
```

In other words, SQL knows from the view definition that the data to be updated is in titles. It also knows that it should increase the prices only in those rows that meet the conditions on the price and advance columns given in the view definition.

Having issued the first update statement—the update to hiprice—you can see its effect either through the view or in the titles table. Conversely, if you had created the view and then issued the second update statement, which operates directly on the base table, the changed prices would also be visible through the view.

If you update a view's underlying table in such a way that more rows qualify for the view, they become visible through the view. For example, suppose you increase the price of the book *You Can Combat Computer Stress* to $25.95. Because this book now meets the qualifying conditions in the view definition statement, it becomes part of the view.

Naming View Columns

An issue to consider in how views work is view column names. Assigning alias names to a view's columns is required when either of these rules is fulfilled:

- One or more of the view's columns is a complex expression: It includes an arithmetic expression, a built-in function, or a constant.
- The view would wind up with more than one column of the same name (the view definition's SELECT statement includes a join, and the columns from the joined tables or views have the same name).

You can assign names to view columns or expressions in two ways:

- Put the names inside parentheses following the view name, separated by commas. Make sure there is a name for every item in the SELECT list. If you do one column name this way, you must do them all the same way.
- Allow the view to inherit names from the columns or display labels in the SELECT clause. Display labels are required for complex expressions and columns with name conflicts. Otherwise, you can leave column names as they are.

Figure 9.3 shows both methods.

Complex Expressions   Assigning column names in the CREATE VIEW clause can be illustrated with the `currentinfo` view discussed earlier in this chapter:

```
SQL
create view currentinfo (PUB#, TYPE, INCOME,
  AVG_PRICE, AVG_SALES)
as
select pub_id, type, sum(price*ytd_sales),
  avg(price), avg(ytd_sales)
from titles
group by pub_id, type
```

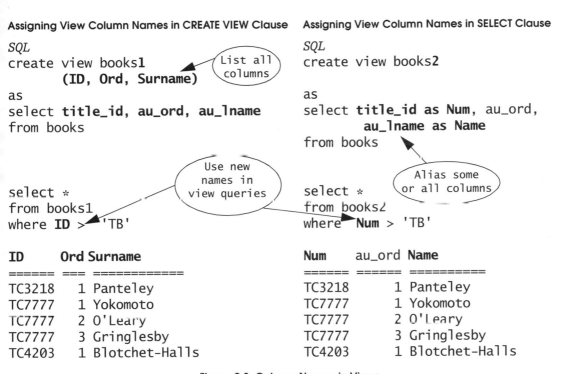

Assigning View Column Names in CREATE VIEW Clause

SQL
```
create view books1          List all
        (ID, Ord, Surname)  columns
as
select title_id, au_ord, au_lname
from books
```

```
                 Use new
                 names in
                 view queries
select *
from books1
where ID > 'TB'
```

ID	Ord	Surname
======	===	============
TC3218	1	Panteley
TC7777	1	Yokomoto
TC7777	2	O'Leary
TC7777	3	Gringlesby
TC4203	1	Blotchet-Halls

Assigning View Column Names in SELECT Clause

SQL
```
create view books2

as
select title_id as Num, au_ord,
            au_lname as Name
from books
```

```
                 Alias some
                 or all columns
select *
from books2
where Num > 'TB'
```

Num	au_ord	Name
======	======	===========
TC3218	1	Panteley
TC7777	1	Yokomoto
TC7777	2	O'Leary
TC7777	3	Gringlesby
TC4203	1	Blotchet-Halls

Figure 9.3 Column Names in Views

The computed columns in the SELECT list don't really have names, so you must give them new names in the CREATE VIEW clause or assign display labels in the SELECT clause. Otherwise, you'd have no way to refer to them. When you work with the view `currentinfo`, always use the new names, like this:

```
SQL
select PUB#, AVG_SALES
from currentinfo
```

Using the old names, such as `pub_id` or `avg(ytd_sales)`, won't work.

Duplicate Column Names The second circumstance in which assigning new column names is required usually arises when there's a join in the SELECT statement and the joining columns have the same name. Even though they are qualified with different table names in the SELECT statement, you have to rename them in order to resolve the ambiguity:

SQL
```
create view cities (Author, Authorcity, Pub, Pubcity)
as
select au_lname, authors.city, pub_name, publishers.city
from authors, publishers
where authors.city = publishers.city
```

Of course, you are free to rename columns in a view definition statement whenever it's helpful to do so. Just remember that when you assign column names in the CREATE VIEW clause, the number and order of column names inside the parentheses has to match the number and order of items in the SELECT list.

Whether you rename a view column, its datatype and null status depend on how it was defined in its base table(s).

Creating Views with Multiple Underlying Objects

Another issue in how views work is the underlying objects. As you've seen, views can be based on one or many underlying objects. The objects can be connected with joins and/or subqueries and can be tables and/or views.

Using Subqueries and Joins   Here is an example of a view definition that includes three joins and a subquery. It finds the author ID, title ID, publisher, and price of each book with a price that's higher than the average of all the books' prices. (Including the author ID means that you'll see more than one row for books with multiple authors.)

SQL
```
create view highaverage
as
select authors.au_id, titles.title_id, pub_name, price
from authors, titleauthors, titles, publishers
where authors.au_id = titleauthors.au_id and
      titles.title_id = titleauthors.title_id and
      titles.pub_id = publishers.pub_id and
      price >
          (select avg(price)
          from titles)
```

Now that the view has been created, you can use it to display the results. In this example, you use the SELECT, WHERE, and ORDER BY clauses to tailor the information you see:

SQL
```
select price as Price, title_id as BookNum, au_id as
               Writer
from highaverage
where pub_name = 'Binnet & Hardley'
order by price, title_id
      Price BookNum Writer
========== ======= ===========
      29.99 MC2222  712-45-1867
      29.99 TC7777  672-71-3249
      29.99 TC7777  267-41-2394
      29.99 TC7777  472-27-2349
      40.95 TC3218  807-91-6654
[5 rows]
```

Deriving Views from Views Let's use `highaverage` to illustrate a view derived from another view. Here's how to create a view that displays all the higher-than-average-priced books published by Binnet & Hardley:

SQL
```
create view highBandH
as
select *
from highaverage
where pub_name = 'Binnet & Hardley'
```

You can structure your SELECT statement to limit columns and order rows.

SQL
```
select price, title_id, au_id
from highBandH
order by price, title_id
      price title_id au_id
========== ======== ===========
      29.99 MC2222   712-45-1867
      29.99 TC7777   672-71-3249
```

```
29.99 TC7777   267-41-2394
29.99 TC7777   472-27-2349
40.95 TC3218   807-91-6654
[5 rows]
```

Resolving Views

The process of combining a query on a view with its stored definition and translating it into a query on the view's underlying tables is called view resolution. Several problems can arise during this process. Be on the alert for issues arising from modifications of underlying tables or views:

- Adding columns to underlying tables or views for a view defined as SELECT * (SQL expands the asterisk shorthand at view creation, not at execution). A query of the view runs without an error message, but results don't include columns added to the underlying object after the view was created.
- Changing underlying tables or views by modifying column names or datatypes or by renaming or dropping the underlying objects. You'll probably get error messages when you query the view.
- Updating through views so that rows in the view become ineligible for it. You can use the WITH CHECK OPTION clause to prevent "hiding" data through a view update.

Adding Columns   A query of the view runs but does not display columns added to underlying objects after the view was created. This is because the asterisk is expanded at view creation, not at execution. In the following example, the addon table starts out with two columns:

```
SQL
create table addon
(name char(5),
num   int)

insert into addon
values ('one' , 1)
```

After a view is created, someone adds a column to the table.

```
SQL
create view addonv
as
select *
from addon

alter table addon
add  status char(1) null
```

A query of the table shows three columns.

```
SQL
select *
from addon

name           num status
===== =========== ======
one              1 (NULL)
[1 row]
```

A query of the view shows only two columns—the two that existed when the view was created.

```
SQL
select *
from addonv

name           num
===== ===========
one              1
[1 row]
```

Breaking Object Chains Because views can be defined in terms of other views and tables, it's possible to wind up with a chain of objects, each dependent on another. Just as an actual chain can break at any link, so can a chain of objects. Any one of the views or tables in the chain might be redefined in such a way that its dependent views no longer make sense.

As an example, three generations of views derived from the `authors` table are shown here:

SQL
```
create view number1
as
select au_lname, phone
from authors
where zip like '94%'
```

SQL
```
select *
from number1
```

au_lname	phone
===	==============
Bennet	415 658-9932
Green	415 986-7020
Carson	415 548-7723
Stringer	415 843-2991
Straight	415 834-2919
Karsen	415 534-9219
MacFeather	415 354-7128
Dull	415 836-7128
Yokomoto	415 935-4228
White	408 496-7223
Hunter	415 836-7128
Locksley	415 585-4620

[12 rows]

SQL
```
create view number2
as
select au_lname, phone
from number1
where au_lname >  'M'
```

SQL
```
select *
from number2
```

au_lname	phone
===	==============
Stringer	415 843-2991
Straight	415 834-2919

```
MacFeather                                 415 354-7128
Yokomoto                                   415 935-4228
White                                      408 496-7223
[5 rows]
```

SQL
```
create view number3
as
select au_lname, phone
from number2
where au_lname = 'MacFeather'
```

SQL
```
select *
from number3
au_lname                                   phone
================================== ============
MacFeather                                 415 354-7128
[1 row]
```

What happens to number3 if you redefine number2 with different selection criteria?

- A condition on a column available in number2's underlying table number1 (either au_fname or phone) works fine. The WHERE clause determines what, if any, data is seen through number3.
- A condition such as a zip code matching "947nn" causes failure in creating number2 or displaying data through it because the zip column exists in neither number1 nor number2. With number2 in trouble, there's not much hope for retrieving data through number3.

Whatever you do to view number2, view number3 still exists and becomes usable again by dropping and re-creating view number2.

In short, some systems allow you to change the definition of an intermediate view without affecting dependent views as long as the *target list* of the dependent views remains valid. If you violate this rule, a query that references the invalid view produces an error message.

Using WITH CHECK OPTION   One of the problems with updating a view is that it is possible to change its values in such a way as to make the values ineligible for the view. For example, consider a view that displays all books with prices greater than $15.00. What happens if you update one of those book prices through the view, changing its price to $14.99? The optional WITH CHECK OPTION clause, which appears after the SELECT statement in the CREATE VIEW syntax, is designed to prevent such a problem:

```
CREATE VIEW view_name [(column_name [, column_name]...)]
AS
SELECT_statement
[WITH CHECK OPTION]
```

SYNTAX

The WITH CHECK OPTION clause tells SQL to reject any attempt to modify a view in a way that makes one or more of its rows ineligible for the view. In other words, if a data modification statement (UPDATE, INSERT, or DELETE) causes some rows to disappear from the view, the statement is considered illegal.

As an example, recall the view hiprice, which includes all titles with price greater than $15 and advance greater than $5,000:

```
SQL
create view hiprice
as
select *
from titles
where price > $15
and advance > $5000


select title, price, advance
from hiprice
```

title	price	advance
Secrets of Silicon Valley	40.00	8000.00
Sushi, Anyone?	29.99	8000.00
But Is It User Friendly?	42.95	7000.00
Life Without Fear	17.00	6000.00
Onions, Leeks, and Garlic: Cooking Secrets of the Mediterranean	40.95	7000.00
Computer Phobic and Non-Phobic Individuals: Behavior Variations	41.59	7000.00

```
[6 rows]
```

This statement updates one of the books visible through `hiprice`, changing its price to $14.99.

```
SQL
update hiprice
set price = $14.99
where title = 'Secrets of Silicon Valley'
```

If WITH CHECK OPTION had been part of the definition of `hiprice`, the UPDATE statement would be rejected because the new price of *Secrets of Silicon Valley* would make it ineligible for the view. Because the definition of `hiprice` does not include the WITH CHECK OPTION clause, the UPDATE statement is accepted. But the next time you look at the data through `hiprice`, you'll no longer see *Secrets of Silicon Valley*.

SQL VARIANTS   In some systems, WITH CHECK OPTION can be included in a CREATE VIEW statement only if the view being defined is otherwise updatable. The `checkv` view is not updatable because it contains an aggregate expression. One system refuses to create it:

```
SQL Server
create view checkv (Type, AvPrice)
as
select type, avg(price)
from titles
group by type
with check option
```

```
Server: Msg 4510, Level 16, State 1, Procedure checkv, Line 1
Could not perform CREATE VIEW because WITH CHECK OPTION was specified
and the view is not updatable.
```

Other systems are more forgiving. The same view is created without problem on ASA. However, you get an error message when you try to update data through it.

```
Adaptive Server Anywhere
update checkv
set type = 'Psychology'
where type = 'psychology'

Error at line 1.
Update operation attempted on non-updatable query.
```

Data Modification Through Views

Changing data through views is a thorny issue. The general problem, as we'll demonstrate here, is that commands to change data in a view sometimes can't be understood by SQL in an unambiguous way. Such updates are disallowed by every version of SQL. In other words, some views are inherently and logically not updatable.

There are other views that are logically updatable but that many versions of SQL rule nonupdatable. Disallowing a wide range of data modification statements makes for more severe restrictions but simplifies the rules about what you can and cannot do. Other SQL implementations go to great lengths to let you make as many kinds of changes as possible, in spite of the complications inevitably introduced into rules about data modification.

The kinds of data modification statements that are allowed vary a great deal from SQL to SQL, so treat the rules we give here as guidelines and check your system's reference manuals for details.

The Rules According to ANSI

The ANSI standard declares that views are read-only (not modifiable) if the CREATE VIEW statement contains any of the following:

- DISTINCT in the select list
- Expressions (computed columns, aggregates, functions, and so on) in the select list
- References to more than one table—in the FROM clause or in a subquery or in a UNION clause
- References to a view that is itself not updatable, either in the FROM clause or in a subquery
- A GROUP BY or HAVING clause

Some dialects of SQL are less restrictive than the ANSI standard; others may be more restrictive. You can consult your reference manual, or you can experiment. When you try to modify data through a view, SQL checks to make sure that no restrictions are violated. If it detects a violation, it rejects the data modification statement and informs you of an error.

The best way to understand the rationale for these restrictions is to look at some examples of nonupdatable views.

Computed Columns   Let's start with the restriction that prohibits updating views with columns derived from computed columns. The gross_sales column in the view accounts is computed from the price and ytd_sales columns of the titles table:

```
SQL
create view accounts (title, advance, gross_sales)
as
select title_id, advance, price * ytd_sales
from titles
where price > 15
   and advance > 5000
```

The rows visible through accounts are these:

```
SQL
select *
from accounts
```

title	advance	gross_sales
======	============	===========
PC8888	8000.00	163800.00
TC7777	8000.00	122809.05
PC1035	7000.00	377101.00
PS2106	6000.00	1887.00
TC3218	7000.00	15356.25
PS1372	7000.00	15596.25

[6 rows]

Think about what it would mean to update the gross_sales column. How could the system deduce the underlying values for price or year-to-date sales from any value you might enter? There's no way for the system to know, and there's no way for you to tell it. Thus updates on this view are illegal.

Theory aside, you may find you can update a column that is not computed
in a view that contains computed expressions, as long as it has a direct relationship to an underlying column and no other rules are broken.

```
SQL
update accounts
set title = 'PC0000'
where title = 'PC8888'

select *
from accounts
title          advance gross_sales
======  ============= ===========
PC0000      8000.00    163800.00
TC7777      8000.00    122809.05
PC1035      7000.00    377101.00
PS2106      6000.00      1887.00
TC3218      7000.00     15356.25
PS1372      7000.00     15596.25
[6 rows]
```

Use an UPDATE to change PC0000 back to PC8888, if this statement suc-
ceeded on your system.

Aggregates Now let's turn to a view with a column derived from an aggregate—that is, a view whose definition includes a GROUP BY clause. Such
views (and any view derived from them) are called **grouped views**. A variety of
restrictions may apply to grouped views, depending on the particular version of
SQL you're using. Here's the view definition statement:

```
SQL

create view categories (Category, Average_Price)
as
select type, avg(price)
from titles
group by type
```

Here's what the view data looks like:

```
SQL
select *
from categories
Category      Average_Price
============ ==============
popular_comp        41.48
business            23.73
psychology          25.70
mod_cook            21.49
trad_cook           30.96
(NULL)              (NULL)
[6 rows]
```

It would make no sense to insert rows into the view `categories`. To what group of underlying rows would an inserted row belong? Updates on the `Average_Price` column cannot be allowed either because there is no way to know from any value you might enter there how the underlying prices should be changed. Theoretically, updates to the `Category` column and deletions could be allowed, but they are not supported by many versions of SQL.

Multiple Underlying Objects   Another restriction on view modifications disallows updates and insertions through a view if the statement would modify columns that are derived from more than one object. This is because updates and insertions on more than one object in a single statement are never allowed.

Some systems allow you to modify the view if you change columns from only one of the underlying tables. For example, if you want to change an author's name through the `oaklanders` view (based on `authors`, `title-authors`, and `titles`), some systems let you do it because the name is stored in one table only. You couldn't write an UPDATE statement that changed one column from `titles` and one column from `authors`.

SQL VARIANTS   Note how Adaptive Server Anywhere and Oracle handle the same query, updating a noncomputed column through a multitable view:

Adaptive Server Anywhere
```
update oaklanders
set FirstName = 'Sylvia'
where FirstName = 'Stearns'

select *
from oaklanders
```

FirstName	LastName	Book
=========	==============	==
Marjorie	Green	The Busy Executive's Database Guide
Sylvia	MacFeather	Cooking with Computers: Surreptitious Balance Sheets
Marjorie	Green	You Can Combat Computer Stress!
Dick	Straight	Straight Talk About Computers
Livia	Karsen	Computer Phobic and Non-Phobic Individuals: Behavior Variations
Sylvia	MacFeather	Computer Phobic and Non-Phobic Individuals: Behavior Variations

[6 rows]

Oracle
```
SQL> update oaklanders
  2  set FirstName = 'Sylvia'
  3  where FirstName = 'Stearns';
```
ERROR at line 3:
ORA-01779: **cannot modify a column** which maps to a non key-preserved table

Reverse the UPDATE to restore MacFeather's first name.

Creating Copies of Data

In this chapter we stressed that views are not copies of data but rather virtual tables with no physical data associated with them. If an independent copy of data is what you want, check to see what your system provides. At a minimum, you can create a new table and then INSERT data from an existing table (your system may use a different datatype for `price`).

```
SQL
create table bizprices
(title_id       char(6)            not null ,
price           numeric(8,2)       null)
[table created]

insert into bizprices
select title_id, price
from titles
where type = 'business'
[4 rows]

select *
from bizprices
title_id       price
======== ==========
BU1032         29.99
BU1111         21.95
BU2075         12.99
BU7832         29.99
[4 rows]
```

This technique is useful for creating test tables, new tables that resemble existing tables, and tables that have some or all of the columns in several other tables. However, it introduces redundancy: Now you have additional copies of title numbers and their prices. As you change values in the original table, values in the new table will not change, unless you add a REFERENCES constraint or the like.

SQL VARIANTS   Some systems offer SQL extensions that allow you to define a table and put data into it (based on existing definitions and data) without going through the usual data definition process.

In Transact-SQL's version, the new table (named in the INTO clause) holds data defined by the columns you specify in the SELECT list, the table(s) you name in the FROM clause, and the rows you choose in the WHERE clause.

```
Transact-SQL
select title_id, price
into bizprices
from titles
where type = 'business'
```

Oracle adds an AS and a SELECT statement to CREATE TABLE.

```
Oracle
SQL>   create table bizprices
   2   as
   3   select title_id, price
   4   from titles
   5   where type = 'business';
```

In either case, the data look like this:

```
Oracle
TITLE_     PRICE
------ ----------
BU1032     29.99
BU1111     21.95
BU2075     12.99
BU7832     29.99
```

Summary

This chapter covered views that allow you to control just how your users see data:

- The familiar CREATE and DROP keywords allow you to set up and remove views. You retrieve data through views with the SELECT statement, treating the view as a kind of table. However, the view does not contain any data: It is simply a way of looking at table data.
- Views allow you to provide focus, simplification, and customization of tables. They also offer a security mechanism (they restrict users from seeing tables but provide access to views based on the tables). In addition, views keep the data independent of the database structure.
- System catalogs hold the view definition. When you query the view, SQL runs the query that created the view. Because of this, you need to make sure any derived or computed columns have names in the view and look out for broken view chains (views based on wounded tables or views).

- Data modification through views is a sticky issue. Because views are often summary data, there may be no way to change data through them. It is important to understand the limitations of your system.

Views out of the way, the chapter moved on to ways of creating copies of data.

The next chapter is a roundup of some remaining database management issues: security, transactions, performance, and integrity.

Chapter 10

Security, Transactions, Performance, and Integrity

In This Chapter

- Database Management in the Real World
- Data Security
- Transactions
- Performance
- Data Integrity

Database Management in the Real World

This chapter is devoted to four issues that are of particular importance in production-oriented, online database applications.

The first of these issues, security, is handled in nearly every relational database management system by two mechanisms: the assignment of permissions (also called **privileges**) with the SQL GRANT and REVOKE commands and the creation of views (through which users can be granted selective access to the database). Some systems also use procedures (sets of extended, often procedural, SQL statements that may accept parameters) as a method to control user actions. Different database management systems deal with the other three issues—transactions, performance, and integrity—in a wide variety of ways. For that reason, this chapter emphasizes concepts rather than syntax details in its discussion of transactions, performance, and integrity.

Security and one aspect of transaction management are primarily of concern in multiuser situations: Granting permissions to other users is an issue only when there are other users. Transaction management allows the database system to run interference among simultaneous requests for the same data from different users (a capability known as **concurrency control**). Database management systems also rely on transaction management for **recovery** purposes—in case of software or media failure. Recovery is important for both single-user and multiuser systems.

The integrity of data is important whether you're in a single-user system or a shared one. Performance is particularly critical in large multiuser database environments, but it also can become a problem in single-user systems.

In the past, performance was considered a weak point of the relational model. Now some relational products perform as well as or better than systems based on other data models. These high-performance relational systems tend to provide tools, some of which are SQL-based, for monitoring and improving the speed and efficiency of data retrieval and modification.

Relational systems have also been criticized for failing to provide adequate assurances of data integrity. Unlike most of the critics of performance, however, the commentators most vocally addressing the integrity issue are strong relational supporters. The ANSI SQL-92 standard includes language for defining some integrity constraints, and most vendors have enhanced their SQLs to meet other integrity needs.

Data Security

Security is an important issue in database management because information is a valuable commodity. Much of the data worth entrusting to a database management system needs to be protected from unauthorized use—that is, from being seen, changed, or removed by anyone not certified to do so.

If you're the sole user of a database, the security issue boils down to figuring out how to protect the database as a whole—a project not in the province of SQL. With a personal computer, for example, your main line of defense may be as low tech as a lock and key.

On the other hand, even if you're the only authorized user of a database, the database management system may be running in a shared environment (on either a multiuser computer or one that's linked into a network). Most such computers provide security facilities at the operating system level. Typically, they require passwords for logging on to the computer in the first place; often they flag each file according to which users have permission to read, write, and execute it.

When you're sharing a database with other users, you turn to SQL and the database management system to meet your security needs with two mechanisms:

- The first is the control of privileges (also called permissions): the use of the SQL GRANT and REVOKE commands to specify which users are allowed to perform which commands on which tables, views, and columns.
- A second security mechanism is the use of views in conjunction with GRANT and REVOKE to provide selective access to subsets of the data.

Both mechanisms assume the database system has a way to know who you are—to recognize its users and verify their identities.

User Identification and Special Users

Database management systems vary widely in their approaches to identifying users, both in basic concept and in detail. Not much can be said that applies across the board; a broad outline of the major variations is about the best that can be done.

Some systems rely on the user's identity at the operating system level: In other words, they recognize as an authorized user anyone who can log on to the computer. That's not to say, however, that anyone who can access the database system will be able to do much of anything in it.

More sophisticated database management systems have their own identification and authorization mechanisms that require each user to have an established name (sometimes called an account or login) and password on the system itself and/or in each database on the system (assuming the system supports the concept of multiple interacting databases). Application programs can supply additional layers of protection.

What happens once the database management system recognizes your identity and verifies it by requesting and receiving your password? At that point, what you can do depends on the kind of user you are and the permissions you've explicitly been granted. Most multiuser database management systems recognize at least two specially privileged categories:

- A super user, often known as the database administrator (DBA) or system administrator
- Owners of database objects

Some database systems recognize additional special users and establish a hierarchy that assigns privileges to execute various commands based on user positions in the hierarchy.

In addition, most systems support groups and/or roles. Groups are collections of users who need the same core permissions. Roles are essentially groups based on specific functions (DBA, operator). The most common group is PUBLIC; it includes all current and future users.

Creating Users and Groups   The mechanisms for creating users and groups vary greatly from system to system. The ANSI standard requires that each user have an authorization identifier; it does not specify how this is done, nor does it insist that a user be an individual person, rather than a group. Creating users and groups may be done with GUI tools, SQL-like commands, special utilities, or stored procedures.

In case you're following along on Adaptive Server Anywhere and want to create some users, use Sybase Central. Click the server name in the left window, and then click the database name in the right window. You'll see a list of functions, including *Users & Groups*. Click it to start adding a user. If you want to stay in the Interactive SQL window, use this code to add and then remove a user named "mary" with a password of "marymary":

SQL VARIANTS

```
Adaptive Server Anywhere
grant connect to mary identified by marymary
[user added]
revoke connect from mary
[user dropped]
```

Alternatively, you can use the Transact-SQL system procedure, SP_ ADDLOGIN. The first argument is a user name; the second is a password:

```
Transact-SQL (and Adaptive Server Anywhere)
execute sp_addlogin mary, marymary
[login added]
```

Remove Mary with `execute sp_droplogin mary`.

In Sybase Adaptive Server Enterprise and Microsoft SQL Server, with their multidatabase systems, you need to enter the SP_ADDLOGIN command from the `master` database. To authorize Mary to use `bookbiz`, enter `execute sp_adduser mary` (no password required) from `bookbiz` after creating the login in `master`.

In Oracle, adding a user entails a SQL-like command:

```
Oracle
SQL> create user mary
  2  identified by marymary;
User created.
```

You can remove Mary from Oracle with `drop user mary`.

Database Administrators   The existence of the database administrator (in some RDBMSs, system administrator, or SA) is established at the time the system is installed. The identity of the DBA is not exactly the same as that of ordinary mortals; DBA is actually a special position that can be (temporarily) filled by any user who knows the correct account name and password. In many database installations, the role of DBA is shared by several people. Each of these users might log in as DBA in order to accomplish administrative tasks but use his or her own name for other functions in the database. Alternatively, the system may support the DBA function through roles or groups. In this way, users can have individual database identities such as "Stacy" and "Tom" and also be assigned functional roles. Under such a plan, users have the power they need to do specialized work, and role activities can be traced to specific individuals.

The DBA typically is blessed with many special privileges and burdened with many responsibilities for the maintenance and smooth operation of the database application. For the purposes of this discussion on security, the DBA (in most systems) automatically holds all permissions that the system recognizes, on all database objects and for all commands. Which of these permissions the DBA can pass along to other users varies from system to system.

Object Owners   The other special category of users that's important for security purposes is the owner of a table or view. In many systems, the user who creates a table or view is its owner. (Some systems support the additional concept of a **database owner**.) A table owner or view owner may automatically be entitled to do anything to the table or view, (usually) including granting permissions on it to other users.

Users other than the owner of a table or view (and the DBA) need explicit permission to perform any operation on it. These permissions are controlled with the SQL GRANT and REVOKE commands that are supported by virtually every multiuser implementation of SQL.

Information about user identification and permissions may be stored in the system catalogs.

PUBLIC Group Ordinarily, you won't need to create the PUBLIC group—it is a system default. All users automatically belong to PUBLIC, which is useful for assigning basic permissions. If you want everyone to have access to a new table, you can grant use to PUBLIC, and all current and future users are covered.

The GRANT and REVOKE Commands

The phrases "granting privileges" or "assigning permissions" are often associated with discussions of GRANT and REVOKE. In most implementations of SQL, you can't do anything for which you don't have explicit authorization—either by being an object owner or a database administrator or by having been granted access with the GRANT command.

The GRANT and REVOKE commands specify which users can perform which operations on which tables, views, or columns. In addition, permission must also be explicitly granted (usually by the database administrator) to execute commands such as CREATE TABLE.

GRANT and REVOKE Syntax The operations associated with GRANT and REVOKE include SELECT, UPDATE, INSERT, DELETE, and REFERENCES; and the objects are tables and views. Authorization to grant these permissions originates with the object owner and is optionally transferable along with the permission itself.

```
GRANT {ALL | privilege_list [(column_list)]}
ON {table_name | view_name}
TO {PUBLIC | user_list}
[WITH GRANT OPTION]
```

`SYNTAX`

The REVOKE command is similar:

```
REVOKE {ALL | privilege_list [(column_list)]}
ON {table_name | view_name}
FROM {PUBLIC | user_list}
[WITH GRANT OPTION]
```

`SYNTAX`

As often the case in SQL, the syntax looks much more complicated than the majority of statements you'll need to write. Before we explain it in detail, here's a simple example that grants Mary permission to insert into and update the `titles` table:

SQL

```
grant insert, update
on titles
to mary
```

Now let's take a closer look at the GRANT and REVOKE syntax. The first line includes the keyword GRANT or REVOKE and either the keyword ALL or a list of (one or more) privileges granted or revoked. If you include more than one privilege in the privilege list, separate them with commas. If the keyword ALL is used, every one of the privileges applicable to the object (that is, every privilege held by the grantor or revoker) is granted or revoked.

Different versions of SQL specify somewhat different sets of privileges. SELECT, UPDATE, DELETE, and INSERT are always in the basic set, and SQL-92 has added REFERENCES (the right to reference a table in the CREATE TABLE statement of another table for foreign keys). Less frequently included privileges are ALTER, INDEX, EXECUTE, AUDIT, and BACKUP. SQLs differ in whether permissions for some, all, or none of these operations can be controlled on the level of columns as well as tables and views. When permissions are being granted on columns, the column name or names are listed in parentheses.

Privileges can be granted for more than one column at a time, but all the columns must be in the same table or in the same view. If you don't include a list of column names, the privilege is being granted or revoked for the entire table or view.

SQL VARIANTS   Don't be thrown by slight variations in SQL dialects. Some allow column name specifications after the SELECT and UPDATE verbs in the first line, some after the object name in the second, some both, and some neither.

Adaptive Server Anywhere

```
revoke update (advance, price)
on titles
from mary
```

```
SQL Server
revoke update
on titles (advance, price)
from mary
```

```
Oracle
SQL> revoke update (advance, price)
  2  on titles
  3  from mary;
ERROR at line 1:
ORA-01750: UPDATE/REFERENCES may only be REVOKEd from the whole
table, not by column
```

The ON clause specifies the table or view for which the privilege is being granted or revoked—one table or one view per statement.

The next line in the syntax begins with the keyword TO (for the GRANT command) or FROM (for the REVOKE command). The keyword PUBLIC refers to all the users of the system.

The alternative to PUBLIC is a list of the names of the users or groups to whom you want to grant the privileges or from whom you want to revoke them. As always, each name in the list is separated from the next by a comma. In SQL dialects that support the concept of user groups, roles, or both, the name of a group or role may be included in the user list.

The optional WITH GRANT OPTION clause governs whether the grantee can, in turn, pass that privilege (with or without the grant option) on to other users. For example, here is a statement that grants Mary permission to SELECT from the authors table and allows her to pass that privilege to other users:

```
SQL
grant select
on authors
to mary
with grant option
```

GRANT and REVOKE Strategies   Whenever you set up permissions on a table or view that you own, it's good practice to issue the GRANT and

REVOKE commands according to a plan to which you've given some thought, rather than to GRANT and REVOKE haphazardly, on the spur of the moment.

Following are some examples that show how to use GRANT and REVOKE statements to set up permissions on a table. Suppose you are the owner of the `titles` table, and you've decided that most of the system's users should be allowed access to the table—except for data modification commands. You want to restrict INSERT, UPDATE, and DELETE to three specific users (Sara, John, and Leslie).

To handle this situation, you can choose between two approaches. The more straightforward is to assign specific permissions to specific users—which in this case would mean writing a GRANT statement with a detailed user list. You'd need one statement to grant all the permissions to Sara, John, and Leslie:

SQL
```
grant select, insert, delete, update
on titles
to sara, john, leslie
```

Now you'd need a statement to grant only SELECT permissions to all those other users:

SQL
```
grant select
on titles
to linda, pat, steve, chris, cathy, peter, lee, carl, karen
```

The list of users could be very long. Because all users are going to be granted SELECT privileges, it's easier to start with the general GRANT and then deal with specific additional permissions for specific users. Here's how: Begin with a statement that grants all users permission to select from `titles`:

SQL
```
grant select
on titles
to public
```

Now, to give Sara, John, and Leslie permission to modify data, you might issue this command:

SQL
```
grant update, insert, delete
on titles
to sara, john, leslie
```

Check your RDBMS documentation to see if REVOKEs to PUBLIC include the object owner. If they do, you'll need to include your name in specific GRANTs that follow general REVOKEs. Also ascertain how GRANT and REVOKE to PUBLIC interact with earlier specific commands involving that object. On some systems, PUBLIC permissions triumph, overruling previous GRANTs and REVOKEs. On other systems, holders of specific permissions are not affected by the general GRANT or REVOKE to PUBLIC.

SQL VARIANTS

Views as Security Mechanisms

The second major security mechanism in most relational database management systems involves using views in conjunction with GRANT and REVOKE. Permission to access the subset of data in a view must be explicitly granted or revoked, regardless of the set of permissions in force on the view's underlying table or tables.

Through a view, users can query and modify only the data they can see. The rest of the database is neither visible nor accessible. For example, you might not want some users to be able to access the `titles` table columns that have to do with money and sales. You could create a view of the `titles` table that omits those columns (call it `bookview`) and then give all users permission on the view, but give only some members of the sales group permission on the table. Here's how to do it on systems where permissions involving PUBLIC override previous specific grants. (To follow along, add more users to your system, or scale back the TO list):

SQL
```
revoke all
on titles
from public
```

```
grant all
on bookview
to public

grant all
on titles
to dba, mary, himmelwright, brady
```

By defining different views and selectively granting permissions on them, a user (or any combination of users) can be restricted to different subsets of data:

- Access can be restricted to a subset of the rows of a base table (a value-dependent subset). For example, you might define a view that contains only the rows for business and psychology books, in order to keep information about other types of books hidden from some users.
- Access can be restricted to a subset of the columns of a base table (a value-independent subset). For example, you might define a view that contains all the rows of the `titles` table but omits the `ytd_sales` and `advance` columns because this information is sensitive.
- Access can be restricted to a row-and-column subset of a base table. For example, you might define a view that contains information about only business and psychology books and then only nonfinancial information about them.
- Access can be restricted to the rows that qualify for a join of more than one base table. For example, you might define a view that joins the `titles`, `authors`, and `titleauthors` tables in order to display the names of the authors and the books they have written. This view would hide personal data about authors and financial information about the books.
- Access can be restricted to a statistical summary of data in a base table. For example, you might define a view that shows the average price of each type of book.
- Access can be restricted to a subset of another view or of some combination of views and base tables. For example, you might define a view on the view described in the previous example, containing the average price of cooking and computer books.

Creating views and setting up authorizations on them and on base tables are tasks often done as part of the data definition process. However, you can change the authorization scheme at any time, defining new views and writing new GRANT and REVOKE statements. For more details on views, you may want to review Chapter 9.

Transactions

A **transaction** is a logical unit of work. Transaction management means ensuring that a set of SQL statements is treated as a unit—as an indivisible entity. In other words, transaction management guarantees either that all the operations within a set (a transaction) are completed or that none of them is completed: A transaction is an all-or-nothing proposition.

Transactions are necessary for the purposes of

- Concurrency control (keeping users who are simultaneously accessing the database from colliding with each other); and
- Recovery (allowing the database system to bring the database back to a consistent state after a software failure).

SQL automatically manages all commands, including single-step change requests, as transactions. Much of the concurrency and recovery work accomplished by transaction management is invisible to ordinary users. You can also group a set of SQL statements into a **user-defined transaction** with transaction commands, discussed later in this chapter.

Transactions and Concurrency

In multiuser systems, more than one user and/or transaction can access the same data at the same time. Preventing simultaneous transactions from interfering with each other—controlling concurrency—means making sure that data is not seen or operated on by another user until a change is complete.

The purchase of airline tickets provides a classic example of one of the situations in which concurrency can be a problem. (It's so classic that it has a name: the **lost-update problem**.)

Suppose you call your favorite airline and ask for a ticket to Tahiti. The ticketing clerk submits a query to the database that selects all the available seats and tells you that there's one seat left on tonight's flight. As you ponder, another desperate tourist calls his travel agent to find out if he can get to Tahiti tonight. The travel agent submits the query to the database—the same query submitted by your ticketing clerk—and gets the same results. The travel agent informs the customer of the availability of a single seat. By now you've made up your mind to buy the ticket, and the airline's ticketing clerk updates the database to reflect the fact that the last seat has been sold. You start packing—unaware that the travel agent, who has no way of knowing about the update made by the ticketing clerk, has just sold the same ticket. In fact, the update made by the travel agent overwrites the update submitted by your ticketing clerk. When you get to the airport, there's no seat on the flight for you.

This example demonstrates one of the dangers posed by concurrency demands in large, shared database systems. Every RDBMS has ways of handling concurrency problems, but the details are outside the scope of this book.

Transactions and Recovery

A transaction is not only a unit of work but also a unit of recovery. Recovery refers to the database system's ability to get the database back on its feet after a system failure—that is, into the most current state of affairs that can be guaranteed to be consistent.

System failures are those that affect all transactions in progress but don't damage the database physically. Physical damage to a database is caused by media failure; protection against this kind of failure is provided by regularly backing up your database. In the case of system failure, the problem facing the database system's recovery mechanism is to figure out two things:

- Which transactions were incomplete at the time of the failure and should, therefore, be undone
- Which transactions were complete at the time of the failure but had not yet been written from the system's internal buffers to the physical database itself and should, therefore, be redone

The recovery mechanism is largely invisible to users.

User-Defined Transactions

User-defined transactions allow users to instruct the database management system to process any number of SQL statements as a single unit and to save or cancel the unit when the work is completed. Why user-defined transactions? A classic illustration of the need for transactions comes from banking—when a customer transfers money from a savings account to a checking account. In database terms, this banking transaction consists of two operations: First updating the savings balance to reflect a debit and then updating the checking balance with the credit. Unless these two updates are treated as a single transaction to the database, the danger exists that some other user might submit a query during the interval between them. If a bank officer happened to submit a query requesting the customer's balance after the money was deducted from the savings account but before it was added to the checking account, the results would be incorrect. Putting the two operations into a user-defined transaction ensures that the transfer of money is either accomplished completely or not at all.

In addition to giving the user control over transaction management, user-defined transactions also improve performance on those RDBMSs in which system overhead is incurred only once for a set of transactions, rather than once for each individual command.

User-defined Transaction Syntax   Syntax varies from system to system, but transaction commands usually contain keywords such as BEGIN, COMMIT, and ROLLBACK.

The SQL commands for beginning and ending transactions can enclose any number of SQL statements. Depending on the syntax your system supports, it'll look something like this:

SYNTAX

```
[begin transaction statement]
   SQL statement
   SQL statement
   SQL statement
commit transaction statement
```

Certain SQL commands cannot be included inside user-defined transactions. Check your system's reference manuals for details.

If a transaction must be canceled before it is committed—either because of some failure or because of a change of heart by the user—all of its statements that have been completed must be undone. A transaction can be canceled or rolled back with the ROLLBACK transaction command at any time before the COMMIT transaction command has been given. You can cancel either an entire transaction or part of it (if you have a savepoint mechanism for marking a savepoint). However, *you can't cancel a transaction after it has been committed.*

In most systems, the syntax of the ROLLBACK transaction command looks something like this:

```
[begin transaction statement]
   SQL statement
   SQL statement
   SQL statement
rollback transaction statement
```

Preventing Data Modification Errors   Here is a simple example of a user-defined transaction. Since you're planning to make some changes to pricing data and want to be sure you don't make any mistakes, you start out with a BEGIN TRANSACTION and then calculate the current average price in the titles table:

```
SQL
begin transaction
[command completed]
select avg(price)
from titles
avg(titles.price)
=================
          27.64
[1 row]
```

Next, you issue a data modification command, and check to see its effect:

```
SQL
update titles
set price = price * 2
[18 rows]
select avg(price)
from titles
avg(titles.price)
=================
          55.28
[1 row]
```

You realize you've made a mistake—you didn't mean to double all the prices. Since you formally began the transaction, you can roll it back, canceling the change:

```
SQL
rollback
[18 rows]
select avg(price)
from titles
avg(titles.price)
==================
           27.64
[1 row]
```

SQL VARIANTS

In many systems, data modification commands are implicit transactions. You can type ROLLBACK or COMMIT without a preceding BEGIN. However, you may cancel all the way back to the most recent COMMIT or ROLLBACK, perhaps unraveling more work than you expected. To avoid this problem, start a new transaction with a COMMIT (or a BEGIN, if it is allowed).

Performance

Performance is a critical issue in relational database management systems. Multiuser, production-oriented applications are especially sensitive to performance problems. Databases running on these systems tend to be larger, their operations more complex. The number of users and transactions puts heavy demands on the system, and the tasks for which the applications are responsible are often time critical. However, performance sometimes becomes a matter of concern even for single-user database systems. No one wants to wait an unreasonable length of time for the results of a query or the execution of a data modification statement.

Unfortunately, many aspects of performance are outside the control of users. Instead, people depend on the features and capabilities built into the system by the vendor. If you're currently shopping for a relational database management system, you'll be particularly interested in the next section: It briefly discusses the use of **benchmarking** to compare the performance of different database systems. Benchmarking can also be used to evaluate how different database designs and indexes affect performance.

Following the discussion of benchmarking, the rest of this section mentions some of the ways that users can influence performance:

- A good logical database design can make a big difference in how well your system performs. Make sure you understand what kind of work your database is tuned for and what it looks like—the tables, views, and other objects in it. An entity-relationship diagram is very helpful. If you don't have one, use system tools to sketch out the major tables.
- The way you structure your queries can affect performance. You get the biggest wins by writing queries that take advantage of indexes.
- Some database systems provide tools for monitoring and fine-tuning performance, including some control of physical design (where and how data is physically stored). You can use these tools to analyze problem queries.

Benchmarking

If you're using a high-volume, production-oriented relational database management system, you've probably heard vendors making claims about the number of transactions per second their systems deliver. The numbers they bandy about are based on the results of benchmarks or tests that measure the performance of a system in a controlled environment using a standard methodology.

Interpreting and analyzing claims about performance benchmarks are notoriously difficult. Benchmarking is technically complex, and the results announced by vendors inevitably reflect the tendency of any interested party to show his or her product at its best. The technical details of benchmark evaluation are the province of database experts and are beyond the scope of this book, but you'll find some suggested readings in Appendix E, Resources.

Here are a few nontechnical questions you can ask about performance claims based on benchmarking:

- Is one of the accepted standard tests used? Or has the vendor selected the test on the basis of how well its product does on it?
- Are the benchmark process and results validated by an independent and reputable organization?
- Is the hardware configuration that was used for the benchmark similar to what you'll be running on? Consider not only the type of computer,

but also how its memory is configured, whether it was in a network, and so on.

- Is the software that was used for the benchmark the commercially available version of the product, or was the benchmark test run on a preproduction or special release?
- Are the results of the benchmark consistent and repeatable?

Benchmarks are typically associated with database systems that will be used for mission-critical applications involving dozens to hundreds of users and very large databases—hundreds or thousands of megabytes. They are used for making performance comparisons among products, for planning the kind of hardware you'll need for a given level of performance, and for making decisions about database design and indexing. Two versions of a database design, for example, can be created and tested against a benchmark to determine which is better for your purposes.

Design and Indexing

You can greatly enhance performance by paying close attention to logical database design. The importance of design for performance (as well as in other areas) belies the often repeated notion that with a relational database system, you need to specify only what you want, not how to get it. The relational database is no smarter than your design.

Chapters 2 and 3 explain how to analyze your data and follow the normalization guidelines in order to wind up with a good, clean database design. You may remember from the discussion in these chapters that indexes speed retrieval considerably while slowing down data modification to some extent and that splitting tables for the purposes of normalization can slow the retrieval of data when a query that could have been answered by looking at one table now requires the system to look at more than one table. Multitable queries can adversely affect performance for several reasons. Because the data is dispersed among several tables, additional disk reads may be required to find it. Then, once the data is located, the system must integrate it. Finally, accessing more tables incurs the overhead of setting more locks.

Thus, with respect to performance, the basic principle is to consider how the database will primarily be used. If the number of queries to be run far surpasses the number of data modification statements, build a lot of indexes and minimize the number of joins that are required by designing fewer and larger tables. For the fastest response to data modification statements, use as few indexes as possible and normalize thoroughly.

Optimizing Queries

When you submit a SQL statement to the database management system, a lot of work that you don't see gets done. In fact, SQL is considered a nonprocedural language precisely because it does not require the user to specify the steps the system must take to execute the command. Instead, the user simply states what is being sought.

The strength of the nonprocedural approach is the same as its drawback. To state it positively, the system does the work for you. The bad news is that once you're committed to a particular database design, you usually have no choice but to trust the system's intelligence rather than your own.

Optimizers   The part of the database management system responsible for analyzing a SQL statement is called the **query optimizer**. The query optimizer decomposes each query into its constituent parts and rearranges it to run as efficiently as possible. It evaluates several search strategies or access paths, deciding on the most useful indexes to use and on the path that requires the smallest number of logical page accesses. In other words, the query optimizer generates a plan, determining the most efficient path between the user's SQL statement and the data needed to carry out the assigned task.

The query optimizers of relational database management systems have two general approaches to optimization: rule-based and cost-based.

- In a rule-based system, the optimizer makes choices based on a set of ranked guidelines.
- In a cost-based system, the optimizer looks at processing options and chooses the one that is "cheapest" in terms of time, according to statistics based on the distribution of key values. These give a much better estimate of retrieval time than simple statistics, which assume that the index's key values are uniformly distributed. If you're using a version of SQL that relies on distribution statistics, it's important to reissue the command that keeps statistics current whenever you've added, deleted, or modified a bunch of new data because those actions are likely to change the distribution of the index keys. If the system's information about key distribution is not kept up-to-date, it uses the old information and may make a bad choice about how to process a query.

Commands related to cost-based optimizers include UPDATE STATISTICS in Transact-SQL and ANALYZE in Oracle. Microsoft SQL Server also supports a command that tells you when the UPDATE STATISTICS command was last run (STAT_DATE).

Rule- or cost-based query optimizers have a library of standard query-processing strategies (for example, to use the column's index) that are applied in various query situations. If none of the strategies known to the system applies to the SQL statement being examined, the system resorts to the default strategy of reading every row of the table or tables referenced by the query (a table scan). Whole-table scans always produce the desired results, but on a table of any size at all, they are horribly slow.

Queries After good design, your best route to efficient queries involves understanding your indexes and constructing WHERE clauses that take advantage of the indexes—or that at least don't prevent the indexes from being used. The easiest elements for an optimizer to work with are comparison operators (=, >, <, and variants) or operators that can be translated to comparison operators (BETWEEN and LIKE clauses that do not begin with a wildcard).

Anything else may make your indexes unavailable. Indexes point to column values. If the column value you provide on the left side of the WHERE clause is unknown or is part of a complex expression or is negative, the index may have no route to follow to find the row. Here is a list of WHERE clause activities that could get you in trouble. Be sure to check your vendor for specifics (Some of the functions may be unfamiliar—they are discussed in a later chapter.)

- Comparing columns in the same table (both values are unknown)
  ```
  select au_id
  from authors
  where au_fname = au_lname
  ```

- Choosing columns with low-selectivity indexes (most rows have the same value, so using the index offers no advantage)
  ```
  select title_id
  from titles
  where contract = 1
  ```

- Doing math on a column before comparing it to a constant
```
select title_id, price
from titles
where (price * ytd_sales) > 150000
```

- Applying a function to a column before comparing it to a constant
```
select au_fname, au_lname
from authors
where substr(au_id, 1, 3) = '213'
```

- Matching with LIKE, when the first character is unknown
```
select au_fname, au_lname, au_id
from authors
where au_id like '%9391%'
```

- Converting column values to another datatype
```
select sonum, stor_id
from sales
where cast ( sonum as varchar(2) ) = '2'
```

- Comparing to NULL
```
select title
from titles
where title_id is null
```

- Negating with NOT
```
select title, price, title_id
from titles
where not title_id < 'PS8888'
```

- Using OR or IN
```
select title, price, title_id
from titles
where title_id in ( 'BU1032',  'BU1111', 'BU2075',
'BU7832')
```

- Using multicolumn indexes when the commonly queried item is not the first element in the query, as if you're looking in the phone book for all the people with the first name Sandy, rather than looking for all the folks surnamed Smith. It doesn't work because the phone book is in last-name order.
```
select au_fname, au_lname
from salesdetails
where au_fname = 'Ann'
```

You can rewrite many of these queries to take advantage of indexes. The IN query, for example, could become a LIKE or range query (in this case, it's not always possible).

Other Tools for Monitoring and Boosting Performance

Relational database management systems that have been developed for production-oriented, multiuser, online applications often provide a variety of tools for monitoring and fine-tuning performance. Many of these features are outside the province of SQL per se; some systems expect you to accomplish these tasks using operating system facilities rather than those provided by the database system.

Logging Most relational database management systems allow you to turn off the logging of database transactions, which speeds updates by saving the time it takes to enter the changes in the log. Of course, in case of a media failure, you can't rely on the database system to recover any of the changes that have been made if there is no log.

It makes sense to suspend logging temporarily before you load a large amount of data into the database—if the operation can be easily repeated in case of a media failure. But remember to make a backup copy before you begin so that you can easily start over.

Monitoring Execution Plans Check to see if your system provides a facility that allows you to monitor a query's execution plan. You can use this tool to check on SQL's work and to see how its plan varies depending on where you put indexes and how you have written the statement.

Other monitoring tools may display information about how a given SQL statement was processed: how many table scans, logical accesses (cache reads), and physical accesses (disk reads) the system did for each table or view that is referenced in a query; how many pages it wrote for each data modification command; and how much CPU time it took to parse and compile each command or to execute each step of the command.

The RDBMS included on the CD, Adaptive Server Anywhere, includes some information about performance in the Interactive SQL Statistics window. You can usually see if the optimizer chose an index or did a table scan. You can also use the PLAN command for more detailed information.

SQL VARIANTS

Adaptive Server Anywhere

select plan ('
          select title_id, sonum
          from salesdetails
          where sonum = 5
          ')
Estimate 4 I/O operations
Scan salesdetails **using unique index sdind**
for rows where sonum equals 5
Estimate getting here 8 times

Transact SQL provides the SET SHOWPLAN ON command. Here's how you use it on SQL Server. The NOEXEC command suppresses results.

SQL Server

set showplan_text on;

set noexec on;

select title_id, sonum
from salesdetails
where sonum = 5

StmtText

Index Seek(OBJECT:([bookbiz].[dbo].[salesdetails].[**sdind**]), SEEK:
([salesdetails].[sonum]=[@1]) ORDERED)
(1 row(s) affected)

With Oracle SQL Plus, use the EXPLAIN PLAN command, or set AUTOTRACE ON. In either case, begin by following directions in your documentation to create the PLAN_TABLE.

Oracle

SQL> **set autotrace on;**

SQL> select title_id, sonum
   2   from salesdetails
   3   where sonum = 5;

TITLE_   SONUM
------ ----------
MC3021   5

```
Execution Plan
-----------------------------------------------------------
   0       SELECT STATEMENT Optimizer=CHOOSE
   1   0   INDEX (RANGE SCAN) OF 'SDIND' (UNIQUE)
Statistics
-----------------------------------------------------------
         0   recursive calls
         0   db block gets
         2   consistent gets
         0   physical reads
         0   redo size
       427   bytes sent via SQL*Net to client
       425   bytes received via SQL*Net from client
         2   SQL*Net roundtrips to/from client
         0   sorts (memory)
         0   sorts (disk)
         1   rows processed
```

Index Management   You may have commands that give you control of how the indexes are set up. For example, indexing options provided by Transact-SQL (FILLFACTOR, MAX_ROWS_PER_PAGE) allow you to control how full to make each page of a new index. This number affects performance because of the time it takes for the system to split index pages when they become completely full.

Data Integrity

Broadly speaking, data integrity refers to the accuracy and consistency of the data in the database. Ideally, database software would provide a variety of mechanisms for checking on data integrity; unfortunately, several important kinds of integrity are unsupported by most relational systems.

In practice, many requirements for integrity are often met through special-purpose application code. The disadvantages of assigning the task of integrity control to application programs include the amount of extra work involved in writing and maintaining integrity-checking code, the potential for both duplicating work and introducing inconsistencies when more than one application uses the same database, and the ease with which constraints coded into applications can be bypassed by users with access to the underlying database.

There are several kinds of data integrity. At the most basic level, all database systems (not just relational ones) should be able to guarantee that a value being entered is the correct datatype and that it's within the range of values supported by the system. Different relational systems provide different assortments of datatypes, but all of them check values being entered and reject the data modification statement if the value is wrong for the specified datatype. The null status of the column is also checked on data entry. Finally, certain datatypes—usually character types—can (or must) be associated with user-specified lengths. Some systems reject data entries that exceed the maximum length for the datatype, others truncate the entered value to fit.

Three kinds of integrity are discussed in this section:

- Domain constraints
- Entity integrity
- Referential integrity

Domain Constraints

A **domain** is the set of logically related values from which the value in a particular column can be drawn. Here are some examples of domains in the bookbiz database:

- The domain of the authors.au_id column is all the Social Security numbers issued by the U.S. government.
- The domain of the authors.city and publishers.city columns is all the cities in the United States; for authors.state and publishers.state, it's all the states in the United States. (Note the assumption that all authors live in the United States.)
- The domain of titles.type is the following set of values: business, popular_comp, psychology, mod_cook, and trad_cook.
- The domain of titles.title_id is the set of values with the following format: The first two characters are capitalized letters of the alphabet from the set BU, PC, PS, MC, TC; the next four characters are integers between 0 and 9, inclusive.
- The domain of titleauthors.royaltyshare is all numbers between 0 and 1, inclusive.

Notice the different kinds of logical relationships among the values in these domains. Some of the domains represent application-determined constraints—that is, business rules and regulations. For example, the constraints on the format of the title ID numbers were determined by someone in the publishing company. The publisher might also decide that the prices of books must be no less than $1.99 and no greater than $99.99; dollars-and-cents amounts between those two values would then be the domain for `titles.price`.

Other domains are based not on business rules but on physical or mathematical constraints. The values in `titleauthors.royaltyshare`, for example, represent percentages, so they must be numbers between 0 and 1. As another example, suppose the publisher wanted to record the gender of each author in the database. The domain for that column would be limited by (widely accepted interpretations of) human biology to the values `female`, `male`, and `unknown`.

The descriptions of the domains in the preceding list were deduced from an examination of the values in the `bookbiz` database. You can use the CHECK constraint in the CREATE TABLE statement to express many of them—lists of values (like the domain for `titles.type`), ranges (like the domain for `titleauthors.royaltyshare`), or format (like the domain for `titles.title_id`).

SQL VARIANTS

Transact-SQL supports an additional mechanism for specifying domains, the CREATE RULE command. A rule is a named database object that can be associated with any number of columns or with all columns of a specified user-defined datatype. The Transact-SQL rule mechanism is limited, however, in that the rule definition cannot reference another column in the database.

One last note: Recall from Chapter 7 that if the values in two columns have the same domains, joins between these columns are usually logical. For example, `publishers.city` and `authors.city` have the same domain (all cities in the United States); therefore it would be meaningful to join on these columns.

Entity Integrity

Entity integrity requires that no component of a primary key be allowed to have a null value. That is, a single-column primary key can't accept nulls, neither can any of the columns in a composite primary key.

The entity-integrity constraint derives from the relational model, not from the requirements of any particular application. And entity integrity is not a concern in other models of database management the way domain constraints are. The requirement that no primary key contain a null value is based on the fact that real-world entities are distinguished from each other by primary keys that serve as unique identifiers. In fact, entity integrity is as much a design issue as it is an integrity issue.

You should guarantee entity integrity by designating a primary key that will not accept null values when you design your database. You can implement it by specifying NOT NULL in the CREATE TABLE statement and using the PRIMARY KEY constraint or by creating a unique index for the column. (See Chapters 2 and 3 for a review of these concepts.)

Referential Integrity

Informally speaking, referential integrity concerns the relationship between the values in logically related tables. In the relational model, it means guaranteeing the logical consistency of the database by making sure that the values of a primary key and the foreign keys that point to it always match.

Chapter 2 explains that foreign key/primary key relationships are planned during the design of a database; they represent the logical relationships among data (although their presence in no way limits the possible access paths among the data). In considering referential integrity, the question is what the database system can do to guarantee the maintenance of matching values between foreign keys and the primary key to which they point (that is, that referential constraints are not violated). Chapter 3 introduces the REFERENCES and FOREIGN KEY constraints in the CREATE TABLE statement. These clauses ensure some referential integrity—they allow you to set up checks that prevent a foreign key from being added if it does not correspond to a primary key. However, this is only one issue in referential integrity.

For example, changing an author ID can present a problem because the alteration would destroy the connection between the authors, titles, and `titleauthors` tables. How do you deal with the primary key—changing the ID in the `authors` table or deleting or updating a publisher ID in the `publishers` table when books in the `titles` table still reference the old ID? One approach is to decide that primary keys should never be changed and, therefore, prevent these updates. The REFERENCES clause prevents this kind of change in the foreign key (`titleauthors.au_id`), and in the primary key (`authors.au_id`).

Another answer is to **cascade** the update or delete operation automatically to the matching foreign keys. For example, if a publisher's ID number changes, the system would change the matching IDs in `titles.pub_id` in exactly the same way, without intervention by the user.

A third possibility is to accept data modification operations to primary key values, even if they upset referential integrity, but first to change the matching foreign key values to NULL. (Of course, if the foreign key has been defined so as not to accept null values, this course of action is out.)

To summarize briefly, there are in general three possible responses to an attempt to delete or update a primary key to which a foreign key points:

- **Restrict**—the delete or update operation on the primary key is rejected unless there are no matching foreign key values.
- **Cascade**—the delete or update operation is automatically applied to the foreign keys whose values matched the "old" value of the deleted or updated primary key.
- **Nullify**—before the delete or update operation on the primary key is committed, the values of matching foreign keys are set to NULL.

Unfortunately, many SQL dialects do not provide mechanisms for controlling primary key referential integrity. In these cases, the closest you can come to guaranteeing referential integrity is to revoke all permissions for deleting and updating a primary key column.

However, as the importance of referential integrity becomes more and more widely recognized, vendors are beginning to address it with special procedures or triggers.

Stored Procedures and Triggers

At present, many RDBMSs offer stored procedures and triggers—named collections of SQL code, usually including non-ANSI SQL extensions, created to handle more complex problems than a CHECK or REFERENCES constraint can take on.

Triggers, for example, are set off ("triggered") by specific SQL operations—most commonly UPDATE, INSERT, or DELETE.

Triggers represent a generalized method for dealing with integrity issues:

- Triggers can enforce restrictions much more complex than those defined with rules, CHECK constraints, or REFERENCES constraints. For example, a trigger can reject updates that attempt to increase a book's price by more than 1 percent of its advance or prevent all price increases greater than 100 percent.
- Triggers can be used to recalculate ongoing tallies. For example, you might write a trigger that updates the `ytd_sales` column in the `titles` table whenever a row is added to the `salesdetails` table.

There is no current standard for stored procedures or triggers, and they vary considerably from system to system, both semantically and syntactically. Many database programmers avoid the problem of porting triggers by using Java code. However, there is hope! The ANSI committee is looking at standardizing trigger functionality. Triggers and stored procedures are included in the forthcoming SQL-3 draft.

Summary

This chapter has brought the discussion of generic SQL closer to the real world by touching on topics such as

- Data Security
- Transactions
- Performance
- Data Integrity

We will not explore these issues further as relational database management systems differ widely from each other in their implementations of backup and recovery tools, transaction control, and access strategies.

The next chapter pulls together many of the SQL statements you have learned so far, presenting more complex pieces of code. It also introduces functions and gives examples of nesting functions inside one another.

Chapter 11

Solving Business Problems

In This Chapter

- Using SQL on the Job
- Thinking Conditionally
- Formatting and Displaying Data
- Playing with Patterns
- Avoiding Mistakes

Using SQL on the Job

When you get right down to it, whatever you know about SQL is useful only to the degree that it helps you get your work done. SQL is a business tool.

Earlier chapters focused on teaching SQL's capabilities; now it's time to look at how people really use SQL on the job. Most of the material in this chapter was collected from discussions (sometimes heated!) on the Internet: Puzzled SQL users submitted SQL questions to the world of network subscribers, often including code samples and background descriptions with their appeals for help. Readers volunteered solutions, added to or vigorously disagreed with previous answers, and occasionally "flamed" the inquirer for poorly analyzed materials.

Out of all this give-and-take, some common themes emerged. Certain questions, such as how to format results, came up over and over. It became clear that a "cookbook" with code "recipes" for dealing with common issues could prove valuable.

This book deals with generic or industry SQL, rather than with any particular vendor's implementation. However, code recipes require attention to the specific if they are going to have any real value, and they need testing. We've used Adaptive Server Anywhere in our examples and have included notes on

Adaptive Server Enterprise, SQL Server, and Oracle as needed. You may need to modify some of the items in the cookbook if you are using a different database system. However, we have avoided questions that are strictly system-specific (for example, stored procedure or trigger code).

In short, this chapter is a collection of brief pieces of as-generic-as-possible SQL code. Each one is based on a real question posted on the Internet. The problems and solutions are modified to work with the sample database, *book-biz*. They are not terribly difficult, but they represent the kind of things typical users get stuck on. The assumption is that if someone had the problem, you may have it too.

Use this chapter as a SQL cookbook, but be a creative chef: Find interesting recipes and modify the ingredients to suit your palate.

Thinking Conditionally

Have you ever wished for a SQL IF? Although that doesn't exist, except as a vendor extension, SQL does support a number of conditional functions. Their names vary from system to system, but what they have in common is the ability to test an expression and take action, based on the result. In this section, you'll examine CASE/DECODE and functions that deal with null values.

CASE/DECODE

The CASE function allows you to use conditional logic pretty much anyplace you can use an expression. CASE is flexible and efficient and comes in two forms. They look like this:

SYNTAX

```
CASE expr
WHEN value1 THEN result1
  [WHEN value2 THEN result2]... [ELSE resultn]
END


CASE
WHEN condition1 THEN result1
   [WHEN condition2 THEN result2]... [ELSE  resultn]
END
```

Let's start with an example that translates succinct codes into more descriptive strings. The `titles` table includes a `contract` column that allows entries of either 0 or 1 to indicate the contract status. But 0 and 1 have no intrinsic meaning for contracts. Looking at a report, you'd be unclear which books were signed up and which were not. CASE examines the `contract` value and assigns different strings, depending on the value. Because the logic is in the SELECT clause, not the WHERE clause, and the table is traversed only once, you get good performance.

SQL

```
select title_id, substr (title, 1, 25) as book,
    case contract
        when 1 then 'contract on file'
        when 0 then 'no contract'
    end as contract
from titles
order by title_id
```

title_id	book	contract
==========	==========================	=================
BU1032	The Busy Executive's Data	contract on file
BU1111	Cooking with Computers: S	contract on file
BU2075	You Can Combat Computer S	contract on file
BU7832	Straight Talk About Compu	contract on file
MC2222	Silicon Valley Gastronomi	contract on file
MC3021	The Gourmet Microwave	contract on file
MC3026	The Psychology of Compute	no contract
PC1035	But Is It User Friendly?	contract on file
PC8888	Secrets of Silicon Valley	contract on file
PC9999	Net Etiquette	no contract
PS1372	Computer Phobic and Non-P	contract on file
PS2091	Is Anger the Enemy?	contract on file
PS2106	Life Without Fear	contract on file
PS3333	Prolonged Data Deprivatio	contract on file
PS7777	Emotional Security: A New	contract on file
TC3218	Onions, Leeks, and Garlic	contract on file
TC4203	Fifty Years in Buckingham	contract on file
TC7777	Sushi, Anyone?	contract on file

[18 rows]

Using the other form of CASE, the query looks like this:

```
SQL
select title_id, substr (title, 1, 25) as book,
 case when contract = 1 then 'contract on file'
      when contract = 0 then 'no contract'
         end as contract
from titles
order by title_id
```

Oracle and Informix support CASE and an earlier non-ANSI form, called DECODE. The syntax is similar.

SQL VARIANTS

```
DECODE (value, if1, then1 [ , if2, then2, ]... , else)
```

Rewriting the previous query with DECODE gives you this:

```
Oracle
SQL> select title_id, substr (title, 1, 25) as book,
  2  decode (contract, 1, 'contract on file',
  3                     0, 'no contract' )
  4    from titles
  5    order by title_id;
```

The results are the same.

In this example, you produce a report that compares sales date and ship date and prints notes depending on the difference. (Date functions vary widely from system to system. DATEDIFF, supported by ASA and Transact-SQL, takes three arguments: the unit, the early date, and the late date.)

```
Adaptive Server Anywhere
select sales.sonum, salesdetails.sonum, sdate,  date_shipped,
 case
   when datediff (dd, sdate , date_shipped)  between 0 and 2 then
      'on time'
```

```
  when datediff (dd, sdate , date_shipped)  < 0 then 'ERROR--
    check dates'
  when datediff (dd, sdate , date_shipped)  > 2  then 'LATE'
  when date_shipped is NULL then 'NO DATE'
 end as note
from sales, salesdetails
where sales.sonum = salesdetails.sonum
```

sonum	sonum	sdate	date_shipped	note
1	1	Sep 13 1998 12:00 am	Sep 15 1998 12:00 am	on time
2	2	Sep 14 1998 12:00 am	Sep 15 1998 12:00 am	on time
3	3	Sep 14 1998 12:00 am	Sep 18 1998 12:00 am	LATE
4	4	Sep 14 1998 12:00 am	Sep 18 1998 12:00 am	LATE
5	5	Sep 14 1998 12:00 am	Sep 14 1998 12:00 am	on time
6	6	Sep 14 1998 12:00 am	Sep 22 1998 12:00 am	LATE
7	7	Sep 13 1998 12:00 am	Sep 20 1998 12:00 am	LATE
8	8	Sep 14 1998 12:00 am	Sep 14 1998 12:00 am	on time
9	9	Mar 11 2001 12:00 am	Mar 28 2001 12:00 am	LATE
19	19	Feb 21 2001 12:00 am	Mar 15 2001 12:00 am	LATE
10	10	Oct 28 2000 12:00 am	Oct 29 2000 12:00 am	on time
11	11	Dec 12 2000 12:00 am	Jan 12 2001 12:00 am	LATE
12	12	May 22 2000 12:00 am	May 24 2000 12:00 am	on time
13	13	May 24 2000 12:00 am	May 24 2000 12:00 am	on time
14	14	May 29 2000 12:00 am	May 29 2000 12:00 am	on time
14	14	May 29 2000 12:00 am	Apr 29 2000 12:00 am	ERROR--check dates
14	14	May 29 2000 12:00 am	May 29 2000 12:00 am	on time
14	14	May 29 2000 12:00 am	Jun 13 2000 12:00 am	LATE
15	15	Jun 15 2000 12:00 am	Jun 15 2000 12:00 am	on time
15	15	Jun 15 2000 12:00 am	May 30 2000 12:00 am	ERROR--check dates
15	15	Jun 15 2000 12:00 am	Jun 17 2000 12:00 am	on time

[21 rows]

A final example provides a spreadsheet display, listing each author associated with a particular book on a single line. The separate CASE statements put the au_ids into the proper cells. Only one book has three authors.

SQL
```
select  title_id,
    min (case au_ord when 1 then au_id end) as A1,
```

```
    min (case au_ord when 2 then au_id end) as A2,
    min (case au_ord when 3 then au_id end) as A3
  from titleauthors
  group by title_id
  order by title_id
  title_id A1            A2           A3
  ======== ============ ============ ============
  BU1032   409-56-7008  213-46-8915  (NULL)
  BU1111   724-80-9391  267-41-2394  (NULL)
  BU2075   213-46-8915  (NULL)       (NULL)
  BU7832   274-80-9391  (NULL)       (NULL)
  MC2222   712-45-1867  (NULL)       (NULL)
  MC3021   722-51-5454  899-46-2035  (NULL)
  PC1035   238-95-7766  (NULL)       (NULL)
  PC8888   427-17-2319  846-92-7186  (NULL)
  PC9999   486-29-1786  (NULL)       (NULL)
  PS1372   756-30-7391  724-80-9391  (NULL)
  PS2091   998-72-3567  899-46-2035  (NULL)
  PS2106   998-72-3567  (NULL)       (NULL)
  PS3333   172-32-1176  (NULL)       (NULL)
  PS7777   486-29-1786  (NULL)       (NULL)
  TC3218   807-91-6654  (NULL)       (NULL)
  TC4203   648-92-1872  (NULL)       (NULL)
  TC7777   672-71-3249  267-41-2394  472-27-2349
  [17 rows]
```

Another form of the same query looks like this:

SQL

```
select  title_id,
 min (case when au_ord = 1  then au_id end) as A1,
 min (case when au_ord =2 then au_id end) as A2,
 min (case when au_ord = 3 then au_id end) as A3
 from titleauthors
 group by title_id
 order by title_id
```

Changing Null Displays

If members of your audience are not database-literate, they might find NULL confusing and decide it means zero. You can prevent trouble by using a function to substitute a value for NULL. On Adaptive Server Anywhere, this function is COALESCE (with two arguments) or ISNULL.

```
COALESCE ( expr, value-to-substitute-if-null)
```

The `type` column in the `titles` table allows NULL. Here's how the data looks

```
SQL
select title_id, type
from titles
title_id type
======== ============
PC8888   popular comp
BU1032   business
PS7777   psychology
PS3333   psychology
BU1111   business
MC2222   mod_cook
TC7777   trad_cook
TC4203   trad_cook
PC1035   popular_comp
BU2075   business
PS2091   psychology
PS2106   psychology
MC3021   mod_cook
TC3218   trad_cook
MC3026   (NULL)
BU7832   business
PS1372   psychology
PC9999   popular_comp
[18 rows]
```

When you add COALESCE, the report is easier to read:

SQL
```
select title_id, coalesce( type, 'UNDECIDED') as type
from titles
title_id type
======== ============
PC8888   popular_comp
BU1032   business
PS7777   psychology
PS3333   psychology
BU1111   business
MC2222   mod_cook
TC7777   trad_cook
TC4203   trad_cook
PC1035   popular_comp
BU2075   business
PS2091   psychology
PS2106   psychology
MC3021   mod_cook
TC3218   trad_cook
MC3026   UNDECIDED
BU7832   business
PS1372   psychology
PC9999   popular_comp
[18 rows]
```

For translating NULL, Transact-SQL also supports ISNULL, and Oracle uses NVL. The syntax is similar.

SQL VARIANTS

Oracle
```
SQL> select title_id, nvl (type, 'UNDECIDED')
  2  from titles;
```

Formatting and Displaying Data

The way you store data isn't always the best way to display it. If you have application programs such as report generators connected to your database, they may provide all the formatting that you need. Sometimes, however, it makes sense to use the string, number, and date functions that most database vendors support. Many of them became part of the ANSI SQL standard in 1992.

But remember: SQL is *not* a display tool! It was designed to retrieve data, not to make it look good. If some of the recipes in this section look convoluted, it's because they are.

This section includes code for

- Displaying one column as two;
- Displaying two columns as one; and
- Converting data from one datatype to another;

Displaying One Column as Two

Sometimes data stored in the database as one column make more sense to users when it appears as two or more separate displays. This is particularly true when the column consists of data that seem to be of mixed types, as in some composite identification fields (a health insurance number, for example, may consist of the familiar nine-digit Social Security number plus an alphabetic company or geographic code).

In the `titles` table, the `title_id` column comes close to this situation. It contains six characters: two letters followed by four digits. Here's some sample data (the WHERE clause limits the rows returned):

```
SQL
select title_id
from titles
where price > 29.99
title_id
========
PC8888
PC1035
TC3218
PS1372
[4 rows]
```

To display the letter part of the column separately from the numeric part, you can use character (also called string) functions in your SELECT. Once you have the data looking the way you want it, create a view. That way, users always see the divided columns instead of the original ones.

The first step is to define the two column subsets with a function called SUBSTR that returns part of a character or binary string. The syntax is this:

```
SUBSTR ( expression, start [ , length ] )
```

SYNTAX

You can see how SUBSTR works by running a SELECT on `title_id`, giving each fragment of the column a new name:

```
SQL
select substr(title_id,1,2) as alpha,
  substr(title_id,3,4) as num
from titles
where price > 29.99

alpha num
===== ====
PC    8888
PC    1035
TC    3218
PS    1372
[4 rows]
```

The optional third argument allows two variants for the second substring. The first counts from the start value to the end of the string. The second (with a negative sign) counts the specified number of characters back from the end of the string.

```
SQL
select substr(title_id,1,2) as alpha,
  substr (title_id, 3, 4) as num,
  substr (title_id, 3) as no3rd,
  substr (title_id, -4) as countback
from titles
where price > 29.99
```

alpha	num	no3rd	countback
=======	=====	=======	===========
PC	8888	8888	8888
PC	1035	1035	1035
TC	3218	3218	3218
PS	1372	1372	1372

[4 rows]

SQL VARIANTS

The ANSI version is slightly different:

```
SUBSTRING (char_expr FROM start [ FOR size ] )
```

In Transact-SQL, the function is called SUBSTRING. The arguments are the same as for SUBSTR, but a length value is required, rather than optional. You must provide all three arguments, and none of them may be negative.

Now that you have split the alphabetic and numeric parts of the code, hide this work from users by creating a view. When users run queries, they'll be unaware that `alpha` and `num` are actually parts of `title_id`. The CREATE VIEW looks like this (once again, the WHERE clause is included only to limit the number of rows returned for this example):

```
SQL
create view split
as
select substr (title_id, 1, 2) as alpha,
    substr (title_id, 3, 4) as num
from titles
where price > 29.99
[view created]
```

After you revoke permission to use the table and grant rights to use the view, users can see the two columns with this query:

SQL
```
select  *
from split
alpha num
===== ====
PC    8888
PC    1035
TC    3218
PS    1372
[4 rows]
```

Displaying Two Columns as One

Another function (concatenate) allows you to put expressions together. It is represented as a double pipe (||). The syntax looks like this:

```
char_expr || char_expr
```

SYNTAX

For example, you can concatenate first and last names into one string:

SQL
```
select au_fname  || au_lname as Writer
from authors
where state > 'CA'
Writer
=======================================================
AlbertRinger
AnneRinger
MichelDeFrance
SylviaPanteley
MorningstarGreene
Innesdel Castillo
ReginaldBlotchet-Halls
MeanderSmith
[8 rows]
```

To make the names more readable, add a space in quotes after the first name and another concatenation symbol after the space:

SQL
```
select au_fname || ' '  || au_lname as Writer
from authors
where state > 'CA'
Writer
====================================================
Albert Ringer
Anne Ringer
Michel DeFrance
Sylvia Panteley
Morningstar Greene
Innes del Castillo
Reginald Blotchet-Halls
Meander Smith
[8 rows]
```

This combination of SUBSTR and concatenation gives you the first initial and the full last name:

SQL
```
select substr ( au_fname, 1, 1) || '.' || ' '  || au_lname as Writer
from authors
where state > 'CA'
Writer
================================================
A. Ringer
A. Ringer
M. DeFrance
S. Panteley
M. Greene
I. del Castillo
R. Blotchet-Halls
M. Smith
[8 rows]
```

Transact-SQL has a different symbol for concatenation, the plus sign (+). **SQL** The previous code looks like this (and remember SUBSTR is SUBSTRING in **VARIANTS** this dialect):

```
SQL Server
select substring ( au_fname, 1, 1) + '.' + ' '  + au_lname as Writer
from authors
where state > 'CA'
```

You can use these functions in the WHERE clause to find rows. For example, you can locate information about M. Greene like this:

```
SQL
select au_id, au_fname,  au_lname, phone
from authors
where substring ( au_fname, 1, 1) + '.' + ' '  + au_lname = 'M. Greene'
au_id          au_fname            au_lname                       phone
===========    ================    ============================   ============
527-72-3246 Morningstar         Greene                         615 297-2723
```

Converting from One Datatype to Another

Some SQL engines do a lot of autoconverting. They allow you to use character functions with numbers or dates and number functions with character datatype numbers. Other systems are not as forgiving. SQL provides convert functions to help when autoconverting isn't available.

For example, the percentage of royalty each author gets is listed as a decimal value. If you want to display it with a percent sign, you can multiply by 100 and convert to an integer. Our sample database uses the ANSI CAST function.

```
CAST (expr AS datatype)
```

SYNTAX

Here is a query that shows both the original format and the CAST result:

SQL
```
select title_id, au_id,  royaltyshare,
    cast ( royaltyshare * 100 as int) || '%' as percent
from titleauthors
order by title_id
title_id au_id       royaltyshare percent
======== =========== ============ ============
BU1032   409-56-7008          .60 60%
BU1032   213-46-8915          .40 40%
BU1111   724-80-9391          .60 60%
BU1111   267-41-2394          .40 40%
BU2075   213-46-8915         1.00 100%
BU7832   274-80-9391         1.00 100%
MC2222   712-45-1867         1.00 100%
MC3021   722-51-5454          .75 75%
MC3021   899-46-2035          .25 25%
PC1035   238-95-7766         1.00 100%
PC8888   427-17-2319          .50 50%
PC8888   846-92-7186          .50 50%
PC9999   486-29-1786         1.00 100%
PS1372   756-30-7391          .75 75%
PS1372   724-80-9391          .25 25%
PS2091   998-72-3567          .50 50%
PS2091   899-46-2035          .50 50%
PS2106   998-72-3567         1.00 100%
PS3333   172-32-1176         1.00 100%
PS7777   486-29-1786         1.00 100%
TC3218   807-91-6654         1.00 100%
TC4203   648-92-1872         1.00 100%
TC7777   672-71-3249          .40 40%
TC7777   267-41-2394          .30 30%
TC7777   472-27-2349          .30 30%
[25 rows]
```

You can dress up the report with the authors' names, pulled from the authors table:

SQL
```
select title_id, au_fname || ' ' || au_lname as name,
    cast ( royaltyshare * 100 as int) || '%' as percent
from titleauthors, authors
```

```
where titleauthors.au_id = authors.au_id
    and title_id <'P'
order by title_id, percent
```

title_id	name	percent
==========	==============================	==============
BU1032	Marjorie Green	40%
BU1032	Abraham Bennet	60%
BU1111	Michael O'Leary	40%
BU1111	Stearns MacFeather	60%
BU2075	Marjorie Green	100%
BU7832	Dick Straight	100%
MC2222	Innes del Castillo	100%
MC3021	Anne Ringer	25%
MC3021	Michel DeFrance	75%

[9 rows]

Although CAST is the ANSI function, RDBMSs have adopted it at different rates. Most had their own functions for converting from one datatype to another and still provide them. Oracle uses a series of special functions in addition to CAST (introduced with version 8.1.7). Here's how you'd use TO_NUMBER or TO_CHAR in this case:

SQL VARIANTS

Oracle
```
SQL> select royaltyshare,
  2    to_number (royaltyshare * 100) || '%' as percent
  3  from titleauthors
  4  where title_id < 'P'
  5  order by title_id;
```

ROYALTYSHARE	PERCENT
.6	60%
.4	40%
.6	60%
.4	40%
1	100%
1	100%
1	100%
.75	75%
.25	25%

9 rows selected.

Transact-SQL uses a general-purpose function, called CONVERT, that is similar to CAST. The first argument is the target datatype; the second is the expression to convert. (Sybase and Microsoft handle a third, optional argument differently.) Because concatenation of numeric and character data is not allowed, you need to convert royaltyshare to CHAR:

SQL Server
```
select royaltyshare,
   convert( char (5), royaltyshare * 100) + '%' as NewPercent
from titleauthors
where title_id < 'P'
order by title_id
```

Playing with Patterns

The following recipes concern retrieving data when there's lots of action in the WHERE clause but the joins are simple. The four queries retrieve data by matching patterns in various ways. Read on to learn how to find

- Character data when you're not sure whether it's uppercase, lowercase, or mixed
- Data within a range with unknown values
- Date data
- Summary values based on date units

Matching Uppercase and Lowercase Letters

Sometimes data is stored in uppercase letters ("COMPUTER"), sometimes in lowercase letters ("computer"), and sometimes in mixed cases ("Computer"). This may reflect the lack of standards when the data was entered and thus the absence of integrity checks.

For example, let's say you want to determine the exact title of a book that is called either *Life Without Fear* or *Life without Fear*. You're unsure of the case of the word *without*. In fact, you suspect that the data is inconsistent throughout and there is no good way to predict how book titles are stored. There are a number of ways to deal with this.

You can use LIKE, as in the following example, if your dialect allows you to mark sets of characters with square brackets—not all do:

```
SQL
select title
from titles
where title
    like '%[Ww][Ii][Tt][Hh][Oo][Uu][Tt]%'
title
================================
Life Without Fear
[1 row]
```

Each bracketed pair allows matches on either upper- or lowercase letters. Another option is to use the UPPER function. It converts lowercase letters to uppercase letters.

The syntax is this:

SYNTAX

```
UPPER (char_expression)
```

Once the data has been changed to uppercase letters, LIKE compares it to the matching pattern:

```
SQL
select title
from titles
where upper(title) like '%WITHOUT%'
```

This is easier to read and understand than the LIKE syntax alone. UPPER's sister function, LOWER, works the same way but converts data to a lowercase string. Use UPPER (or LOWER) twice to match any combination of upper- and lowercase letters:

```
SQL
select title
from titles
where upper(title) like upper("%wiTHout%)
```

It may appear that the simplest answer to the problem of case is to enter the data in one case only and avoid this kind of work. But be careful! You may lose important information that you'll need later. Many names use both upper- and lowercase letters internally. Consider the names Blotchett-Halls, DeFrance, O'Leary, MacFeather, and del Castillo from the bookbiz database. You've probably seen them written with irregular distributions of capital letters. If you've stored them in a one-case style, you may find yourself trying to re-create distinctions you once had but then eliminated.

Finding Data Within a Range When You Don't Know the Values

To find all the books with prices between $40.95 and $50.00, you can run a query like this:

```
SQL
select substr( title, 1, 30) as book,  title_id, price
from titles
where price between 40.95 and 50.00
order by price
book                           title_id    price
============================== ========    ==========
Onions, Leeks, and Garlic: Coo TC3218        40.95
Computer Phobic and Non-Phobic PS1372        41.59
But Is It User Friendly?       PC1035        42.95
[3 rows]
```

If you want to see all books with prices between those of two particular books but you don't know the prices of the books, try something like this:

```
SQL
select title, title_id, price
from titles
where price between
   (select price
    from titles
    where title like 'Onions%')
  and
    (select price
     from titles
     where title like 'But Is%')
```

As long as you put the book with the lower price first in the BETWEEN clause, you're fine. But if you put them in higher-to-lower order (not knowing what the prices are), you'll get zero rows returned or an error message. One way to avoid this possibility is to use an OR and include both combinations:

SQL
```
select title, title_id, price
from titles
where price between
    (select price
    from titles
    where title like 'Onion%')
    and
    (select price
    from titles
    where title like 'But Is%')
or price between
    (select price
    from titles
    where title like 'But Is%')
    and
    (select price
    from titles
    where title like 'Onion%')
```

Another way to cover both cases is to find the minimum and maximum prices. As a variant, you can use the identification numbers of the books instead of the titles:

SQL
```
select title, title_id, price
from titles
where price between
    (select min(price)
    from titles
    where title_id in ('TC3218', 'PC1035') )
and
    (select max(price)
    from titles
    where title_id in ('TC3218', 'PC1035') )
```

Without subqueries, the code is something like this:

```SQL
select t1.title, t1.title_id, t1.price
from titles t1, titles onion, titles izit
where onion.title like 'Onion%'
    and izit.title like 'But Is%'
    and (t1.price between onion.price and izit.price
        or t1.price between izit.price and onion.price)
```

You include the OR clause because you don't know which price is higher. The parentheses ensure that the OR works correctly; they are needed to limit the rows returned since there are no joins in this three-table query.

Locating Date Data

Date data can be hard to retrieve because of the variety of possible ways it can be stored. In many systems, date columns include the month, day, year, and time of day (the first three fields can be displayed in a number of ways).

This presents some problems in matching the time part of the column. One example is a query like this:

```SQL
select price, pubdate
from titles
where pubdate = 'Oct 21 1998'

     price pubdate
========== ====================
     40.95 Oct 21 1998 12:00 am
     41.59 Oct 21 1998 12:00 am
[2 rows]
```

This query finds records with a date of October 21, 1998, and a time of 12:00 A.M. To get all records from *any* time on that date, you must add some more code. To test the solutions, first change one of the dates:

```SQL
update titles
set pubdate = 'Oct 21 1998 2:30PM'
where pubdate = 'Oct 21 1998' and price = 40.95
```

Although the ANSI standard includes date functions, most vendors still use **SQL** their own, and there is a lot of variation. To update `pubdate` in Oracle with its **VARIANTS** native functions, you'd have to do something like this:

```
Oracle
SQL> update titles
  2  set pubdate = to_date ( '21-OCT-98 02:30PM', 'DD-MON-YY HH:MIPM')
  3  where price = 40.95 and pubdate = '21-OCT-98';
1 row updated.
```

Now the query returns only one row:

```
SQL
select price, pubdate
from titles
where pubdate = 'Oct 21 1998'
     price pubdate
========== ====================
     41.59 Oct 21 1998 12:00 am
[1 row]
```

One simple method for finding all rows entered on one day is to spell out the full minimum and maximum time values for the day and use BETWEEN to find everything within those parameters:

```
SQL
select price, pubdate
from titles
where pubdate
     between 'Oct 21 1998 00:00'
         and 'Oct 21 1998 23:59'
     price pubdate
========== ====================
     40.95 Oct 21 1998 02:30 pm
     41.59 Oct 21 1998 12:00 am
[2 rows]
```

Another idea is to use the keyword LIKE to find everything that matches the known part of the date. Here the percent sign (%) wildcard stands for whatever follows the month, day, and year part of the date:

SQL

```
select price, pubdate
from titles
where pubdate like 'Oct 21 1998%'
```

You could also use convert functions to change the date into a shorter character string and then search for the string:

SQL

```
select price, pubdate
from titles
where cast ( pubdate as char(11) ) = 'Oct 21 1998'
       price pubdate
========== ====================
    40.95 Oct 21 1998 02:30 pm
    41.59 Oct 21 1998 12:00 am
```

SQL VARIANTS

ASA supports DATEFORMAT and CONVERT in addition to CAST.

Adaptive Server Anywhere

```
select price, pubdate
from titles
where dateformat( pubdate, 'Mmm dd yyyy' ) =
'Oct 21 1998'
```

Transact-SQL provides CONVERT (SQL Server offers both CAST and CONVERT). The CONVERT syntax is not identical for Sybase and Microsoft.

Transact-SQL

```
select price, pubdate
from titles
where convert( char(11), pubdate ) = 'Oct 21 1998'
```

Oracle offers TO_CHAR as well as CAST. Whichever you use, make sure the date format is the current default.

```
Oracle
SQL> select price, pubdate
   2  from titles
   3  where to_char (pubdate )  = '21-OCT-98';
```

A different approach involves date functions. Check to see what your system provides. This example uses DATEPART, a Transact-SQL function that matches each known part (month, day, and year) of the full date value against its numeric representation (October is 10). The time part of the date becomes irrelevant.

```
DATEPART (datepart, date)
```

SYNTAX

Here's how the query looks:

```
SQL
select price, pubdate
from titles
where datepart(mm, pubdate) = 10 and
      datepart(dd, pubdate) = 21 and
      datepart(yy, pubdate) = 1998
```

DATEADD is a similar function. Set it up to add one day to the known date. Then you can retrieve all the data between the parameters without worrying about the time, as shown in the following example:

```
SQL
select price, pubdate
from titles
where pubdate between 'Oct 21 1998' and
      dateadd(day, 1, 'Oct 21 1998')
```

This finds all records with a date between 10/21/98 and one day later, 10/22/98.

SQL VARIANTS

The Oracle TO_CHAR/TO_DATE version of these queries look like this:

```
Oracle
SQL> select price, pubdate
  2  from titles
  3  where to_char (pubdate, 'DD') = '21' and
  4     to_char (pubdate, 'MON') = 'OCT' and
  5     to_char (pubdate, 'YY' ) = '98';

SQL> select price, pubdate
  2  from titles
  3  where pubdate between to_date('21-OCT-98')
  4     and to_date('21-OCT-98') + 1;
```

Displaying Data by Time Units

How do you get statistics on event per time unit? GROUP BY is the answer to this interesting problem. For example, what is the distribution by month of books published during the year? Check your vendor for functions similar to DATEPART, which displays a specified date part, such as month or year, for a complete date. The results show a cluster of books published during the sixth month:

```
SQL
select datepart(month, pubdate), count(title_id)
from titles
group by datepart(month, pubdate)
datepart(month,titles.pubdate  count(titles.title_id)
=============================  ======================
                           6                        13
                          10                         3
                      (NULL)                         2
   [3 rows]
```

For readability, add column names as in the following query:

```
SQL
select datepart(month, pubdate) as month#,
   count(title_id) as books
from titles
group by datepart(month, pubdate)
      month#          books
   =========== ===========
             6           13
            10            3
        (NULL)            2
[3 rows]
```

The TO_CHAR version looks like this (Oracle and Informix use different date unit names):

SQL VARIANTS

```
Oracle
SQL> select to_char ( pubdate, 'MON') as Month,
         count (title_id) as books
   2  from titles
   3  group by to_char ( pubdate, 'MON');
MON       BOOKS
---   ---------
JUN          13
OCT           3
              2
3 rows selected.
```

Avoiding Mistakes

SQL is an unusual computer language: It's not just for experts. There are still relatively few SQL mavens. Many users, in fact, are really C programmers or accountants or technical marketing whizzes. They pick up SQL on their own and learn by doing. They develop some skill but remain only occasional users. When they hit a snag, they don't have the luxury of appealing to a nearby guru.

Let's face it: SQL can be confusing. The code samples that follow are based on real-life problems submitted via the Internet, transposed to work on the now-familiar `bookbiz` database. In this case, though, they aren't examples to model or copy—they are illustrations of common misuses and misunderstandings.

This section doesn't contain complete explanations or full syntax diagrams. Refer to earlier parts of the book and to your vendor's manuals when you encounter a topic for which you need more detailed information.

Topics include:

- Distinguishing DISTINCTs
- Creating report-style output
- Finding the "first" row

Distinguishing DISTINCTs

Given a table with two identifying columns, how do you find all the unique combinations? DISTINCT seems like an obvious answer, but more than one user on the Internet complained of getting nothing but syntax errors or confusing results from what seemed like straightforward DISTINCT queries.

This is probably because DISTINCT occurs in two unique forms:

- With columns or expressions
- With aggregates

The syntax of these two cases differs just enough to cloud the occasional user's judgment.

With column names and expressions, you use DISTINCT just once, and it applies to everything that comes after it. It is the first word in the select list and requires no parentheses. When you opt to use DISTINCT this way, you're locked in; you can't specify a non-DISTINCT value for anything in the select list.

There are exceptions, however. When you use DISTINCT with an aggregate (AVG, SUM, and so on), it goes inside the aggregate parentheses and applies to the elements in that particular aggregate clause only. In some systems you can use more than one aggregate DISTINCT in a select list.

These two variants are similar enough to instill fear, uncertainty, and doubt. How many DISTINCTs can you use in a select list? Should they or shouldn't they be inside parentheses?

The safest way to avoid errors is to remember that there are really two DISTINCTs.

DISTINCT with Columns and Expressions   Here is an example that may help to clarify the difference between the two DISTINCTs. Suppose you want to look at the distribution of prices and advances in the *titles* table for books costing under $25.00. Getting separate lists of unique prices and unique advances is easy.

SQL
```
select distinct price
from titles
where price < $25.00
       price
==========
      17.99
      21.95
      12.99
      17.00
[4 rows]
```

SQL
```
select distinct advance
from titles
where price < 25.00
       advance
=============
     4000.00
     5000.00
    10125.00
     2275.00
     6000.00
    15000.00
[6 rows]
```

There are four distinct prices and six different advance amounts.

To find the distinct *combinations* of these values, resist the temptation to use DISTINCT with each column: DISTINCT must be the first word in the

SELECT clause, and it applies to everything after it. The following query finds the unique combinations of price and advance for books under $25.00:

SQL
```
select distinct price, advance
from titles
where price < 25.00
```
price	advance
==========	============
17.99	4000.00
21.95	5000.00
21.95	4000.00
12.99	10125.00
21.95	2275.00
17.00	6000.00
12.99	15000.00

[7 rows]

The results show seven different combinations of price and advance. One price ($21.95) appears three times, and another ($12.99) appears twice. One advance ($4,000.00) is listed twice.

DISTINCT with Aggregates   Now let's examine how DISTINCT is used in aggregates. More than one SQL neophyte has puzzled over how to get a *count* of distinct values in a table. The code offered for comment often resembles the following:

SQL
```
select count (distinct *)
from titles
```

The result is syntax errors.

In this instance, DISTINCT isn't legal with COUNT(*). If you think it through, it's clear why. Because COUNT(*) tallies all rows, there's no way to distinguish which duplicates you're trying to eliminate. Copies of particular column values? Which ones? Copies of duplicate rows?

For a similar reason, DISTINCT doesn't do you much good with MIN or MAX. The minimum (or maximum) value for a column is as distinct as it's going to get.

You could get the answer—the number of distinct values—in two steps:

1. Store distinct values in a temporary table or view:

    SQL
    ```
    create view temp_table
    as
    select distinct pub_id
    from titles
    [view created]
    ```

2. Tally the rows in the temporary table or view:

    SQL
    ```
    select count(*) as Num
    from temp_table
              Num
    ===========
                3
    [1 row]
    ```

However, there is an easier way. DISTINCT works fine for counting unique values when you specify the column by name. Here's some code that'll do the job:

```
SQL
select count (distinct pub_id)
from titles
    count(*)
===========
            3
[1 row]
```

You use DISTINCT with other aggregates in the same way. To find the average of distinct prices under $25.00, you'd write a query like this:

```
SQL
select avg (distinct price)
from titles
where price < 25
avg(distinct titles.price)
==========================
                     17.48
[1 row]
```

If your system permits multiple DISTINCTs with aggregates, you can try this type of maneuver to find the average of distinct advances as well as price:

```
SQL Server
select avg (distinct price), avg( distinct advance)
from titles
where price < 25

-------------------- --------------------
17.4825                    7066.6666
(1 row(s) affected)
```

Notice that you use DISTINCT twice, once in each aggregate. If you don't, you're likely to get results of disputable meaning.

DISTINCT and DISTINCT In some database systems, it's possible to mix the two kinds of DISTINCTs, but be alert! Combining column names and aggregates can be tricky. Your system might forbid the mixture unless the column name is a grouping column. Even if this is allowed, the results may not make sense.

Removing Duplicates

It's true—SQL is *not* a formatting tool. There are some things it just can't do or can't do without expensive gyrations. Sometimes you simply have to give up and turn your results over to a good report writer. Removing duplicated elements from output to produce a nicely formatted display is one of those cases.

But hope springs eternal: More than one Internet respondent has wondered if there is any SQL method for cleaning up these kinds of results:

SQL
```
select pub_id, type
from titles
order by pub_id

pub_id type
====== ============
0736   psychology
0736   psychology
0736   business
0736   psychology
0736   psychology
0736   psychology
0877   mod_cook
0877   trad_cook
0877   trad_cook
0877   mod_cook
0877   trad_cook
0877   (NULL)
1389   popular_comp
1389   business
1389   business
1389   popular_comp
1389   business
1389   popular_comp
[18 rows]
```

Ideally, you'd rather have a display like this:

SQL
```
pub_id type
====== ============
0736   psychology
       psychology
       business
       psychology
       psychology
       psychology
```

```
0877    mod_cook
        trad_cook
        trad_cook
        mod_cook
        trad_cook
        (NULL)
1389    popular_comp
        business
        business
        popular_comp
        business
        popular_comp
[18 rows]
```

In fact, there's no easy way to construct that display with SQL. Instead, you should turn to a front-end formatter or report writer to reformat the unwieldy results. If a spreadsheet format meets your needs, try a CASE statement. In the following example, the two cooking types are classified together:

SQL
```
select pub_id,
  min (case type when 'business' then 'yes' end )  as biz ,
  min (case type when 'psychology' then 'yes' end ) as psych ,
  min (case type  when 'popular_comp' then 'yes' end ) as nerd,
  min (case when type like  '%_cook' then 'yes' end ) as cook,
  min (case when type is null then 'yes' end ) as undecided
from titles
group by pub_id
pub_id biz psych nerd cook undecided
====== === ===== ==== ==== =========
1389   yes (NULL yes  (NUL (NULL)
0736   yes yes   (NUL (NUL (NULL)
0877   (NU (NULL (NUL yes  yes
[3 rows]
```

Finding the "First" Entry

Here's a problem based on more than a syntax error: It's a misunderstanding of what a relational database can do.

The question, like others in this chapter, is based on mail sent via the Internet. Given a table with a limited number of codes, each possibly having multiple identification entries, the submitter asked, How do you find the *first* entry for each code?

There are a couple of odd things about this question. It implies a built-in order, and it assigns a special status to the first entry for each code. Both of these concepts are foreign to relational databases and hence meaningless in SQL.

If you find yourself needing to construct such a query, you should probably start by reexamining your database design. Maybe the table is lacking a time-stamp or some kind of sequential column that would save information about when or in what order data were entered. Once you add that, you'll be able to find entries in sequence. Without it, you have to make a series of questionable assumptions about what "firstness" means.

Summary

This chapter has introduced some real-world SQL as well as cautions on common mistakes. The first section includes the following:

- Thinking conditionally—using CASE, COALESCE, and variants of these two keywords to make IF-like choices
- Formatting and displaying data—learning how to split columns, how to join columns, and how to convert columns from one datatype to another
- Playing with patterns—handling uppercase/lowercase issues, using complex expressions in predicates, and working with date data

The second section gives examples of common mistakes:

- Mixing up DISTINCTs
- Creating report-style displays
- Finding the "first" row

For more information on these topics, see Appendix E, Resources.

Appendix A

Syntax Summary for the SQL Used in This Book

In This Appendix

- Formatting
- Syntax Conventions
- Statement List

Formatting

SQL is a free-form language; that is, there are no rules about how many words you can put on a line or where you need to break a line. However, for readability, all examples and syntax statements in this book are formatted so that each clause of a statement begins on a new line. Clauses that have more than one part extend to additional lines, which are indented.

SYNTAX

```
SELECT column_name
FROM table_name
WHERE search_conditions
```

In syntax statements in this book, keywords (commands) are in uppercase letters, and identifiers and user-supplied words are in lowercase letters. Type the keywords just as you see them, disregarding case. (Keywords with some uppercase and some lowercase letters mean you can use either the full word or abbreviate by using only the uppercase part of it.)

Case significance for identifiers and user-supplied words depends on your RDBMS and the character set and collating sequence used when it was set up. For greatest portability, assume that case matters.

Syntax Conventions

Key

BIG	Caps means it's a keyword (command).
MIXed	Caps mixed with lowercase letters means it's a keyword and you can type either the full word or just the part in caps.
little	Lowercase words are variables; supply your own.
{ }	Curly braces mean you must choose at least one of the enclosed options.
[ ]	Brackets mean choosing one or more of the enclosed options is optional.
( )	Parentheses are actually typed as part of the command (unlike curly braces and brackets, which are syntax symbols).
|	The vertical bar means you choose a maximum of one option.
,	The comma means you choose as many options as you like and separate your choices with commas that you type as part of the command.
. . .	The ellipses mean you can do it again, whatever it was.

Statement List

The following SQL statements are discussed in *The Practical SQL Handbook:*

ALTER DATABASE	DROP INDEX
ALTER TABLE	DROP TABLE
BEGIN TRANsaction	DROP VIEW
COMMIT TRANsaction	GRANT
CREATE DATABASE	INSERT
CREATE INDEX	REVOKE
CREATE TABLE	ROLLBACK TRANsaction
CREATE VIEW	SELECT
DELETE	UPDATE
DROP DATABASE	UPDATE STATISTICS

Appendix B

Industry SQL Equivalents

In This Appendix

- Comparisons
- Naming Convention Comparison
- Datatype Comparison
- Function Comparison

Comparisons

In this appendix, you'll find a comparison of naming conventions and datatypes, as well as the most common SQL functions for Sybase Adaptive Server Enterprise, Sybase Adaptive Server Anywhere, Microsoft SQL Server, Informix, and Oracle. All of the versions are represented with the syntax conventions described in this book, although in some cases the syntax has been simplified to make the entries easier to read and to compare. For example, we shorten all types of expressions (`constant_expression`, `non_aggregate_expression`, and so on) to "expr" and substitute "INT" for "INTEGER."

Naming Convention Comparison

Figure B.1 shows how naming conventions compare in the five example systems. In the syntax comparison tables, these object names have been stripped down and reduced to their simplest forms.

RDBMS	Naming Format
SQL Anywhere	[owner.]table_name
Microsoft SQL Server	[[[server_name.]db_name.]owner.]table_name
Adaptive Server Enterprise	[[[server_name.]db_name.]owner.]table_name
Informix	[[db_name[@server_name];]owner.]table_name
Oracle	[owner.]table_name[@dblink]

Figure B.1 Naming Conventions

Datatype Comparison

The datatype comparison chart (Figure B.2) shows datatype names used in the bookbiz database by vendor. Where a particular datatype is used for compatibility with one offered by another vendor, it is in italics. Some names have long and short versions (DECIMAL and DEC): They are noted here with mixed case (DECimal). However, precision and scale for numeric datatypes are not included. Don't assume the same name means identical characteristics; check your documentation for details.

Adaptive Server Anywhere treats CHAR, VARCHAR, and LONG VARCHAR columns all as the same type.

Oracle's base real numeric datatype is NUMBER for whole numbers and NUMBER (precision, scale) for decimal numbers. However, Oracle accepts most numeric datatype names used by other systems, such as INT, SMALLINT, DECIMAL, FLOAT, REAL, and DOUBLE PRECISION, translating each into the appropriate NUMBER. Oracle has a VARCHAR datatype but urges customers to use VARCHAR2. VARCHAR is reserved for other uses.

* Oracle is introducing a full range of date and time datatypes, including TIMESTAMP, TIME, and INTERVAL, along with the ANSI EXTRACT function. The Oracle 8.1.7 version used for this book requires a special ALTER SESSION SET EVENTS command to use these features, so they are not included in this list. Check your documentation for details.

Element	ASA	ASE	MS SQL Server	Oracle	Informix
fixed character, max size *n*	CHAR(n)	CHAR(n)	CHAR(n)	CHAR(n)	CHAR(n)
variable character, max size *n*	VARCHAR(n)	VARCHAR(n)	VARCHAR(n)	VARCHAR2(n)	VARCHAR(n)
date and time information	*DATETIME SMALLDATE TIME* TIMESTAMP	DATETIME SMALLDATE-TIME	DATETIME SMALLDATE-TIME	*DATE	DATETIME
date information	DATE			*	DATE
time information	TIME			*	INTERVAL
whole numbers	INTeger SMALLINT TINYINT	INTeger SMALLINT TINYINT	INTeger SMALLINT TINYINT	*INTeger SMALLINT* NUMBER	INTeger SMALLINT
exact decimal	DECimal NUMERIC	DECimal NUMERIC	DECimal NUMERIC	*DECimal NUMERIC* NUMBER	DECimal NUMERIC
approximate numeric	FLOAT REAL DOUBLE PRECISION	FLOAT REAL DOUBLE PRECISION	FLOAT REAL DOUBLE PRECISION	*FLOAT* *REAL* *DOUBLE* *PRECISION* NUMBER	FLOAT SMALLFLOAT REAL DOUBLE PRECISION DECimal
currency	*MONEY SMALLMONEY*	MONEY SMALLMONEY	MONEY SMALLMONEY		MONEY

Figure B.2 Comparing Datatypes in Five RDBMSs

Function Comparison

Following are SQL functions mentioned in the earlier chapters, divided into three groups. This material is meant to be a starting place, not a final reference. Even when functions look the same, there may be underlying semantic content that makes two apparently identical commands rather different in meaning (for example, the definitions of terms such as `expression`). Vendors modify existing SQL commands and add new ones as they refine their products; items on this list may not represent the latest version.

In short, this appendix can help you get an idea of the similarities and differences among vendors, but you should consult your system manuals for exact, up-to-date information.

Character Functions

Figure B.3 provides a list of SQL functions used with character (string) expressions. It is limited to functions mentioned in earlier chapters.

ANSI	ASA	ASE	MS SQL Server	Oracle	Informix
CHARacter_LENGTH (expr)	LENGTH (expr) DATALENGTH (expr)	DATALENGTH (expr)	LEN(expr) DATALENGTH (expr)	LENGTH (expr)	LENGTH (expr)
expr || expr	expr + expr expr || expr	expr + expr	expr + expr	expr || expr	expr || expr
SUBSTRING (char_expr FROM start [FOR size])	SUBSTR (expr, start [, size]) SUBSTRING (expr, start, size)	SUBSTRING (expr, start, size)	SUBSTRING (expr, start, size)	SUBSTR (expr, start [, size])	SUBSTRING (expr FROM start [FOR size]) SUBSTR (char_expr, start [, size])
UPPER(expr) LOWER(expr)	UPPER(expr) LOWER(expr)	UPPER(expr) LOWER(expr)	UPPER(expr) LOWER(expr)	UPPER(expr) LOWER(expr)	UPPER(expr) LOWER(expr)

Figure B.3　Character Functions

ANSI	ASA	ASE	SQL Server	Oracle	Informix
CASE	CASE	CASE	CASE	CASE DECODE	CASE DECODE
NULLIF	NULLIF	NULLIF	NULLIF		
COALESCE	COALESCE	COALESCE	COALESCE		
	ISNULL	ISNULL	ISNULL	NVL	NVL

Figure B.4 Conditional Functions

Conditional Functions

CASE and DECODE, plus related functions are shown in Figure B.4.

Date and Time Functions

Date and time functions are the most troublesome because they vary a great deal by vendor and version. The following (shown in Figure B.5) is far from complete. It includes only those date functions that appeared in the book.

ANSI	ASA	ASE	MS SQL Server	Oracle	Informix
CURRENT_DATE CURRENT_TIME CURRENT_TIME- STAMP	CURRENT DATE CURRENT TIME		CURRENT_TIME -STAMP		TODAY
	GETDATE	GETDATE	GETDATE	SYSDATE	CURRENT
date_expr + INTERVAL n unit date_expr – INTERVAL n unit	date_expr + n date_expr – n		date_expr + n date_expr – n	date_expr + n date_expr – n	date_expr + INTERVAL n unit date_expr – INTERVAL n unit
	DATEADD DATEDIFF	DATEADD DATEDIFF	DATEADD DATEDIFF		

Figure B.5 Date and Time Functions

ANSI	ASA	ASE	MS SQL Server	Oracle	Informix
CAST (expr AS [datatype | domain])	CAST (expr AS datatype) CONVERT (target datatype, expr [, datestyle])	CONVERT (target datatype, expr [, datestyle])	CAST (expr AS datatype) CONVERT (target datatype. expr [,datestyle])	CAST (expr AS datatype)	CAST (expr AS datatype) expr :: datatype
	DATEFORMAT (expr, 'pattern') DATE ('expr')			TO_CHAR (expr, 'format') TO_DATE (expr, 'format')	TO_CHAR (expr, 'format') TO_DATE (expr, 'format') DATE ('expr')

Figure B.5 Date and Time Functions (Continued)

Appendix C

Glossary

access strategy
The method by which a database management system locates physical data.

aggregate functions
Often used with the GROUP BY and HAVING clauses, aggregate functions generate one summary value from a group of values in a specified column. Aggregate functions include AVG, SUM COUNT, COUNT(*), MIN, and MAX.

alias
A temporary name given to a table (in the FROM clause). Here are two examples of how it can be used:

```
select au_id, a.city, p.city, pub_id
from authors a, publishers p
where au_lname like 'P%'

select a.au_id, b.au_id
from authors a, authors b
where a.zip = b.zip
```

In the first example, the alias eliminates the need to type the whole table name as a qualifier for each column name that could belong to either table in the FROM clause. In the second example, aliases allow a self-join—the `authors` table takes on two identities, a and b.

anti-join
Oracle's name for a query that returns results based on a nonmatch, as in a NOT IN or NOT EXISTS subquery or a MINUS query.

argument

A value (also called "parameter") supplied to a function.

arithmetic operators

Addition (+), subtraction (–), multiplication (*), and division (/) are arithmetic operators. They can be used with all numeric columns. Some systems also supply modulo (%), for finding the integer remainder after a division operation on two integers.

association

A many-to-many relationship between entities.

attribute

A data value that describes one characteristic of an entity. It is also called a "field" or a "column."

base table

A permanent database table on which a view (also called a virtual table) is based.

benchmarking

The process of testing a piece of hardware or software to determine its general or specific performance characteristics.

binary datatype

A datatype provided by some systems for storing bit patterns.

bit datatype

A datatype provided by some systems for storing true/false data.

Boolean operators

The logical operators AND, OR, and NOT.

Cartesian product

All the possible combinations of rows from the tables. Such a result is generally caused by not including all the necessary joins.

cascade

Propagation of an update or delete through related tables in a database.

character datatype
A datatype used to store character data such as letters, numbers, and special characters.

character set
A list of letters and special characters (repertoire) and its internal mapping to computer codes (form-of-use).

clustered index
An index in which the bottom, or leaf, level is the data itself. A table can have only one clustered index.

collating sequence
See **sort order**.

collation
See **sort order**.

column
One particular attribute or characteristic of the entity that is the subject of a table—also called a "field."

column alias
See **display label**.

command
Any SQL statement, such as INSERT or CREATE DATABASE.

comparison operators
Operators used for comparing one expression to another in a WHERE or HAVING clause. Comparison operators include equal to (=), greater than (>), less than (<), greater than or equal to (>=), less than or equal to (<=), and not equal to (<> or !=).

composite indexes
Indexes based on more than one column in a table.

comprehensive data sublanguage
A single language that handles all communications with the database.

concurrency control
 Strategies that prevent two or more users from changing the same piece of data at the same time.

connecting column
 A column that participates in a join, allowing one table to link with another or with itself. Connecting columns are columns from one or more tables that contain similar values.

constraints
 Clauses in the CREATE TABLE statement (CHECK, PRIMARY KEY, UNIQUE, REFERENCES, FOREIGN KEY) that help enforce referential integrity and business rules.

correlated subquery
 A subquery that cannot be evaluated independently but that depends on the outer query for its results. Also called a "repeating subquery," since the subquery is executed once for each row that might be selected by the outer query.

data administration
 One of the three general categories for which SQL is used. The other two are data definition and data manipulation. Data administration includes activities such as granting and revoking permissions to users.

data control
 Another term for data administration.

data definition
 The process of creating (or removing) a database and its objects.

data manipulation
 Retrieving and modifying data through SQL statements SELECT, INSERT, DELETE, and UPDATE.

data modification
 Changing data through SQL statements INSERT, DELETE, and UPDATE.

data retrieval
 Finding and displaying data in the database via queries (SELECT statements).

data structure diagram

A diagram that shows how the objects in a database fit together. It is also called an "entity-relationship (E-R) diagram."

database

A collection of related tables containing data and definitions of database objects.

database administrator

See **system administrator**.

database design

The process of setting up the objects in the database (principally, but not exclusively, tables and their columns).

database device

The physical or logical device on which a database is stored.

database owner

The creator or owner of a database, a concept most useful in systems that allow more than one database.

date datatype

A datatype used for storing date information.

DDL

Data definition language, SQL commands for creating and dropping database objects.

decimal datatype

A datatype used for storing decimal data.

default

A value entered by the system for specificd columns when the user supplies no explicit value.

derived tables

A name sometimes applied to views, also known as "virtual tables."

detail table

See **master table**.

difference
A set operation that displays rows that two tables do not have in common.

display label
Heading added to query results to make them easier to understand. Also called column alias or column heading.

distinguished nulls
Unknown pieces of information, the values of which are not precisely known, although some things about the values are known.

DML
Data manipulation language, SQL commands for querying or changing data in the database (SELECT, INSERT, DELETE, UPDATE).

domain
The set of all legal or valid values for a particular column.

dummy values
False values you enter as placeholders or tests.

entity
The object or thing that a table describes—the subject of the table.

entity integrity
An integrity rule requiring that each row have a primary key and that no primary key allow nulls.

entity-relationship diagram
See **data structure diagram**.

entity-relationship modeling
Identifying the important subjects about which information will be stored, their attributes, and the relationships among these entities—also known as "entity modeling."

equijoin
Joining columns on the basis of equality, where values match exactly; see also **natural join**.

escape character
> A character used in a LIKE clause with the ESCAPE keyword to strip a wild-card of its magic meaning and force SQL to interpret it as a literal.

expression
> A constant, column name, function, or any combination thereof connected by arithmetic (and sometimes bitwise) operators.

field
> An attribute of an entity, a column of a table.

file
> Often used as equivalent to "table."

first normal form
> First of the five normal forms. It requires that tables have a fixed number of columns and that there be no repeating groups.

fixed length
> Some datatypes can have either fixed or variable length. Choosing the correct one may have storage and performance implications.

foreign key
> A column in a table that matches a primary key column in another table.

form-of-use
> See **character set**.

form system
> A user-interface screen with places where you can type data.

free-form language
> A computer language with no requirements for line length or line breaks.

grouped view
> A view with a GROUP BY clause in its definition.

identifier
> The name of a database or database object.

inclusive range
A range, specified with the keyword BETWEEN, in which you search for the lower value and upper value of the range as well as the values included in the range.

indcx
A mechanism for locating data.

instance
Each row in a table represents an occurrence, or instance, of the entity.

integrity
Data consistency and correctness.

intersection
A set operation that displays rows that two or more tables have in common.

join
Selecting from more than one table by comparing values in specified columns.

join column
A column used to set conditions for a join.

join-compatible columns
Columns holding similar kinds of data values.

key values
Primary keys uniquely identify a row, while foreign keys provide a way to refer to those unique values from another table.

keyword
A word used as part of SQL syntax, also called a "reserved word."

logical independence
The concept that relationships among tables, columns, and rows can change without impairing the function of application programs and ad hoc queries.

logical operators
AND (joins two or more conditions and returns results when all the conditions are true), OR (connects two or more conditions and returns results when any of the conditions is true), and NOT (negates a condition).

lookup table
A table used primarily for reference purposes rather than for data entry or modification.

lost-update problem
Multiuser updates can overwrite each other if a database has no concurrency control.

many-to-many
Relationships such as those between *authors* and *titles,* in which an author can have several books and a book can have several authors.

master table
A database table that holds the top level of information (such as the `bookbiz sales` table) for a particular activity and is associated with one or more detail tables (such as the `bookbiz salesdetails` table).

MIS specialist
See **system administrator.**

money datatype
A datatype used for representing decimal currency values.

natural join
A display of only one from each pair of columns whose matching values created the join on the basis of equality. See also **equijoin.**

nested query
See **subquery.**

nested sort
A sort within another sort.

noncorrelated subquery
A subquery that can be evaluated independently of the outer SQL statement—also called a simple subquery.

non-loss decomposition
The process of splitting a table into smaller tables without losing any information.

nonprocedural language
> A language that allows you to specify the results you want without describing the method for getting them.

normal forms
> See **normalization**.

normalization
> Normalization guidelines are a set of data design standards called the **normal forms**. Five normal forms are widely accepted, although more have been proposed.

null
> A null represents a missing or inapplicable value in a column of a database table.

occurrence
> Each row in a table is an occurrence or instance of the entity.

one-to-many
> A master-detail relationship in which one row in the first table may relate to many in the second, but a row in the second table can relate to only one row in the first.

outer join
> A join that displays nonjoining rows from either one or the other of a pair of joined tables.

owner
> The creator of a database object is the owner of that object and usually has full privileges on that object.

permissions
> Authority to run certain actions on certain database objects or to run certain commands.

physical data independence
> The independence of the physical storage of data from a database's logical design.

primary key
The column or columns whose values uniquely identify a row in a table.

privileges
See **permissions**.

projection
Listing the columns that will be included in the results of a selection from the database.

qualifications
Conditions on the rows to be retrieved, described in the WHERE or HAVING clause.

queries
Requests for retrieval of data from the database; sometimes also used to refer to SQL statements in general.

query optimizer
The part of the DBMS that calculates the most efficient way to perform a given query.

record
A set of related fields that describes a specific entity. Also called "tuple" or "row."

recovery
Restoring the database to a consistent state after a software or hardware failure.

referential integrity
The rules governing data consistency, specifically the requirement that a foreign key must either match its primary key exactly or be completely null.

relation
   Synonym for **table**.

repeating subquery
   See **correlated subquery**.

repertoire
   See **character set**.

restriction
   One of the basic query operations in a relational system, also called selection. A restriction determines which rows will be selected from a table.

row
   The set of data values associated with one instance of the entity that the table describes: one set of columns.

rule
   A specification that controls what data may be entered in a particular column.

scalar aggregate
   An aggregate function that produces a single value from a SELECT statement. See also **vector aggregate**.

schema
   In SQL-92 terms, a collection of database objects belonging to a single user. The term is also used for the overall database design. ("Let me see the schema.")

second normal form
   Requires that all the nonprimary key columns relate to the entire primary key and not just to one of its components.

selection
   Specifying conditions for retrieving rows from a table. See also **restriction**.

select list
   The asterisk (for all columns) or a list of columns and expressions to be included in the query results.

self-join
Selecting from a table by comparing values in one or more columns of the same table.

serial datatype or property
A facility to maintain a sequentially increasing number.

sets
Groups of rows to which aggregates apply.

simple subquery
A subquery that can be evaluated independently of the outer SQL statement.

sort order
A collating sequence (or collation) for a character set, determining which characters come before and after other characters.

SQL
A unified language for defining, querying, modifying, and controlling the data in a relational database (originally an acronym for Structured Query Language).

statement
A SQL data definition, data manipulation, or data administration command.

stored procedures
Named collections of SQL code, usually containing non-ANSI elements.

strings
Groups of one or more letters, numbers, or special characters (such as the question mark or asterisk).

subquery
A SELECT statement that nests inside the WHERE clause of another SELECT statement.

system administrator
The person who has overall responsibility for the data in the database and for its consistency and integrity.

system catalog
  The system tables containing descriptions of the database objects and how they are structured.

system tables
  See **system catalog**.

table
  A rectangular display of data values as rows and columns.

table list
  The list of tables, views, or both following the FROM keyword in a SELECT statement.

table scan
  Reading each row in a table rather than using an index to locate a particular data element. (For small tables, a table scan can be the most efficient access method.)

terminator
  A character, word, or menu option marking the end of a SQL statement.

third normal form
  Third normal form requires that each non-key column give information about the key column. A non-key column may not describe another non-key column.

time datatype
  A datatype that stores time information.

transaction
  A mechanism for ensuring that a set of actions is treated as a single unit of work.

transaction management
  Ensuring that transactions are either completed or canceled so that the database is never left in an inconsistent state.

trigger
Stored SQL code that goes into effect when a user gives a data modification command on a specified table or column.

trigger conditions
The conditions that cause a trigger to take effect.

tuple
A set of related attributes that describes a specific entity. Also called "row" or "record."

unique indexes
An index with no duplicate primary keys.

unmodified comparison operator
A comparison operator not followed by ANY or ALL.

user-defined transaction
Transactions you define with transaction commands such as BEGIN TRANSACTION and COMMIT TRANSACTION.

user tables
Tables that contain the information that is the database management system's reason for existing.

validation rules
A rule specifies what data may be entered in a particular column: It is a way of defining the domain of the column. Rules are sometimes referred to as "validation rules" because they allow the system to check whether a value being entered in a column falls within the column's domain.

value
A single data element, such as the contents of one column-row intersection.

vector aggregate
An aggregate that returns an array of values, one per set.

view
An alternative way of looking at the data in one or more tables.

viewed table

Another term for "view" (as opposed to "base" table).

virtual table

See **view**.

whole-number datatype

A datatype that holds whole numbers (number, integer, int, smallint).

wildcards

Characters used with the SQL LIKE keyword that can represent one character (underscore, _) or any number of characters (percent sign, %).

Appendix D

The bookbiz **Sample Database**

In This Appendix

- Database Details
- Table Charts
- CREATE Statements for the bookbiz Database
- INSERT Statements
- CREATE VIEW Statements

Database Details

This appendix shows details for the sample database bookbiz. The names of the tables are authors, publishers, roysched, titleauthors, titles, editors, titleditors, sales, and salesdetails. The information is shown first as a chart for each table and then as scripts, with CREATE and INSERT statements.

Table Charts

The header for each column lists the datatypes and the column null/not null status. Indexes have underlined names below the column or columns they point to.

publishers **Table**

The publishers table has three rows, representing three publishing lines in bookbiz. The pub_id and state columns are fixed character datatype. All the other columns are variable character datatype. There is a unique index on pub_id called pubind.

pub_id not null pubind	pub_name null	address null	city null	state null
======	======================	===============	===================	=====
0736	New Age Books	1 1st St.	Boston	MA
0877	Binnet & Hardley	2 2nd Ave.	Washington	DC
1389	Algodata Infosystems	3 3rd Dr.	Berkeley	CA

authors Table

The authors table describes writers associated with the three publishing lines in bookbiz. There are 23 authors. Four columns (au_id, phone, state, zip) are fixed-length character datatype. The other columns are all variable-length character datatype. There is a unique index on au_id and another index (non-unique) on the author last and first name.

au_id not null auidind	au_lname not null	au_fname not null aunmind	phone null	address null	city null	state null	zip null
===========	===============	===========	============	=====================	===============	=====	=====
172-32-1176	White	Johnson	408 496-7223	10932 Bigge Rd.	Menlo Park	CA	94025
213-46-8915	Green	Marjorie	415 986-7020	309 63rd St. #411	Oakland	CA	94618
238-95-7766	Carson	Cheryl	415 548-7723	589 Darwin Ln.	Berkeley	CA	94705
267-41-2394	O'Leary	Michael	408 286-2428	22 Cleveland Av. #14	San Jose	CA	95128
274-80-9391	Straight	Dick	415 834-2919	5420 College Av.	Oakland	CA	94609
341-22-1782	Smith	Meander	913 843-0462	10 Misisipi Dr.	Lawrence	KS	66044
409-56-7008	Bennet	Abraham	415 658-9932	6223 Bateman St.	Berkeley	CA	94705
427-17-2319	Dull	Ann	415 836-7128	3410 Blonde St.	Palo Alto	CA	94301
472-27-2349	Gringlesby	Burt	707 938-6445	PO Box 792	Covelo	CA	95428
486-29-1786	Locksley	Chastity	415 585-4620	18 Broadway Av.	San Francisco	CA	94130
527-72-3246	Greene	Morningstar	615 297-2723	22 Graybar House Rd.	Nashville	TN	37215
648-92-1872	Blotchet-Halls	Reginald	503 745-6402	55 Hillsdale Bl.	Corvallis	OR	97330
672-71-3249	Yokomoto	Akiko	415 935-4228	3 Silver Ct.	Walnut Creek	CA	94595
712-45-1867	del Castillo	Innes	615 996-8275	2286 Cram Pl. #86	Ann Arbor	MI	48105
722-51-5454	DeFrance	Michel	219 547-9982	3 Balding Pl.	Gary	IN	46403
724-08-9931	Stringer	Dirk	415 843-2991	5420 Telegraph Av.	Oakland	CA	94609
724-80-9391	MacFeather	Stearns	415 354-7128	44 Upland Hts.	Oakland	CA	94612
756-30-7391	Karsen	Livia	415 534-9219	5720 McAuley St.	Oakland	CA	94609
807-91-6654	Panteley	Sylvia	301 946-8853	1956 Arlington Pl.	Rockville	MD	20853
846-92-7186	Hunter	Sheryl	415 836-7128	3410 Blonde St.	Palo Alto	CA	94301
893-72-1158	McBadden	Heather	707 448-4982	301 Putnam	Vacaville	CA	95688
899-46-2035	Ringer	Anne	801 826-0752	67 Seventh Av.	Salt Lake City	UT	84152
998-72-3567	Ringer	Albert	801 826-0752	67 Seventh Av.	Salt Lake City	UT	84152

titles **Table**

The titles table stores information about books put out by **bookbiz** publishers. There are 18 books. The title_id, type and pub_id columns are fixed-length character datatype. The title and notes columns are variable-length datatype. The price and advance columns hold money values (decimal datatypes for systems that do not support a currency datatype). There is a unique index on title_id and a nonunique one on title.

title_id not null titleidind	title not null titlcind	type null	pub_id null	price null	advance null	ytd_sales null	contract not null	notes null	pubdate null
PC1035	But Is It User Friendly?	popular_comp	1389	42.95	7000.00	8780	1	A survey of software for the naive user, focusing on the 'friendliness' of each.	Jun 30 1998 12:00 am
BU1032	The Busy Executive's Database Guide	business	1389	29.99	5000.00	4095	1	An overview of available data-base systems with emphasis on common business applications. Illustrated.	Jun 12 1998 12:00 am
BU1111	Cooking with Computers: Surrepti-tious Bal-ance Sheets	business	1389	21.95	5000.00	3876	1	Helpful hints on how to use your electronic resources to the best advantage.	Jun 09 1998 12:00 am
BU2075	You Can Combat Computer Stress!	business	0736	12.99	10125.00	18722	1	The latest medical and psychological techniques for living with the electronic office. Easy-to-understand explanations.	Jun 30 1998 12:00 am
BU7832	Straight Talk About Computers	business	1389	29.99	5000.00	4095	1	Annotated analy-sis of what computers can do for you: a no-hype guide for the critical user.	Jun 22 1998 12:00 am

title_id	title	type	pub_id	price	advance	ytd_sales	contract	notes	pubdate
not null	not null	null	null	null	null	null	not null	null	null
titleidind	titleind								
==========	===========	============	======	======	========	=========	========	================	=======
MC2222	Silicon Valley Gastronomic Treats	mod_cook	0877	29.99	0.00	2032	1	Favorite recipes for quick, easy, and elegant meals tried and tested by people who never have time to eat, let alone cook.	Jun 09 1998 12:00 am
MC3021	The Gourmet Microwave	mod_cook	0877	12.99	15000.00	22246	1	Traditional French gourmet recipes adapted for modern microwave cooking.	Jun 18 1998 12:00 am
MC3026	The Psychology of Computer Cooking	(NULL)	0877	(NULL)	(NULL)	(NULL)	0	(NULL)	(NULL)
PC1035	But Is It User Friendly?	popular_comp	1389	42.95	7000.00	8780	1	A survey of software for the naive user, focusing on the 'friendliness' of each.	Jun 30 1998 12:00 am
PC8888	Secrets of Silicon Valley	popular_comp	1389	40.00	8000.00	4095	1	Muckraking reporting on the world's largest computer hardware and software manufacturers.	Jun 12 1998 12:00 am
PC9999	Net Etiquette	popular_comp	1389	(NULL)	(NULL)	(NULL)	0	A must-read for computer conferencing debutantes!	(NULL)
PS1372	Computer Phobic and Non-Phobic Individuals: Behavior Variations	psychology	0736	41.59	7000.00	375	1	A must for the specialist, this book examines the difference between those who hate and fear computers and those who think they are swell.	Oct 21 1998 12:00 am

title_id not null titleidind	title not null titleind	type null	pub_id null	price null	advance null	ytd_sales null	contract not null	notes null	pubdate null
PS2091	Is Anger the Enemy?	psychology	0736	21.95	2275.00	2045	1	Carefully researched study of the effects of strong emotions on the body. Metabolic charts included.	Jun 15 1998 12:00 am
PS2106	Life Without Fear	psychology	0736	17.00	6000.00	111	1	New exercise, meditation, and nutritional techniques that can reduce the shock of daily interactions. Popular audience. Sample menus included, exercise video available separately.	Oct 05 1998 12:00 am
PS3333	Prolonged Data Deprivation: Four Case Studies	psychology	0736	29.99	2000.00	4072	1	What happens when the data runs dry? Searching evaluations of information-shortage effects.	Jun 12 1998 12:00 am
PS7777	Emotional Security: A New Algorithm	psychology	0736	17.99	4000.00	3336	1	Protecting yourself and your loved ones from undue emotional stress in the modern world. Use of computer and nutritional aids emphasized	Jun 12 1998 12:00 am
TC3218	Onions, Leeks, and Garlic: Cooking Secrets of the Mediterranean	trad_cook	0877	40.95	7000.00	375	1	Profusely illustrated in color, this makes a wonderful gift book for a cuisine-oriented friend.	Oct 21 1998 12:00 am

title_id not null titleidind	title not null titleind	type null	pub_id null	price null	advance null	ytd_sales null	contract not null	notes null	pubdate null
TC4203	Fifty Years in Bucking-ham Palace Kitchens	trad_cook	0877	21.95	4000.00	15096	1	More anecdotes from the Queen's favorite cook describing life among English royalty. Recipes, tech-niques, tender vignettes.	Jun 12 1998 12:00 am
TC7777	Sushi, Anyone?	trad_cook	0877	29.99	8000.00	4095	1	Detailed instructions on improving your position in life by learning how to make authen-tic Japanese sushi in your spare time. 5-10% increase in number of friends per recipe reported from beta test	Jun 12 1998 12:00 am

titleauthors Table

Because authors can write multiple books and books can have one or several authors, the relationship between authors and books is many-to-many. The titleauthors table links authors and their books showing the associations between authors and books (both au_id and title_id are fixed-length charac-ter datatype and their combinations are indexed). The table also contains information related to the title-author associations: the order of the author's name on the cover of the book (a whole number) and the percentage of royalties the author receives (a decimal number). There are 25 rows in titleauthors.

To see book titles and author names, do a three-way join including titles, authors, and titleauthors.

au_id not null taind	title_id not null	au_ord null	royaltyshare null
172-32-1176	PS3333	1	1.00
213-46-8915	BU1032	2	.40
213-46-8915	BU2075	1	1.00
238-95-7766	PC1035	1	1.00
267-41-2394	BU1111	2	.40
267-41-2394	TC7777	2	.30
274-80-9391	BU7832	1	1.00
409-56-7008	BU1032	1	.60
427-17-2319	PC8888	1	.50
472-27-2349	TC7777	3	.30
486-29-1786	PC9999	1	1.00
486-29-1786	PS7777	1	1.00
648-92-1872	TC4203	1	1.00
672-71-3249	TC7777	1	.40
712-45-1867	MC2222	1	1.00
722-51 5454	MC3021	1	.75
724-80-9391	BU1111	1	.60
724-80-9391	PS1372	2	.25
756-30-7391	PS1372	1	.75
807-91-6654	TC3218	1	1.00
846-92-7186	PC8888	2	.50
899-46-2035	MC3021	2	.25
899-46-2035	PS2091	2	.50
998-72-3567	PS2091	1	.50
998-72-3567	PS2106	1	1.00

sales **Table**

The **sales** table holds the top-level sales order information: **sonum** is the sales order number (whole number), **stor_id** identifies the store that originated the order (fixed-length character), **ponum** is the purchase order number of the store (variable-length character), and **sdate** is the date the sale was entered (date or timestamp). The 16 rows each have a unique index on **sonum**.

For full information on sales orders, join **sales** to **salesdetails** on **sonum**.

sonum not null <u>salesind</u>	stor_id not null	ponum not null	sdate null
1	7066	QA7442.3	Sep 13 1998 12:00 am
2	7067	D4482	Sep 14 1998 12:00 am
3	7131	N914008	Sep 14 1998 12:00 am
4	7131	N914014	Sep 14 1998 12:00 am
5	8042	423LL922	Sep 14 1998 12:00 am
6	8042	423LL930	Sep 14 1998 12:00 am
7	6380	722a	Sep 13 1998 12:00 am
8	6380	6871	Sep 14 1998 12:00 am
9	8042	P723	Mar 11 2001 12:00 am
10	7896	QQ2299	Oct 28 2000 12:00 am
11	7896	TQ456	Dec 12 2000 12:00 am
12	8042	QA879.1	May 22 2000 12:00 am
13	7066	A2976	May 24 2000 12:00 am
14	7131	P3087a	May 29 2000 12:00 am
15	7067	P2121	Jun 15 2000 12:00 am
19	7896	X999	Feb 21 2001 12:00 am

salesdetails Table

In this table, you'll find the line-item entries for each sales order. The order numbers are integers, as are `qty_ordered` and `qty_shipped`. The title identification number is fixed-length character. There is a unique composite index on the combination of `sonum` and `title_id`, and there are 21 rows.

sonum not null <u>sdind</u>	title_id not null	qty_ordered not null	qty_shipped null	date_shipped null
1	PS2091	75	75	Sep 15 1998 12:00 am
2	PS2091	10	10	Sep 15 1998 12:00 am
3	PS2091	20	720	Sep 18 1998 12:00 am
4	MC3021	25	20	Sep 18 1998 12:00 am
5	MC3021	15	15	Sep 14 1998 12:00 am
6	BU1032	10	3	Sep 22 1998 12:00 am
7	PS2091	3	3	Sep 20 1998 12:00 am
8	BU1032	5	5	Sep 14 1998 12:00 am

9	BU1111	25	5	Mar	28	2001	12:00	am
10	BU7832	15	15	Oct	29	2000	12:00	am
11	MC2222	10	10	Jan	12	2001	12:00	am
12	PC1035	30	30	May	24	2000	12:00	am
13	PC8888	50	50	May	24	2000	12:00	am
14	PS1372	20	20	May	29	2000	12:00	am
14	PS2106	25	25	Apr	29	2000	12:00	am
14	PS3333	15	10	May	29	2000	12:00	am
14	PS7777	25	25	Jun	13	2000	12:00	am
15	TC3218	40	40	Jun	15	2000	12:00	am
15	TC4203	20	20	May	30	2000	12:00	am
15	TC7777	20	10	Jun	17	2000	12:00	am
19	BU2075	35	35	Mar	15	2001	12:00	am

editors **Table**

This table contains information about editors. Four columns (ed_id, phone, state, zip) are fixed-length character datatype. The other columns are all variable-length character datatype. There is a unique index on ed_id and another index (nonunique) on the combination of editor last and first name. The ID and name columns do not allow NULL—the others do.

ed_id	ed_lname ed_fname	ed_pos	phone	address	city state zip	ed_boss
not null edidind	not null ednmind	null	null	null		null
===========	================	===========	============	=================	==============	===========
321-55-8906	DeLongue Martinella	project	415 843-2222	3000 6th St.	Berkeley CA 94710	993-86-0420
527-72-3246	Greene Morningstar	copy	615 297-2723	22 Graybar Rd.	Nashville TN 37215	826-11-9034
712-45-1867	del Castillo Innes	copy	615 996-8275	2286 Cram Pl. #86	Ann Arbor MI 48105	826-11-9034
777-02-9831	Samuelson Bernard	project	415 843-6990	27 Yosemite	Oakland CA 94609	993-86-0420
777-66-9902	Almond Alfred	copy	312 699-4177	1010 E. Devon	Chicago IL 60018	826-11-9034
826-11-9034	Himmel Eleanore	project	617 423-0552	97 Bleaker	Boston MA 02210	993-86-0420
885-23-9140	Rutherford-Hayes Hannah	project	301 468-3909	32 Rockbill Pike	Rockbill MD 20852	993-86-0420
943-88-7920	Kaspchek Christof	acquisition	415 549-3909	18 Severe Rd.	Berkeley CA 94710	(NULL)
993-86-0420	McCann Dennis	acquisition	301 468-3909	32 Rockbill Pike	Rockbill MD 20852	(NULL)

`titleditors` Table

The `titleditors` table keeps track of associations between editors and the books they work on and there is a unique index on the combination of editor and title. There are 35 rows. The ID columns are fixed-length character datatype; the order column is an integer.

ed_id not null teind	title_id not null	ed_ord null
============	========	======
321-55-8906	BU1032	2
321-55-8906	BU1111	2
321-55-8906	BU2075	3
321-55-8906	BU7832	2
321-55-8906	PC1035	2
321-55-8906	PC8888	2
777-02-9831	PC1035	3
777-02-9831	PC8888	3
826-11-9034	BU2075	2
826-11-9034	PS1372	2
826-11-9034	PS2091	2
826-11-9034	PS2106	2
826-11-9034	PS3333	2
826-11-9034	PS7777	2
885-23-9140	MC2222	2
885-23-9140	MC3021	2
885-23-9140	TC3281	2
885-23-9140	TC4203	2
885-23-9140	TC7777	2
943-88-7920	BU1032	1
943-88-7920	BU1111	1
943-88-7920	BU2075	1
943-88-7920	BU7832	1
943-88-7920	PC1035	1
943-88-7920	PC8888	1
993-86-0420	MC2222	1
993-86-0420	MC3021	1
993-86-0420	PS1372	1
993-86-0420	PS2091	1
993-86-0420	PS2106	1

```
993-86-0420 PS3333        1
993-86-0420 PS7777        1
993-86-0420 TC3218        1
993-86-0420 TC4203        1
993-86-0420 TC7777        1
```

roysched **Table**

The roysched table is a lookup table. Publishers use it for calculating author royalties, which are based on sales. As the sales increase, the royalty rate also increases. The title_id column is fixed-length character, the low and high ranges are integers, and royalty is a decimal value. The nonunique index is on title_id, and there are 51 rows.

title_id not null rstidind	lorange null	hirange null	royalty null
BU1032	0	5000	.10
BU1032	5001	50000	.12
PC1035	0	2000	.10
PC1035	2001	4000	.12
PC1035	4001	50000	.16
BU2075	0	1000	.10
BU2075	1001	5000	.12
BU2075	5001	7000	.16
BU2075	7001	50000	.18
PS9999	0	50000	.10
PS2091	0	1000	.10
PS2091	1001	5000	.12
PS2091	5001	50000	.14
PS2106	0	2000	.10
PS2106	2001	5000	.12
PS2106	5001	50000	.14
MC3021	0	1000	.10
MC3021	1001	2000	.12
MC3021	2001	6000	.14
MC3021	6001	8000	.18
MC3021	8001	50000	.20
TC3218	0	2000	.10

TC3218	2001	6000	.12
TC3218	6001	8000	.16
TC3218	8001	50000	.16
PC8888	0	5000	.10
PC8888	5001	50000	.12
PS7777	0	5000	.10
PS7777	5001	50000	.12
PS3333	0	5000	.10
PS3333	5001	50000	.12
MC3026	0	1000	.10
MC3026	1001	2000	.12
MC3026	2001	6000	.14
MC3026	6001	8000	.18
MC3026	8001	50000	.20
BU1111	0	4000	.10
BU1111	4001	8000	.12
BU1111	8001	50000	.14
MC2222	0	2000	.10
MC2222	2001	4000	.12
MC2222	4001	8000	.14
MC2222	8001	12000	.16
TC7777	0	5000	.10
TC7777	5001	15000	.12
TC4203	0	2000	.10
TC4203	2001	8000	.12
TC4203	8001	16000	.14
BU7832	0	5000	.10
BU7832	5001	50000	.12
PS1372	0	50000	.10

CREATE Statements for the bookbiz Database

The CREATE and INSERT statements for creating the bookbiz database are provided for your reference in re-creating this database on your system. There are four versions of the CREATE script (to cover datatype differences):

- Adaptive Server Anywhere
- Transact-SQL (Adaptive Server Enterprise and SQL Server)
- Oracle
- Informix

If you're using the Adaptive Server Anywhere software on the CD, you don't need to run the CREATE or INSERT scripts. The bookbiz database is already set up and loaded. Just follow the directions in the CD *readPSH4* file. However, in case you want to create similar tables or reload data, the ASA files are available.

Be sure to drop tables before you try to re-create them, or change the table names in the script. SQL does not allow multiple tables with the same name. If you are keeping the table structure but refreshing the data, remove all data (with a DELETE statement without a WHERE clause) from a table before reloading the data for that table.

Depending on what tool you are using, you may need to change the terminators (go or semicolon in these scripts) to work in your environment.

There is only one script for INSERTs; it works on all the systems tested here. There is also a single script for creating all the views.

All of these scripts are available on the CD.

Adaptive Server Anywhere CREATEs

```
/*
**LOGIN is DBA
**PASSWORD is SQL
*/
--DROP TABLE and CREATE TABLE commands
drop table authors;
create table authors
(au_id char(11) not null,
au_lname varchar(40) not null,
au_fname varchar(20) not null,
phone char(12) null,
address varchar(40) null,
city varchar(20) null,
state char(2) null,
zip char(5) null);
grant select on authors to public
;
drop table publishers;
create table publishers
(pub_id char(4) not null,
pub_name varchar(40) null,
address varchar(40) null,
```

```
city varchar(20) null,
state char(2) null);
grant select on publishers to public
;
drop table roysched;
create table roysched
(title_id char(6) not null,
lorange int null,
hirange int null,
royalty dec(5,2) null);
grant select on roysched to public;
;
drop table titleauthors;
create table titleauthors
(au_id char(11) not null,
title_id char(6) not null,
au_ord tinyint null,
royaltyshare dec(5,2) null);
grant select on titleauthors to public
;
drop table titles;
create table titles
(title_id char(6) not null,
title varchar(80) not null,
type char(12) null,
pub_id char(4) null,
price numeric(8,2) null,
advance numeric(10,2) null,
ytd_sales int null,
contract bit not null,
notes varchar(200) null,
pubdate date null);
grant select on titles to public
;
drop table editors;
create table editors
(ed_id char(11) not null,
ed_lname varchar(40) not null,
ed_fname varchar(20) not null,
ed_pos varchar(12) null,
phone char(12) null,
```

```
address varchar(40) null,
city varchar(20) null,
state char(2) null,
zip char(5) null,
ed_boss char(11) null );
grant select on editors to public
;
drop table titleditors;
create table titleditors
(ed_id char(11) not null,
title_id char(6) not null,
ed_ord tinyint null);
grant select on titleditors to public
;
drop table sales;
create table sales
(sonum int not null,
stor_id char(4) not null,
ponum varchar(20) not null,
sdate date null);
grant select on sales to public
;
drop table salesdetails;
create table salesdetails
(sonum int not null,
qty_ordered smallint not null,
qty_shipped smallint null,
title_id char(6) not null,
date_shipped date null);
grant select on salesdetails to public
;
--CREATE INDEX commands
create unique index pubind on publishers (pub_id);
create unique index auidind on authors (au_id);
create index aunmind on authors (au_lname, au_fname);
create unique index titleidind on titles (title_id);
create index titleind on titles (title);
create unique index taind on titleauthors (au_id, title_id);
create unique index edind on editors (ed_id);
create index ednmind on editors (ed_lname, ed_fname);
create unique index teind on titleditors (ed_id, title_id);
```

```
create index rstidind on roysched (title_id);
create unique index sdind on salesdetails (sonum, title_id) ;
create unique index salesind on sales (sonum);
```

Transact-SQL CREATEs

```
/*
1. Create database with GUI tools or with CREATE DATABASE command.
2. Connect to bookbiz database with GUI tools or with USE command.
3. Load entire script. Ignore error messages for DROP commands.
4. Use the INSERT script to add data.
*/
--create database bookbiz
--go
--use bookbiz
--go
--DROP TABLE and CREATE TABLE commands
drop table authors
go
create table authors
(au_id char(11) not null,
au_lname varchar(40) not null,
au_fname varchar(20) not null,
phone char(12) null,
address varchar(40) null,
city varchar(20) null,
state char(2) null,
zip char(5) null)
go
grant select on authors to public
go
drop table publishers
go
create table publishers
(pub_id char(4) not null,
pub_name varchar(40) null,
address varchar(40) null,
city varchar(20) null,
state char(2) null)
go
```

```
grant select on publishers to public
go
drop table roysched
go
create table roysched
(title_id char(6) not null,
lorange int null,
hirange int null,
royalty float null)
go
grant select on roysched to public
go
drop table titleauthors
go
create table titleauthors
(au_id char(11) not null,
title_id char(6) not null,
au_ord tinyint null,
royaltyshare float null)
go
grant select on titleauthors to public
go
drop table titles
go
create table titles
(title_id char(6) not null,
title varchar(80) not null,
type char(12) null,
pub_id char(4) null,
price money null,
advance money null,
ytd_sales int null,
contract bit not null,
notes varchar(200) null,
pubdate smalldatetime null)
go
grant select on titles to public
go
drop table editors
go
```

```
create table editors
(ed_id char(11) not null,
ed_lname varchar(40) not null,
ed_fname varchar(20) not null,
ed_pos varchar(12) null,
phone char(12) null,
address varchar(40) null,
city varchar(20) null,
state char(2) null,
zip char(5) null,
ed_boss char(11) null )
go
grant select on editors to public
go
drop table titleditors
go
create table titleditors
(ed_id char(11) not null,
title_id char(6) not null,
ed_ord tinyint null)
go
grant select on titleditors to public
go
drop table sales
go
create table sales
(sonum int not null,
stor_id char(4) not null,
ponum varchar(20) not null,
sdate smalldatetime null)
go
grant select on sales to public
go
drop table salesdetails
go
create table salesdetails
(sonum int not null,
qty_ordered smallint not null,
qty_shipped smallint null,
title_id char(6) not null,
date_shipped smalldatetime null)
```

```
go
grant select on salesdetails to public
go
--CREATE INDEX commands
create unique index pubind
on publishers(pub_id)
go
create unique index auidind
on authors (au_id)
go
create index aunmind
on authors (au_lname, au fname)
go
create unique index titleidind
on titles (title_id)
go
create index titleind
on titles (title)
go
create unique index taind
on titleauthors (au_id, title_id)
go
create unique index edind
on editors (ed_id)
go
create index ednmind
on editors (ed_lname, ed_fname)
go
create unique index teind
on titleditors (ed_id, title_id)
go
create index rstidind
on roysched (title_id)
go
create unique index sdind
on salesdetails (sonum, title_id)
go
create unique index salesind
on sales (sonum)
go
```

```
/* check to make sure the 9 tables were completed with this query:
select name
from sysobjects
where type = 'U'
*/
```

Oracle CREATEs

```
--read in at SQL Plus as
--connect name/password (substitute yours);
--start filename.txt;
-- DROP TABLE and CREATE TABLE commands
drop table authors;
create table authors
 (au_id char(11) not null,
  au_lname varchar2(40) not null,
  au_fname varchar2(20) not null,
  phone char(12) null,
  address varchar2(40) null,
  city varchar2(20) null,
  state char(2) null,
  zip char(5) null);
grant select on authors to public
;
drop table publishers;
create table publishers
   (pub_id char(4) not null,
    pub_name varchar2(40) null,
    address varchar2(40) null,
    city varchar(20) null,
    state char(2) null);
grant select on publishers to public
;
drop table roysched;
create table roysched
 (title_id char(6) not null,
  lorange number null,
  hirange number null,
  royalty number(5,2) null);
```

```
grant select on roysched to public
;
drop table titleauthors;
create table titleauthors
 (au_id char(11) not null,
 title_id char(6) not null,
 au_ord number not null,
 royaltyshare number (5,2) null);
grant select on titleauthors to public
;
drop table titles;
create table titles
   (title_id char(6) not null,
   title varchar2(80) not null,
   type char(12) null,
   pub_id char(4) null,
   price number(9,2) null,
   advance number(9,2) null,
   ytd_sales int null,
   contract char(1) not null,
   notes varchar2(200) null,
   pubdate date null);
grant select on titles to public
;
drop table sales;
create table sales
   (sonum number not null,
   stor_id char(4) not null,
   ponum varchar2(20) not null,
   sdate date null);
grant select on sales to public
;
drop table editors;
create table editors
 (ed_id char(11) not null,
 ed_lname varchar2(40) not null,
 ed_fname varchar2(20) not null,
 ed_pos varchar2(12) null,
 phone char(12) null,
 address varchar2(40) null,
 city varchar2(20) null,
```

```
 state char(2) null,
 zip char(5) null,
 ed_boss char(11) null );
grant select on editors to public
;
drop table titleditors;
create table titleditors
 (ed_id char(11) not null,
 title_id char(6) not null,
 ed_ord number null);
grant select on titleditors to public
;
drop table salesdetails;
create table salesdetails
  (sonum number not null,
  qty_ordered number not null,
  qty_shipped number null,
  title_id char(6) not null,
  date_shipped date null);
grant select on salesdetails to public
;
--CREATE INDEX commands
create unique index pubind on publishers(pub_id);
create unique index auidind on authors (au_id);
create index aunmind on authors (au_lname, au_fname);
create unique index titleidind on titles (title_id);
create index titleind on titles (title);
create unique index taind on titleauthors (au_id, title_id);
create unique index edind on editors (ed_id);
create index ednmind on editors (ed_lname, ed_fname);
create unique index teind on titleditors (ed_id, title_id);
create index rstidind on roysched (title_id);
create unique index sdind on salesdetails (sonum, title_id);
create unique index salesind on sales (sonum);
```

Informix CREATEs

```
--CREATE TABLE and DROP TABLE commands
drop table authors;
create table authors
```

```
(au_id    char(11) not null,
au_lname varchar(40) not null,
au_fname varchar(20) not null,
phone    char(12),
address  varchar(40),
city     varchar(20),
state    char(2) ,
zip      char(5)  );
grant select on authors to public
;
drop table publishers;
create table publishers
( pub_id char(4) not null,
pub_name varchar(40) ,
address varchar(40) ,
city varchar(20) ,
state char(2)  );
grant select on publishers to public
;
drop table titleauthors;
create table titleauthors
(au_id char(11) not null,
title_id char(6) not null,
au_ord smallint ,
royaltyshare decimal );
grant select on titleauthors to public
;
drop table roysched;
create table roysched
(title_id char(6) not null,
lorange int   ,
hirange int   ,
royalty decimal   );
grant select on roysched to public
;
drop table titles;
create table titles
( title_id char(6) not null,
title varchar(80) not null,
type char(12)   ,
pub_id char(4)   ,
```

```
price money ,
advance money   ,
ytd_sales int ,
contract char(1) not null,
notes varchar(200)   ,
pubdate date);
grant select on titles to public
;
drop table sales;
create table sales
(sonum int not null,
stor_id char(4) not null,
ponum varchar(20) not null,
sdate date   );
grant select on sales to public
;
drop table salesdetails;
create table salesdetails
(sonum int not null,
qty_ordered smallint not null,
qty_shipped smallint ,
title_id char(6) not null,
date_shipped date   );
grant select on salesdetails to public
;
drop table editors;
create table editors
 (ed_id char(11) not null,
 ed_lname varchar(40) not null,
 ed_fname varchar(20) not null,
 ed_pos varchar(12) ,
 phone char(12) ,
 address varchar(40) ,
 city varchar(20) ,
 state char(2) ,
 zip char(5),
 ed_boss char(11)   );
grant select on editors to public
;
drop table titleditors;
create table titleditors
```

```
(ed_id char(11) not null,
 title_id char(6) not null,
 ed_ord int );
grant select on titleditors to public
;
--CREATE INDEX commands
create unique index auidind on authors(au_id);
create index aunmind on authors (au_lname, au_fname);
create unique index pubind on publishers(pub_id);
create unique index titleidind on titles (title_id);
create index titleind on titles (title);
create unique index taind on titleauthors (au_id, title id);
create index rstidind on roysched (title_id);
create unique index salesind on sales (sonum) ;
create unique index sdind on salesdetails (sonum, title_id);
create unique index edind on editors (ed_id);
create index ednmind on editors (ed_lname, ed_fname);
```

INSERT Statements

Once you've built the tables, it is easy to fill them with data, although you may need to change or remove the statement terminator. After running the INSERT statements, check rows in tables with a command like the following:

> *SQL*
> ```
> select count(*)
> from authors
> ```

The target results for each table are shown in Figure D.1.

For Oracle, the ampersand (&) is the variable marker. When you insert rows into **publisher**, avoid problems with & in either of these ways:

- Change the & in "Binnet & Hardley" so that the company name becomes "Binnet and Hardley" or "Binnet + Hardley"
- Turn off variable substitution with SET SCAN OFF. Turn it back on with SET SCAN ON after the INSERT (the code is in the script; just remove the double dash comment sign).

Table	Rows
authors	23
titleauthors	25
titles	18
roysched	51
publishers	3
sales	16
salesdetails	21
titleditors	35
editors	9

Figure D.1 Number of Rows in Each Table

Other venders also require minor modifications as noted in the commented script.

```
--ORACLE modifications
--& is variable substitution sign for Oracle. Turn it off with
--set scan off;
--turn it back on with set scan on
--set date format for Oracle with alter session:
--alter session set nls_date_format = 'mm/dd/YYYY';

--ADAPTIVE SERVER ANYWHERE modifications
--define the date part order
--set option date_order = 'MDY';
--if you want, change the format with a command such as
--set option date_format= 'Mmm dd yyyy hh:mm aa';
--set option precision= 8;
--set option scale = 2;
```

```
--ADAPTIVE SERVER ENTERPRISE modifications
--either change the terminator to semicolon (;) in your tool
--or change the semicolon in the script to "go"

insert into authors
values('409-56-7008', 'Bennet', 'Abraham',
'415 658-9932', '6223 Bateman St.', 'Berkeley', 'CA', '94705')
;
insert into authors
values ('213-46-8915', 'Green', 'Marjorie',
'415 986-7020', '309 63rd St. #411', 'Oakland', 'CA', '94618')
;
insert into authors
values('238-95-7766', 'Carson', 'Cheryl',
'415 548-7723', '589 Darwin Ln.', 'Berkeley', 'CA', '94705')
;
insert into authors
values('998-72-3567', 'Ringer', 'Albert',
'801 826-0752', '67 Seventh Av.', 'Salt Lake City', 'UT', '84152')
;
insert into authors
values('899-46-2035', 'Ringer', 'Anne',
'801 826-0752', '67 Seventh Av.', 'Salt Lake City', 'UT', '84152')
;
insert into authors
values('722-51-5454', 'DeFrance', 'Michel',
'219 547-9982', '3 Balding Pl.', 'Gary', 'IN', '46403')
;
insert into authors
values('807-91-6654', 'Panteley', 'Sylvia',
'301 946-8853', '1956 Arlington Pl.', 'Rockville', 'MD', '20853')
;
insert into authors
values('893-72-1158', 'McBadden', 'Heather',
'707 448-4982', '301 Putnam', 'Vacaville', 'CA', '95688')
;
insert into authors
values('724-08-9931', 'Stringer', 'Dirk',
'415 843-2991', '5420 Telegraph Av.', 'Oakland', 'CA', '94609')
;
insert into authors
```

```
values('274-80-9391', 'Straight', 'Dick',
'415 834-2919', '5420 College Av.', 'Oakland', 'CA', '94609')
;
insert into authors
values('756-30-7391', 'Karsen', 'Livia',
'415 534-9219', '5720 McAuley St.', 'Oakland', 'CA', '94609')
;
insert into authors
values('724-80-9391', 'MacFeather', 'Stearns',
'415 354-7128', '44 Upland Hts.', 'Oakland', 'CA', '94612')
;
insert into authors
values('427-17-2319', 'Dull', 'Ann',
'415 836-7128', '3410 Blonde St.', 'Palo Alto', 'CA', '94301')
;
insert into authors
values('672-71-3249', 'Yokomoto', 'Akiko',
'415 935-4228', '3 Silver Ct.', 'Walnut Creek', 'CA', '94595')
;
insert into authors
values('267-41-2394', 'O''Leary', 'Michael',
'408 286-2428', '22 Cleveland Av. #14', 'San Jose', 'CA', '95128')
;
insert into authors
values('472-27-2349', 'Gringlesby', 'Burt',
'707 938-6445', 'PO Box 792', 'Covelo', 'CA', '95428')
;
insert into authors
values('527-72-3246', 'Greene', 'Morningstar',
'615 297-2723', '22 Graybar Rd.', 'Nashville', 'TN', '37215')
;
insert into authors
values('172-32-1176', 'White', 'Johnson',
'408 496-7223', '10932 Bigge Rd.', 'Menlo Park', 'CA', '94025')
;
insert into authors
values('712-45-1867', 'del Castillo', 'Innes',
'615 996-8275', '2286 Cram Pl. #86', 'Ann Arbor', 'MI', '48105')
;
insert into authors
values('846-92-7186', 'Hunter', 'Sheryl',
```

```
'415 836-7128', '3410 Blonde St.', 'Palo Alto', 'CA', '94301')
;
insert into authors
values('486-29-1786', 'Locksley', 'Chastity',
'415 585-4620', '18 Broadway Av.', 'San Francisco', 'CA', '94130')
;
insert into authors
values('648-92-1872', 'Blotchet-Halls', 'Reginald',
'503 745-6402', '55 Hillsdale Bl.', 'Corvallis', 'OR', '97330')
;
insert into authors
values('341-22-1782', 'Smith', 'Meander',
'913 843-0462', '10 Misisipi Dr.', 'Lawrence', 'KS', '66044')
;
insert into publishers
values('0736', 'New Age Books', '1 1st St','Boston', 'MA')
;
insert into publishers
values('0877', 'Binnet & Hardley','2 2nd Ave.', 'Washington', 'DC')
;
insert into publishers
values('1389', 'Algodata Infosystems', '3 3rd Dr.','Berkeley', 'CA')
;
insert into roysched
values('BU1032', 0, 5000, .10)
;
insert into roysched
values('BU1032', 5001, 50000, .12)
;
insert into roysched
values('PC1035', 0, 2000, .10)
;
insert into roysched
values('PC1035', 2001, 4000, .12)
;
insert into roysched
values('PC1035', 4001, 50000, .16)
;
insert into roysched
values('BU2075', 0, 1000, .10)
;
```

```
insert into roysched
values('BU2075', 1001, 5000, .12)
;
insert into roysched
values('BU2075', 5001, 7000, .16)
;
insert into roysched
values('BU2075', 7001, 50000, .18)
;
insert into roysched
values('PS9999', 0, 50000, .10)
;
insert into roysched
values('PS2091', 0, 1000, .10)
;
insert into roysched
values('PS2091', 1001, 5000, .12)
;
insert into roysched
values('PS2091', 5001, 50000, .14)
;
insert into roysched
values('PS2106', 0, 2000, .10)
;
insert into roysched
values('PS2106', 2001, 5000, .12)
;
insert into roysched
values('PS2106', 5001, 50000, .14)
;
insert into roysched
values('MC3021', 0, 1000, .10)
;
insert into roysched
values('MC3021', 1001, 2000, .12)
;
insert into roysched
values('MC3021', 2001, 6000, .14)
;
insert into roysched
values('MC3021', 6001, 8000, .18)
;
```

```
insert into roysched
values('MC3021', 8001, 50000, .20)
;
insert into roysched
values('TC3218', 0, 2000, .10)
;
insert into roysched
values('TC3218', 2001, 6000, .12)
;
insert into roysched
values('TC3218', 6001, 8000, .16)
;
insert into roysched
values('TC3218', 8001, 50000, .16)
;
insert into roysched
values('PC8888', 0, 5000, .10)
;
insert into roysched
values('PC8888', 5001, 50000, .12)
;
insert into roysched
values('PS7777', 0, 5000, .10)
;
insert into roysched
values('PS7777', 5001, 50000, .12)
;
insert into roysched
values('PS3333', 0, 5000, .10)
;
insert into roysched
values('PS3333', 5001, 50000, .12)
;
insert into roysched
values('MC3026', 0, 1000, .10)
;
insert into roysched
values('MC3026',1001, 2000, .12)
;
insert into roysched
values('MC3026', 2001, 6000, .14)
;
```

```
insert into roysched
values('MC3026', 6001, 8000, .18)
;
insert into roysched
values('MC3026', 8001, 50000, .20)
;
insert into roysched
values('BU1111', 0, 4000, .10)
;
insert into roysched
values('BU1111', 4001, 8000, .12)
;
insert into roysched
values('BU1111', 8001, 50000, .14)
;
insert into roysched
values('MC2222', 0, 2000, .10)
;
insert into roysched
values('MC2222', 2001, 4000, .12)
;
insert into roysched
values('MC2222', 4001, 8000, .14)
;
insert into roysched
values('MC2222', 8001, 12000, .16)
;
insert into roysched
values('TC7777', 0, 5000, .10)
;
insert into roysched
values('TC7777', 5001, 15000, .12)
;
insert into roysched
values('TC4203', 0, 2000, .10)
;
insert into roysched
values('TC4203', 2001, 8000, .12)
;
insert into roysched
values('TC4203', 8001, 16000, .14)
;
```

```
insert into roysched
values('BU7832', 0, 5000, .10)
;
insert into roysched
values('BU7832', 5001, 50000, .12)
;
insert into roysched
values('PS1372', 0, 50000, .10)
;
insert into titleauthors
values('409-56-7008', 'BU1032', 1, .60)
;
insert into titleauthors
values('486-29-1786', 'PS7777', 1, 1.00)
;
insert into titleauthors
values('486-29-1786', 'PC9999', 1, 1.00)
;
insert into titleauthors
values('712-45-1867', 'MC2222', 1, 1.00)
;
insert into titleauthors
values('172-32-1176', 'PS3333', 1, 1.00)
;
insert into titleauthors
values('213-46-8915', 'BU1032', 2, .40)
;
insert into titleauthors
values('238-95-7766', 'PC1035', 1, 1.00)
;
insert into titleauthors
values('213-46-8915', 'BU2075', 1, 1.00)
;
insert into titleauthors
values('998-72-3567', 'PS2091', 1, .50)
;
insert into titleauthors
values('899-46-2035', 'PS2091', 2, .50)
;
insert into titleauthors
values('998-72-3567', 'PS2106', 1, 1.00)
;
```

```
insert into titleauthors
values('722-51-5454', 'MC3021', 1, .75)
;
insert into titleauthors
values('899-46-2035', 'MC3021', 2, .25)
;
insert into titleauthors
values('807-91-6654', 'TC3218', 1, 1.00)
;
insert into titleauthors
values('274-80-9391', 'BU7832', 1, 1.00)
;
insert into titleauthors
values('427-17-2319', 'PC8888', 1, .50)
;
insert into titleauthors
values('846-92-7186', 'PC8888', 2, .50)
;
insert into titleauthors
values('756-30-7391', 'PS1372', 1, .75)
;
insert into titleauthors
values('724-80-9391', 'PS1372', 2, .25)
;
insert into titleauthors
values('724-80-9391', 'BU1111', 1, .60)
;
insert into titleauthors
values('267-41-2394', 'BU1111', 2, .40)
;
insert into titleauthors
values('672-71-3249', 'TC7777', 1, .40)
;
insert into titleauthors
values('267-41-2394', 'TC7777', 2, .30)
;
insert into titleauthors
values('472-27-2349', 'TC7777', 3, .30)
;
insert into titleauthors
values('648-92-1872', 'TC4203', 1, 1.00)
;
```

```
insert into titles
values ('PC8888', 'Secrets of Silicon Valley',
'popular_comp', '1389', 40.00, 8000.00, 4095,1,
'Muckraking reporting on the world''s largest computer hardware and
software manufacturers.',
'06/12/1998')
;
insert into titles
values ('BU1032', 'The Busy Executive''s Database Guide',
'business', '1389', 29.99, 5000.00, 4095, 1,
'An overview of available database systems with emphasis on common
business applications.  Illustrated.',
'06/12/1998')
;
insert into titles
values ('PS7777', 'Emotional Security: A New Algorithm',
'psychology', '0736', 17.99, 4000.00, 3336, 1,
'Protecting yourself and your loved ones from undue emotional stress
in the modern world.  Use of computer and nutritional aids
emphasized.',
'06/12/1998')
;
insert into titles
values ('PS3333', 'Prolonged Data Deprivation: Four Case Studies',
'psychology', '0736', 29.99, 2000.00, 4072,1,
'What happens when the data runs dry?  Searching evaluations of
information-shortage effects.',
'06/12/1998')
;
insert into titles
values ('BU1111', 'Cooking with Computers: Surreptitious Balance
Sheets',
'business', '1389', 21.95, 5000.00, 3876, 1,
'Helpful hints on how to use your electronic resources to the best
advantage.',
'06/09/1998')
;
insert into titles
values ('MC2222', 'Silicon Valley Gastronomic Treats',
'mod_cook', '0877', 29.99, 0.00, 2032, 1,
```

```
    'Favorite recipes for quick, easy, and elegant meals tried and tested
by people who never have time to eat, let alone cook.',
    '06/09/1998')
;
insert into titles
values ('TC7777', 'Sushi, Anyone?',
'trad_cook', '0877', 29.99, 8000.00, 4095, 1,
'Detailed instructions on improving your position in life by learning
how to make authentic Japanese sushi in your spare time. 5-10%
increase in number of friends per recipe reported from beta test. ',
'06/12/1998')
;
insert into titles
values ('TC4203', 'Fifty Years in Buckingham Palace Kitchens',
'trad_cook', '0877', 21.95, 4000.00, 15096, 1,
'More anecdotes from the Queen''s favorite cook describing life among
English royalty.  Recipes, techniques, tender vignettes.',
'06/12/1998')
;
insert into titles
values ('PC1035', 'But Is It User Friendly?',
'popular_comp', '1389', 42.95, 7000.00, 8780, 1,
'A survey of software for the naive user, focusing on the
''friendliness'' of each.',
'06/30/1998')
;
insert into titles
values('BU2075', 'You Can Combat Computer Stress!',
'business', '0736', 12.99, 10125.00, 18722, 1,
'The latest medical and psychological techniques for living with the
electronic office.  Easy-to-understand explanations.',
'06/30/1998')
;
insert into titles
values('PS2091', 'Is Anger the Enemy?',
'psychology', '0736', 21.95, 2275.00, 2045, 1,
'Carefully researched study of the effects of strong emotions on the
body. Metabolic charts included.',
'06/15/1998')
;
```

```
insert into titles
values('PS2106', 'Life Without Fear',
'psychology', '0736', 17.00, 6000.00, 111, 1,
'New exercise, meditation, and nutritional techniques that can reduce
the shock of daily interactions. Popular audience.  Sample menus
included, exercise video available separately.',
'10/05/1998')
;
insert into titles
values('MC3021', 'The Gourmet Microwave',
'mod_cook', '0877', 12.99, 15000.00, 22246, 1,
'Traditional French gourmet recipes adapted for modern microwave
cooking.',
'06/18/1998')
;
insert into titles
values('TC3218',
'Onions, Leeks, and Garlic: Cooking Secrets of the Mediterranean',
'trad_cook', '0877', 40.95, 7000.00, 375, 1,
'Profusely illustrated in color, this makes a wonderful gift book for
a cuisine-oriented friend.',
'10/21/1998')
;
insert into titles (title_id, title, pub_id, contract)
values('MC3026', 'The Psychology of Computer Cooking', '0877', 0)
;
insert into titles
values ('BU7832', 'Straight Talk About Computers',
'business', '1389', 29.99, 5000.00, 4095, 1,
'Annotated analysis of what computers can do for you: a no-hype guide
for the critical user.',
'06/22/1998')
;
insert into titles
values('PS1372',
'Computer Phobic and Non-Phobic Individuals: Behavior Variations',
'psychology', '0736', 41.59, 7000.00, 375, 1,
'A must for the specialist, this book examines the difference between
those who hate and fear computers and those who think they are
swell.',
'10/21/1998')
;
```

```
insert into titles (title_id, title, type, pub_id, contract, notes)
values('PC9999', 'Net Etiquette', 'popular_comp', '1389', 0,
'A must-read for computer conferencing debutantes!.')
;
insert into editors
values ( '321-55-8906', 'DeLongue', 'Martinella', 'project',
'415 843-2222', '3000 6th St.', 'Berkeley', 'CA', '94710',
'993-86-0420' )
;
insert into editors
values ( '527-72-3246', 'Greene', 'Morningstar', 'copy',
'615 297-2723', '22 Graybar House Rd.', 'Nashville', 'TN','37215',
'826-11-9034' )
;
insert into editors
values ( '712-45-1867', 'del Castillo', 'Innes', 'copy',
'615 996-8275', '2286 Cram Pl. #86', 'Ann Arbor', 'MI', '48105',
'826-11-9034' )
;
insert into editors
values ('777-02-9831', 'Samuelson', 'Bernard', 'project',
'415 843-6990', '27 Yosemite', 'Oakland', 'CA', '94609',
'993-86-0420' )
;
insert into editors
values ('777-66-9902', 'Almond', 'Alfred', 'copy',
'312 699-4177', '1010 E. Devon', 'Chicago', 'IL', '60018',
'826-11-9034' )
;
insert into editors
values ('826-11-9034', 'Himmel', 'Eleanore', 'project',
'617 423-0552', '97 Bleaker', 'Boston', 'MA', '02210', '993-86-0420' )
;
insert into editors
values ('885-23-9140', 'Rutherford-Hayes', 'Hannah', 'project',
'301 468-3909', '32 Rockbill Pike', 'Rockbill', 'MD', '20852',
'993-86-0420' )
;
insert into editors
values ('993-86-0420', 'McCann', 'Dennis', 'acquisition',
'301 468-3909', '32 Rockbill Pike', 'Rockbill', 'MD', '20852', null )
;
```

```
insert into editors
values ('943-88-7920', 'Kaspchek', 'Christof', 'acquisition',
'415 549-3909', '18 Severe Rd.', 'Berkeley', 'CA', '94710', null)
;
insert into titleditors values
('826-11-9034', 'BU2075', 2)
;
insert into titleditors values
('826-11-9034', 'PS2091', 2)
;
insert into titleditors values
('826-11-9034', 'PS2106', 2)
;
insert into titleditors values
('826-11-9034', 'PS3333', 2)
;
insert into titleditors values
('826-11-9034', 'PS7777', 2)
;
insert into titleditors values
('826-11-9034', 'PS1372', 2)
;
insert into titleditors values
('885-23-9140', 'MC2222', 2)
;
insert into titleditors values
('885-23-9140', 'MC3021', 2)
;
insert into titleditors values
('885-23-9140', 'TC3281', 2)
;
insert into titleditors values
('885-23-9140', 'TC4203', 2)
;
insert into titleditors values
('885-23-9140', 'TC7777', 2)
;
insert into titleditors values
('321-55-8906', 'BU1032', 2)
;
```

```
insert into titleditors values
('321-55-8906', 'BU1111', 2)
;
insert into titleditors values
('321-55-8906', 'BU7832', 2)
;
insert into titleditors values
('321-55-8906', 'PC1035', 2)
;
insert into titleditors values
('321-55-8906', 'PC8888', 2)
;
insert into titleditors values
('321-55-8906', 'BU2075', 3)
;
insert into titleditors values
('777-02-9831', 'PC1035', 3)
;
insert into titleditors values
('777-02-9831', 'PC8888', 3)
;
insert into titleditors values
('943-88-7920', 'BU1032', 1)
;
insert into titleditors values
('943-88-7920', 'BU1111', 1)
;
insert into titleditors values
('943-88-7920', 'BU2075', 1)
;
insert into titleditors values
('943-88-7920', 'BU7832', 1)
;
insert into titleditors values
('943-88-7920', 'PC1035', 1)
;
insert into titleditors values
('943-88-7920', 'PC8888', 1)
;
insert into titleditors values
('993-86-0420', 'PS1372', 1)
;
```

```
insert into titleditors values
('993-86-0420', 'PS2091', 1)
;
insert into titleditors values
('993-86-0420', 'PS2106', 1)
;
insert into titleditors values
('993-86-0420', 'PS3333', 1)
;
insert into titleditors values
('993-86-0420', 'PS7777', 1)
;
insert into titleditors values
('993-86-0420', 'MC2222', 1)
;
insert into titleditors values
('993-86-0420', 'MC3021', 1)
;
insert into titleditors values
('993-86 0420', 'TC3218', 1)
;
insert into titleditors values
('993-86-0420', 'TC4203', 1)
;
insert into titleditors values
('993-86-0420', 'TC7777', 1)
;
insert into sales
values(1,'7066', 'QA7442.3', '09/13/1998')
;
insert into sales
values(2,'7067', 'D4482', '09/14/1998')
;
insert into sales
values(3,'7131', 'N914008', '09/14/1998')
;
insert into sales
values(4,'7131', 'N914014', '09/14/1998')
;
insert into sales
values(5,'8042', '423LL922', '09/14/1998')
;
```

```
insert into sales
values(6,'8042', '423LL930', '09/14/1998')
;
insert into sales
values(7, '6380', '722a', '09/13/1998')
;
insert into sales
values(8,'6380', '6871', '09/14/1998')
;
insert into sales
values(9,'8042','P723', '03/11/2001')
;
insert into sales
values(19,'7896','X999', '02/21/2001')
;
insert into sales
values(10,'7896','QQ2299', '10/28/2000')
;
insert into sales
values(11,'7896','TQ456', '12/12/2000')
;
insert into sales
values(12,'8042','QA879.1', '5/22/2000')
;
insert into sales
values(13,'7066','A2976', '5/24/2000')
;
insert into sales
values(14,'7131','P3087a', '5/29/2000')
;
insert into sales
values(15,'7067','P2121', '6/15/2000')
;
insert into salesdetails
values(1, 75, 75,'PS2091', '9/15/1998')
;
insert into salesdetails
values(2, 10, 10,'PS2091', '9/15/1998')
;
insert into salesdetails
values(3, 20, 720,'PS2091', '9/18/1998')
;
```

```
insert into salesdetails
values(4, 25, 20,'MC3021', '9/18/1998')
;
insert into salesdetails
values(5, 15, 15,'MC3021', '9/14/1998')
;
insert into salesdetails
values(6, 10, 3,'BU1032', '9/22/1998')
;
insert into salesdetails
values(7, 3, 3,'PS2091', '9/20/1998')
;
insert into salesdetails
values(8, 5, 5,'BU1032', '9/14/1998')
;
insert into salesdetails
values(9, 25, 5,'BU1111', '03/28/2001')
;
insert into salesdetails
values(19, 35, 35,'BU2075', '03/15/2001')
;
insert into salesdetails
values(10, 15, 15,'BU7832', '10/29/2000')
;
insert into salesdetails
values(11, 10, 10,'MC2222', '1/12/2001')
;
insert into salesdetails
values(12, 30, 30,'PC1035', '5/24/2000')
;
insert into salesdetails
values(13, 50, 50,'PC8888', '5/24/2000')
;
insert into salesdetails
values(14, 20, 20,'PS1372', '5/29/2000')
;
insert into salesdetails
values(14, 25, 25,'PS2106', '4/29/2000')
;
insert into salesdetails
values(14, 15, 10,'PS3333', '5/29/2000')
;
```

```
insert into salesdetails
values(14, 25, 25,'PS7777', '6/13/2000')
;
insert into salesdetails
values(15, 40, 40,'TC3218', '6/15/2000')
;
insert into salesdetails
values(15, 20, 20,'TC4203', '5/30/2000')
;
insert into salesdetails
values(15, 20, 10,'TC7777', '6/17/2000')
;
```

CREATE VIEW Statements

Because views are based on tables, there are no problems with datatypes or NULL status. The only adjustment you may need to make involves column headings, if they happen to include characters illegal on your system. (You may also need to modify view names if they are used by some other object in the RDBMS.) Be sure to change the terminator (;) for systems that require a different symbol.

```
drop view titleview;
create view titleview
as
select title, au_ord, au_lname,
price, ytd_sales, pub_id
from authors, titles, titleauthors
where authors.au_id = titleauthors.au_id
and titles.title_id = titleauthors.title_id
;
drop view oaklanders;
create view oaklanders (FirstName, LastName, Book)
as
select au_fname, au_lname, title
from authors, titles, titleauthors
where authors.au_id = titleauthors.au_id
  and titles.title_id = titleauthors.title_id
  and city = 'Oakland'
;
```

```
drop view books;
create view books
as
select titles.title_id, au_ord, au_lname, au_fname
from authors, titles, titleauthors
where authors.au_id=titleauthors.au_id and
     titles.title_id = titleauthors.title_id
;
drop view royaltychecks;
create view royaltychecks
as
select au_lname, au_fname,
sum(price*ytd_sales*royalty*royaltyshare) as Total_Income
from authors, titles, titleauthors, roysched
where authors.au_id=titleauthors.au_id
  and titles.title_id = titleauthors.title_id
  and titles.title_id = roysched.title_id
  and ytd_sales between lorange and hirange
group by au_lname, au_fname
;
--may need to modify column name if # is illegal
drop view currentinfo;
create view currentinfo (PUB#, TYPE, INCOME,
AVG_PRICE, AVG_SALES)
as
select pub_id, type, sum (price * ytd_sales),
  avg(price), avg(ytd_sales)
from titles
group by pub_id, type
;
drop view hiprice;
create view hiprice
as
select *
from titles
where price > 15
  and advance > 5000
;
drop view cities;
create view cities (Author, Authorcity, Pub, Pubcity)
as
```

```
select au_lname, authors.city, pub_name, publishers.city
from authors, publishers
where authors.city = publishers.city
;
drop view highaverage;
create view highaverage
as
select authors.au_id, titles.title_id, pub_name, price
from authors, titleauthors, titles, publishers
where authors.au_id = titleauthors.au_id and
      titles.title_id = titleauthors.title_id and
      titles.pub_id = publishers.pub_id and
      price >
            (select avg(price)
            from titles)
;
drop view highBandH;
create view highBandH
as select *
from highaverage
where pub_name = 'Binnet & Hardley'
;
drop view number1;
create view number1
as
select au_lname, phone
from authors
where zip like '94%'
;
drop view number2;
create view number2
as
select au_lname, phone
from number1
where au_lname > 'M'
;
drop view number3;
create view number3
as select au_lname, phone
from number2
where au_lname = 'MacFeather'
;
```

```
drop view accounts;
create view accounts (title, advance, gross_sales)
as
select title_id, advance, price * ytd_sales
from titles
where price > 15
  and advance > 5000
;
drop view categories;
create view categories (Category, Average_Price)
as select type, avg(price)
from titles
group by type
;
```

Appendix E

Resources

In This Appendix

Here you'll find lists of resources, including the following:

- Books
- Web Sites
- Newsgroups

Books

Books on SQL and other database topics are divided into categories: general or vendor specific. For your easy reference, books are listed alphabetically by title.

General

- *Database Design for Mere Mortals: A Hands-On Guide to Relational Database Design*, by Michael J. Hernandez (1997: Addison-Wesley).
- *A Guide to the SQL Standard: A User's Guide to the Standard Database Language SQL*, 4th edition, by Chris J. Date and Hugh Darwen (1997: Addison-Wesley).
- *Joe Celko's SQL for Smarties: Advanced SQL Programming*, by Joe Celko (1995: Morgan Kaufmann).
- *Practical SQL: The Sequel*, by Judith S. Bowman (2000: Addison-Wesley).
- *SQL: The Complete Reference*, by James R. Groff and Paul N. Weinberg (1999: McGraw-Hill).
- *SQL for Dummies*, by Allen G. Taylor (1995: IDG Books).

- *SQL: Implementing the SQL Foundation Standard,* by Paul J. Fortier (1999: Osborne McGraw-Hill).
- *SQL Queries for Mere Mortals,* by Michael J. Hernandez and John L. Viescas (2000: Addison-Wesley).
- *Understanding the New SQL: A Complete Guide,* by Jim Melton and Alan R. Simon (1993: Morgan Kaufmann).

Informix

- *Administering Informix Dynamic Server on Windows NT,* by Carlton Doe (1999: Prentice Hall).
- *Informix Basics,* by Glenn Miller (1998: Prentice Hall).
- *INFORMIX DBA Survival Guide,* 2nd edition, by Joe Lumbley (1999: Prentice Hall).
- *Informix Guide to SQL: Reference and Syntax,* 2nd edition, by Informix Software (1999: Prentice Hall).
- *Informix Performance Tuning,* 2nd edition, by Elizabeth Suto (1997: Prentice Hall).
- *Informix Power Reference,* by Art Taylor (1998: Prentice Hall).
- *Programming Informix SQL/4GL,* 2nd edition, by Cathy Kipp (1998: Prentice Hall).

Microsoft SQL Server

- *SQL Server 7 Developer's Guide,* by Michael Otey and Paul Conte (1998: McGraw-Hill).

(See "Transact-SQL" for more books on SQL Server.)

mSQL/MySQL

- *MySQL and mSQL,* by Randy Jay Yarger and George Reese (1999: O'Reilly & Associates).

Oracle

- *Oracle 8: The Complete Reference,* by George Koch and Kevin Loney (1997: Osborne McGraw-Hill).
- *Oracle 8 DBA Handbook,* by Kevin Loney (1998: Osborne McGraw-Hill).
- *Oracle Performance Tuning,* by Mark Gurry and Peter Corrigan (1996: O'Reilly & Associates).
- *Oracle SQL High-Performance Tuning,* by Guy Harrison (1997: Prentice Hall).
- *Oracle SQL Plus: The Definitive Guide,* by Jonathan Gennick (1999: O'Reilly & Associates).

Sybase

- *Sybase Performance Tuning,* by Shaibal Roy and Marc Sugiyama (1996: Prentice Hall).
- *Sybase SQL Server Performance and Tuning Guide,* by Karen Paulsell (1996: International Thomson Publishing).
- *Sybase SQL Server Survival Guide,* by Jim Panttaja, Mary Panttaja, and Judy Bowman (1996: John Wiley and Sons).

(See "Transact-SQL" for more books on Sybase.)

Transact-SQL

- *The Guru's Guide to Transact-SQL,* by Ken Henderson (2000: Addison-Wesley).
- *Optimizing Transact-SQL: Advanced Programming Techniques,* by David Rozenshtein, Anatoly Abramovich, and Eugene Birger (1997: The Coriolis Group).
- *Transact-SQL Programming,* by Kevin Kline, Lee Gould, and Andrew Zanevsky (1999: O'Reilly & Associates).

Web Sites

Vendor Sites

http://www.informix.com
http://www.microsoft.com/sql
http://www.oracle.com
http://www.sybase.com
http://www.technet.oracle.com

Other Links

The following are other Web sites visited during the work on the book:

http://www.sql-server-performance.com
http://www.VB2theMax.com
http://www.iiug.org (the Informix Users' Group site)
http://www.geocities.com/SiliconValley/File/2306/TechDesk.html
http://www.TDAN.com (the Data Administration Newsletter)
http://www.orafaq.com (frequently asked questions on Oracle)

Newsgroups

You can read newsgroup discussions from your Web browser by visiting www.deja.com.

The main newsgroup forum for discussions on database systems is:

comp.databases

comp.databases has 28 subgroups, ranging from comp.databases.adabase to comp.databases.xbase.

For example:

comp.databases.sybase
comp.databases.informix
comp.databases.ms-sqlserver
comp.databases.oracle with subgroups marketplace, misc, server, and tools.

Index

Practical SQL

The Sequel

Judith S. Bowman

Written by the co-author of the best-selling *Practical SQL Handbook, Practical SQL: The Sequel* picks up where the first book leaves off. It goes beyond basic SQL query structure to explore the complexities of using SQL for everyday business needs. It will help you make the transition from classroom to reality, where you must design, fix, and maintain imperfect SQL systems. For those who are working with SQL systems—or preparing to do so—this book offers information organized by use rather than by feature. Readers can turn to specific business problems and learn how to solve them with the appropriate SQL features. In particular, the sequel focuses on the real-world challenges of dealing with legacy systems, inherited problematic code, dirty data, and query tuning for better performance.

0-201-61638-6 • Paperback with CD-ROM • 352 pages • ©2001

SQL Queries for Mere Mortals

A Hands-On Guide to Data Manipulation in SQL

Michael J. Hernandez, John L. Viescas

If you are accessing corporate information from the Internet or from an internal network, you are probably using SQL. *SQL Queries for Mere Mortals* will help new users learn the foundations of SQL queries, and will prove to be an essential reference guide for intermediate and advanced users. The accompanying CD contains five sample databases used for the example queries throughout the book, plus an evaluation copy of Microsoft SQL Server version 7.

0-201-43336-2 • Paperback with CD-ROM • 528 pages • ©2000

Database Design for Mere Mortals

A Hands-On Guide to Relational Database Design

Michael J. Hernandez

Sound design can save you hours of development time before you write a single line of code. Based on the author's years of experience teaching this material, *Database Design for Mere Mortals* is a straightforward, platform-independent tutorial on the basic principles of relational database design. Database design expert Michael J. Hernandez introduces the core concepts of design theory and method without the technical jargon. *Database Design for Mere Mortals* will provide any developer with a commonsense design methodology for developing databases that work.

0-201-69471-9 • Paperback • 480 pages • ©1997

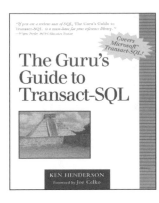

The Guru's Guide to Transact-SQL

Ken Henderson

Since its introduction more than a decade ago, the Microsoft SQL Server query language, Transact-SQL, has become increasingly popular and more powerful. The current version sports advanced features such as OLE Automation support, cross-platform querying facilities, and full-text search management. This book is the consummate guide to Microsoft Transact-SQL. From data type nuances to complex statistical computations to the bevy of undocumented features in the language, *The Guru's Guide to Transact-SQL* imparts the knowledge you need to become a virtuoso of the language as quickly as possible. This book contains the information, explanations, and advice needed to master Transact-SQL and develop the best possible Transact-SQL code. Some 600 code examples not only illustrate important concepts and best practices, but also provide working Transact-SQL code that can be incorporated into your own real-world DBMS applications.

0-201-61576-2 • Paperback • 592 pages • ©2000

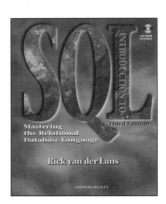

Introduction to SQL, Third Edition

Mastering the Relational Database Language
Rick van der Lans

According to Ian Cargill of Soliton Software, Rick van der Lans has written "a first class book. A thorough and well-written introduction to a complex subject. I wish this book had been available when I was learning SQL." SQL was, is, and always will be the database language for relational database systems such as Oracle, DB2, Sybase, Informix, and Microsoft SQL Server. *Introduction to SQL* describes, in depth, the full capacity of SQL as it is implemented by the commercial databases, without neglecting the most recent changes to the standard, bringing the book up to date and fully compliant with SQL3. Unique in the extent of its coverage, this book takes you from the beginning to the end of SQL, the concepts to the practice, the apprentice to the master.

0-201-59618-0 • Paperback • 720 pages • ©2000

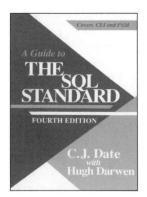

A Guide to the SQL Standard, Fourth Edition

C.J. Date with Hugh Darwen

The SQL language has established itself as the lingua franca for database management; it provides the basis for systems interoperability, application portability, client/server operation, distributed databases, and more. SQL is supported by just about every DBMS on the market today. SQL2—or, to give it its official name, the International Standard Database Language SQL (1992)—represents a major set of extensions to the earlier SQL standard. For a start, the new specification is well over 600 pages, compared with less than 100 for the original version. No database professional can afford to ignore it. This Fourth Edition of *A Guide to the SQL Standard* covers extensive integrity support, powerful new operators, and national and international character data support—all features of SQL2; comprehensive date and time support and a clear explanation of the complexities of Dynamic SQL—features of SQL. This book provides a tutorial treatment of SQL2.

0-201-96426-0 • Paperback • 544 pages • ©1997

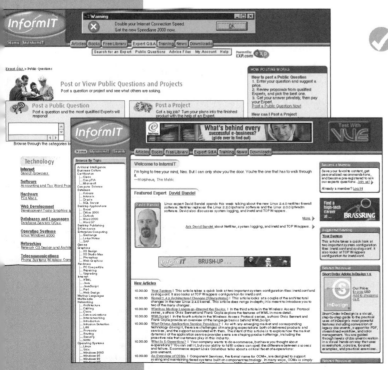

USING THE PRACTICAL SQL HANDBOOK CD

1. This CD contains

   - a 60-day trial version of Sybase Adaptive Server Anywhere
   - the bookbiz sample database used in the book
   - the *readPSH4.txt* file with these instructions
   - files to create the bookbiz tables on other DBMS systems (MS SQL Server, Oracle, Informix, and Sybase Adaptive Server Enterprise—software for these DBMSs is not, however, supplied on the CD)

2. To load Adaptive Server Anywhere, insert the CD into your drive. If an installation program does not come up immediately, choose the correct platform directory from the Anywhere directory (CE, Netware, Win16, or Win32) and start the *setup.exe* file. Follow the installation directions. For those short of space, Personal Server is the minimum. Sybase Central and Help files are useful additions.

3. Once you have installed Adaptive Server Anywhere, use the Windows Explorer (or similar utility) to copy the *bookbiz.db* file from the CD to your hard drive. (For a copy of these instructions, print the *readPSH4.txt* file from the CD.)

4. Start Adaptive Server Anywhere/Interactive SQL (from the "Programs" menu on Windows, or according to the customs of your system.)

5. The "Connect to Adaptive Server Anywhere" window opens. (If it does not, type "connect" in the "Command" pane at the bottom third of the Interactive SQL window and click "Execute". This will bring up the "Connect to Adaptive Server Anywhere" window.)

6. Type "DBA" (must be uppercase) in the login line, and "SQL" in the password line.

7. Without clicking the "OK" button, click the "Database" tab at the top of the form.

8. Type "bookbiz" in the "Database name" line. Give the full path name of *bookbiz.db* in the "Database file" line. (See step 3. If you copied the *bookbiz.db* file to C:/SQL, for example, the address for "Database file" is *C:/SQL/bookbiz.db*.).

9. Click "OK" at the bottom of the form. The heading in the top border of the "Interactive SQL" window indicates you are DBA, on bookbiz. The bookbiz database is already built and ready to go.

10. Type a sample query, such as "select * from publishers" in the Interactive SQL "Command" pane. When you click the "Execute" button, the results appear in the "Data" pane at the top of the "Interactive SQL" window.

11. Use Sybase Central (it may be listed as "Manage Adaptive Server Anywhere" in the "Programs" menu) for adding users, checking table column definitions, etc. Log into Sybase Central by picking the "Connect" option on the Sybase Central "Tools" menu. The "Connect to Adaptive Server Anywhere" window opens. Follow the process described in steps 6-9 above.

12. Scripts to create table, add data, and create views are included in the CREATEs, INSERTs, and VIEWs directories on the CD and directions for using them are in the scripts and in Appendix A. Use these files if you want to restore after removing tables or deleting data.

13. Scripts for creating bookbiz tables for other RDBMSs (Oracle, SQL Server, Informix, and Sybase ASE) are also included on the CD in the CREATEs, INSERTs, and VIEWs folders.